African Studies
History, Politics, Economics, and Culture

Edited by
Molefi Asante
Temple University

A Routledge Series

African Studies
History, Politics, Economics, and Culture

Molefi Asante, *General Editor*

Kwame Nkrumah's Contribution to
Pan-Africanism
An Afrocentric Analysis
D. Zizwe Poe

Nyansapo (The Wisdom Knot)
*Toward an African Philosophy of
Education*
Kwadwo A. Okrah

The Athens of West Africa
*A History of International Education
at Fourah Bay College, Freetown,
Sierra Leone*
Daniel J. Paracka, Jr.

The Yorùbá Traditional Healers of
Nigeria
Mary Olufunmilayo Adekson

The 'Civil Society' Problematique
*Deconstructing Civility and Southern
Nigeria's Ethnic Radicalization*
Adedayo Oluwakayode Adekson

Maat, the Moral Ideal in Ancient
Egypt
A Study in Classical African Ethics
Maulana Karenga

Igbo Women and Economic
Transformation in Southeastern
Nigeria, 1900–1960
Gloria Chuku

Kwame Nkrumah's Politico-Cultural
Thought and Policies
*An African-Centered Paradigm for the
Second Phase of the African Revolution*
Kwame Botwe-Asamoah

Non-Traditional Occupations,
Empowerment and Women
A Case of Togolese Women
Ayélé Léa Adubra

Contending Political Paradigms
in Africa
*Rationality and the Politics of
Democratization in Kenya and Zambia*
Shadrack Wanjala Nasong'o

Law, Morality and International
Armed Intervention
*The United Nations and ECOWAS in
Liberia*
Mourtada Déme

The Hidden Debate
*The Truth Revealed about the Battle
over Affirmative Action in South Africa
and the United States*
Akil Kokayi Khalfani

Britain, Leftist Nationalists and the
Transfer of Power in Nigeria,
1945–1965
Hakeem Ibikunle Tijani

Western-Educated Elites in Kenya,
1900–1963
The African American Factor
Jim C. Harper, II

Western-Educated Elites in Kenya, 1900–1963
The African American Factor

Jim C. Harper, II

Routledge
Taylor & Francis Group
NEW YORK AND LONDON

Published in 2006 by
Routledge
Taylor & Francis Group
711 Third Avenue
New York, NY 10017

Published in Great Britain by
Routledge
Taylor & Francis Group
2 Park Square
Milton Park, Abingdon
Oxon OX14 4RN

© 2006 by Taylor & Francis Group, LLC
Routledge is an imprint of Taylor & Francis Group

First issued in paperback 2012

International Standard Book Number-13: 978-0-415-65322-0 (Paperback)
International Standard Book Number-13: 978-0-415-97730-2 (Hardcover)
Library of Congress Card Number 2005024512

No part of this book may be reprinted, reproduced, transmitted, or utilized in any form by any electronic, mechanical, or other means, now known or hereafter invented, including photocopying, microfilming, and recording, or in any information storage or retrieval system, without written permission from the publishers.

Trademark Notice: Product or corporate names may be trademarks or registered trademarks, and are used only for identification and explanation without intent to infringe.

Library of Congress Cataloging-in-Publication Data

Harper, Jim C.
    Western-educated elites in Kenya, 1900-1963 : the African American factor / Jim C. Harper, II.
        p. cm. -- (African studies)
    Includes bibliographical references (p.　) and index.
    ISBN 0-415-97730-4
    1. Elite (Social sciences)--Kenya--History--20th century. 2. Education--Kenya--History--20th century. 3. Kenya--History--1895-1963. I. Title. II. Series: African studies (Routledge (Firm))

HN793.Z9E43 2006
306.43096762'0904--dc22   2005024512

Taylor & Francis Group
is the Academic Division of Informa plc.

Visit the Taylor & Francis Web site at
http://www.taylorandfrancis.com

and the Routledge Web site at
http://www.routledge-ny.com

Contents

Acknowledgments	vii
Chapter One Introduction	1
Chapter Two Traditional and Islamic Education in Kenya	21
Chapter Three The Rise of the *Asomi*	33
Chapter Four The Quest for Higher Education in the United States, 1945–1963	59
Chapter Five American-Educated *Asomi* Return Home, 1958–1963	91
Chapter Six Conclusion	125
Appendix	129
Notes	157
Bibliography	177
Index	187

Acknowledgments

This book was made possible through the support and generosity of a number of individuals and institutions in the United States and Africa. The principle research was conducted in the following repositories: Morland-Spingarn Research Center at Howard University, Perkins and Divinity libraries at Duke University Library, National Archives II, National Archives, Library of Congress, Ralph J. Bunche Department of State library and in Kenya, the Kenya National Archives. I would like to thank the many librarians and curators who rendered me special services and I hope that they will forgive me if I have omitted their name(s). They include Joellen ElBashir and Walter Hill.

I would like to acknowledge Dr. Aziz Batran, my friend and mentor, for giving me invaluable assistance in a critical and exceptional way at every phase of my research. He spent countless hours reading and editing the manuscript to the completion of the project. I would also like to recognize Dr. Emory Tolbert, Dr. Selwyn H. Carrington, Dr. J.Ayodele Langley, and Dr. Freddie Parker all of whom gave advice and time while reading and commenting on my work. I would also like to thank the faculty and staff at Howard University and North Carolina Central University for their support.

Intensive work on this book began in 1999 when I was a graduate student at Howard University. I received a fellowship from the Department of State to work and conduct research in Kenya. While in Kenya, I was able to interview Dr. Julius Gikonyo Kiano, Dr. Godfrey Muriuki, and Dr. Macharia Munene. The interviews provided me with the perspective needed to conduct further research on western-educated elites in Kenya. During my research trip to Kenya, I benefited from the kindness and counsel of these Kenyan scholars. Their advice led me to extend the scope of my research. I learned much about the links between African

Americans and Kenyans, the Civil Rights Movement, and African Liberation Movements.

The manuscript was completed and revised while I was a Visiting Lecturer at North Carolina Central University. I wish to thank Dr. Sylvia M. Jacobs and the faculty of the Department of History for their support and direction as well as the encouragement and opportunity to present my research at lyceums, seminars, and historical conferences to insightful and critical audiences.

I would like to thank my wife, Rosalind, for accepting kindly the distractions in our life that pursuit of this task necessitated and for her inspiration, devotion, and proofreading of my manuscript. I would also like to thank my children, Antonio and Kamaria, my parents Jim and Doris, and my siblings, Sheila, Darneise, and Stephon, for their encouragement, patience, love, and support throughout this process. Finally yet importantly, I owe a debt of gratitude to many friends and colleagues whose comments, suggestions, and technical expertise were invaluable. They include Dr. P. Masila Mutisya, Dr. Charles D. Johnson, Charmaine Dominique, and Thomas Massey. For your support, I am eternally grateful.

Chapter One
Introduction

HISTORICAL OVERVIEW

"America, and I must say, particularly our African brothers in America, came to our help in that crucial time in our history . . . Independence was coming fast to Kenya and we needed highly qualified personnel to run the country once the British departed. We realized that there was a problem. Kenya needed well-trained personnel very quickly, and so we contacted our friends in the United States. Tom Mboya contacted trade unionists and politicians. Yes, Britain gave us a few scholarships . . . India, France, and the Soviet Union too. But America gave us the majority of needed scholarships."[1] Such were the words of the late Dr. Julius Gikonyo Kiano, graduate of American universities, as I interviewed him in his office that overlooked Harry Thuku Street in Nairobi in the morning of June 23, 1999. Independent Kenya, in 1963, was in dire need of highly educated cadre to replace the British who staffed the Civil Service and the private sector, as well as highly trained labor officers to run the nascent trade unions in the country. Although Kenya had received scholarships from Britain and other nations including India, the Soviet Block, Germany, and France, the number of these scholarships was far from adequate. Hence, the Kenyan nationalists approached the United States to provide hundreds of urgently needed scholarships. Tom Mboya, Dr. Julius Gikonyo Kiano, and Hon. Kariuki Karanja Njiiri contacted the African-American leadership, majority and minority colleges and universities, politicians, black entertainers and sportsmen, all of whom embraced the "Kenya Education Drive." Hundreds of scholarships were offered and funds to transport Kenyan students from Nairobi by air were secured. Thus, Kenyan students began to flow to America in large numbers in the late 1950s and early 1960s. These American-educated students formed the core of the Africanization process of independent Kenya.[2]

However, the arrival of Kenyan students to study in black institutions of higher learning in the United States can be traced back to the early decades of the twentieth century when missionary schools dispatched a few of their Kenyan graduates to America to attend Black Theological Colleges. Evidently, none of these early Kenyan ministers remained permanently in the United States. They all went back home to Africanize the white run Church in the country. On the other hand, the first Kenyan students who pursued Liberal Arts education in America were either sons of wealthy, powerful chiefs who had the means to send their children abroad or were sons of the common folk sponsored by their local communities. Their number was very small and they were almost all men. But thanks to the untiring campaign of Tom Mboya, Dr. Kiano and Hon. Kariuki Njiiri, and their Pan-Africanist counterparts in the United States, the trickle of Kenyan students to America turned into a flood. Although few students stayed permanently in the United States after graduation, the overwhelming majority returned home to occupy leadership positions in the country. It is the contribution of the United States, particularly its African-American leadership, its black colleges and universities and black organizations in the "creation" of the Kenyan *Asomi* or *Jasomi* (*Kiswahili* word meaning western educate elites) that managed Kenya following *Madaraka Day*, that is, independence from Britain in 1963, that will be the main focus of this book.

According to historical records, the region now known as Kenya had contact with foreigners since the 4th century AD. This is verified by the recovery of Roman coins from that period. It is not known for certain who brought the coins to Kenya. It could have been Persian, Indian, Indonesian, Chinese or more probable Arab traders. From ancient times, Arab sailors from the regions of Southern Arabia had active commercial dealings with the coast of East Africa. As a result, extensive permanent Arab trading posts or settlements, such as Mombasa and Malindi, were established along the coastal strip of Kenya. It was from these outposts that Arab merchants conducted their trade with the hinterland and across the Indian Ocean. The settled Arabs intermarried with the local Bantu population and learned to speak their language and eventually mixed the local language with Arabic.[3] This interrelationship gave birth to what came to be known as the *Swahili* culture and the *Kiswahili* language.

It was not however until the 16th century that the Portuguese explorer, Vasco de Gama, arrived at Mombasa on his way to India. In 1553, the Portuguese constructed Fort Jesus in Mombasa to protect their sea route to India and their interests in East Africa. Fort Jesus represented the first European stronghold on the coast of East Africa. Later, it became a launching pad for European penetration of the hinterland. The British however turned the fort into a prison upon their colonization of the region.[4]

On the other hand, the first European missionaries to reach the interior of Kenya were Reverend Johann Krapf and Reverend Johann Rebmann. Both were evangelists of the Anglican Church Missionary Society (CMS). They set up the first missionary school in Kenya in 1847 at Rabai near Mombasa. Krapf and Rebmann were then followed by the Holy Ghost Fathers who established their own missionary school in Mombasa. This was the start of formal western education in Kenya. In time, other white missionaries entered Kenya and founded their missions across the face of the country. The primary purpose of missionary schools was to promote evangelism. However, with the establishment of colonization and the alienation of Kenyan fertile land to white settlers, the schools were used as an agent to produce semi-skilled labor for settler farms and clerical staff for the British colonial administration.[5] In other words, missionary education led to the establishment of a vocational oriented system for Kenyans. Furthermore, the colonial administration founded a handful of government schools for the same purpose. At any rate, one cannot but notice, at the same time, the intentional neglect of higher education in the country by both the missionaries and the colonial government. Consequently, Kenyan students who sought higher education were forced to turn to overseas colleges and universities in India, Great Britain, the Soviet Block, France, Germany but mainly in the United States of America. It was the development of communism and the Cold War that redirected the foreign policy of the United States toward the emerging African nations. All assistance must now be extended to the African countries that were on their way to independence before they fell into the hands of communism. Hence, the interest of the United States in Kenya, and in all the other African countries for that matter, became very real and urgent. It was the general belief in the United States that Kenyan students educated in American institutions of higher learning would more than likely espouse democratic ideals rather than lean towards communism. In fact, the United States education of Kenyan students who eventually became the leaders of their nation played an important role in the development of that solid, seemingly everlasting relationship between the two countries and had certainly stood in the way of the spread of communism in Kenya.

The collaboration between the Kenyan nationalists, led by Tom Mboya, Dr. Kiano, and Hon. Kariuki Njiiri with the leadership of Africans in the Diaspora was not surprising in the least. The flames of Pan-Africanism and of Mau Mau Revolution were then sweeping the Black World. The African-American trade union leaders, such as Asa Philip Randolph, leaders of the Civil Rights movement, such as Martin Luther King Jr. and Congressmen Charles Diggs, educators, such as Dr. Horace Bond and Gwen Carter, entertainers, such as Sidney Poitier and Harry Belafonte, and sportsmen, such as, Jackie Robinson, worked tirelessly to secure scholarships for Kenyan students in the United States. In addition, help was extended by white activists, such as William X. Scheinman and George Houser, and politicians, such as John F. Kennedy, all of whom had cultivated intimate personal friendship with Tom Mboya. Thus, it was individuals, private organizations, universities, and colleges more so than the American Government that shouldered most of the burden of educating Kenyan students in the United States at the time when Kenya was on its way to gain her independence. It was not until 1960/1961 and thereafter that the Department of State, after a long period of ineffective cooperation, threw its weight behind the "Kenya Education Drive" and began to sponsor any significant number of Kenyan students.

The first Kenyan student to arrive in America was sponsored by the African Inland Mission. That was Molonkett Ole Sempele, a Maasai, who arrived in America in 1908 and attended black theological schools in Virginia and North Carolina. Inspired by his experiences and contacts with black America, Ole Sempele returned to his homeland to break away from his white missionary mentors to found the first Independent African Church in Kenya. But active collaboration between Kenyans and African-Americans was practiced on the ground in Kenya when the Phelps-Stokes Commission arrived in the country in 1924 and established its Jeanes School at Kabete. From that time on, the Phelps-Stokes Commission occupied an effective place in the development of the Kenyan *Asomi*. The Commission brought with it to Kenya the illustrious Dr. James Aggrey who campaigned very hard for African-American missionaries' entry into the country. His drive was shared and strongly supported by Bishop Turner, W.E.B. DuBois, and Carter G. Woodson. Besides, young missionary educated nationalists, such as Harry Thuku, the father of Kenya nationalism, *Mzee* Jomo Kenyatta, the first Prime Minister, and Hon. Mbiyu Koinange, the second most powerful Kenyan politician, were exposed to and cultivated close relationship with Pan-Africanists in the Diaspora including Marcus Garvey, W.E.B. DuBois, Ralph Bunch and Thurgood Marshall, as well as with Tuskegee and Hampton Institutes. Further still, copies of the *Negro World* were circulated widely amongst the nationalists in East Africa.

That Kenyans reached out for Africans in America to assist in building a cadre of educated elites was also in response to British sterile high education policy, and the reluctance of British trade unions to help train Kenyan trade union personnel. On the one hand, the British did establish

Introduction

three "colleges," Makerere in Kampala, Uganda, the Royal Technical College in Nairobi, and Dar Es-Salam College in Tanganyika (Tanzania) for their entire East Africa Protectorate, in 1922, 1956, and 1961 respectively. These two-year training colleges offered the equivalent of High School certificates to a small number of students. Students seeking university degrees had to travel and attend colleges and universities abroad. Even so, the association of British trade unions with the Colonial Labor Advisory Committee forced them to work with the Colonial machinery and consequently tied their hands.[6] The foot-dragging of the British trade unions was apparent to Tom Mboya as he received a cold shoulder when he visited the leading British trade union institution, Ruskin College at Oxford, in 1956. In contrast, Mboya was received with great enthusiasm and comradeship by American trade unionists, particularly black trade unionists. Herein lays the reason behind Mboya's efforts to seek scholarships and trade union training programs in the United States rather than in Britain. Furthermore, Tom Mboya was encouraged and assisted in his efforts by influential Kenyan nationalists, Dr. Julius Kiano, Hon. Kariuki Njiiri, and Hon. Mbiyu Koinange, who had been educated in America at Lincoln and other universities, and had established friendships and contacts with both black and white American academicians, politicians, and organizations. They corresponded with their American friends and successfully sought their help.[7] The result was the enrollment of a large number of Kenyan students in American colleges and universities. Over the years, the Kenyan student body in the United States surpassed by far the number of their colleagues who attended colleges and universities in other countries including Britain, the colonial power in the region. These Asomi graduates of American colleges participated fully in the nationalist movement and provided much of the needed highly educated and trained personnel that held the future of the country in its hands once the colonial forces and settler communities evacuated the land.

THEORETICAL OVERVIEW

The book offers an examination of the collaboration between Africans in Africa and Africans in the Diaspora within the context of Pan-Africanism, African Nationalism, and Black Nationalism.[8] Pan-Africanism moved from theory to practical application as black intellectuals called for the unifying of all people of African decent to fight colonialism and racial discrimination. Notable intellectuals of the Diaspora, including W.E.B. DuBois, Martin R. Delany, Alexander Crummell, Edward Blyden, George Padmore, Henry Sylvester Williams, and Marcus Garvey, initiated the movement. Their counterparts in Africa including Léopold Sédar Senghor of Senegal,

Kwame Nkrumah of Ghana, Sékou Touré of Guinea, as well as the East African nationalists, such as Julius Nyerere of Tanzania, Joseph Kamulegeya of Uganda, Harry Thuku, Tom Mboya, Jomo Kenyatta, and Dr. Julius Kiano of Kenya strengthened the linkages between African-Americans and Africans in the motherland.

In 1933, W.E.B. DuBois wrote in the *Crisis* newspaper that Pan - Africanism was a movement that fostered intellectual understanding and co-operation among all groups of African descent in order to bring about "the industrial and spiritual Emancipation of Negro People." Recently, Ronald Walters elaborated on this saying that Pan-African relationships may be divided into five types. First, there are those relationships among African states. Second, there are relationships between African states and states of Africa origin such as those in the Caribbean. Third, there are relationships between African states and peoples of African origin in the Diaspora. Fourth, there are relationships among African-origin states in the Diaspora and African-origin communities in the Diaspora. Fifth, there are relations among African-origin communities in the Diaspora.[9] In other words, the individual or collective relations among Africans in the Diaspora, among African-origin communities outside the African continent or between them and those on the continent are important varieties of Pan-Africanism. It is within this framework that we intend to view the collaboration between African-Americans and the Kenyan nationalists with regard to the education of Kenyan students in the United States. On the other hand, George Sherpperson, saw Pan-Africanism as a struggle against the capitalist, colonial, and dictatorial power of the bourgeoisie.[10]

J. Ayodele Langley in Pan-Africanism and Nationalism in West Africa, 1900–1945, argued that Pan-Africanism was a form of protest, a refusal, a demand, and a utopia born of centuries of contact with Europeans. St. Clair Drake, made a distinction between two kinds of Pan-Africanism. First, there was the pan-africanism with a lower case "p" and the Pan-Africanism with a capital "P." The lower case "p" pan-africanism had no political connotations and referred to linkages between peoples throughout the African Diaspora, while Pan-Africanism with a capital "P" denoted political movements within the Diaspora. P. Olisanwuche Esedebe's work, Pan-Africanism: The Idea and Movement, 1776–1963, suggested that there was still no specific definition of the term as different scholars used it in varying ways. Nonetheless, he defined Pan-Africanism as a political and cultural phenomenon that regarded Africa, Africans and their descendants abroad as a unit. It sought to regenerate and unify Africa and promote a feeling of oneness among the African people of the world.[11] Furthermore, Kenneth King extended the term to include the search of Africans for Western Education by attending missionary schools in Africa or abroad, as well as enrollment in educational institutions run by black Americans in the United States.[12]

Initially, these educational opportunities were often the result of the desire of missionaries and philanthropists to provide Kenyan students with the opportunity to attend colleges and universities in the United States. Even politicians, like ex-president Theodore Roosevelt, joined the campaign and went out of his way to assist a Kenyan student to study in America. Hakim Adi also examined Pan-Africanism and education as he studied West Africans in Great Britain and the development of the West African Students Union in England.

To illustrate the all-embracing spirit of Pan-Africanism among African students in Britain, Adi maintained that the West African Student movement in Great Britain in collaboration with the British Communist Party, as well as with organizations in Africa articulated anti-colonial sentiment and helped pave the way for successful independence movements in Africa. Education was one of the pillars of Pan-Africanism. DuBois' philosophy of attaining Higher Education for social change and self-assertion was a driving force behind the co-operation between Kenyans and African-Americans in the Diaspora in the field of education. Kenyans as well as other Africans, forced by the need for highly educated and well-trained personnel, were quick to heed the call. They took full advantage of all educational opportunities extended to them by black colleges and universities, and by black trade unions in the United States. That collaboration testifies to the success of Pan-Africanism as an instrument that unified and solidified relationships between Africans in Africa and the sons and daughters of Africa in their homelands overseas. Pan-Africanism was the instrument that Africans everywhere used to fight colonialism and racism and to build Africa by their own hands. In other words, Pan-Africanism, African Nationalism, and Black Nationalism combined to create the environment necessary that prepared Kenyan students to use Higher Education as a vehicle for liberation and the reconstruction of their homeland. Kenyans educated in black institutions in America or helped by African-Americans to attend majority colleges and universities, as well as those indigenous *Asomi* came under the influence of Garveyism. The Negro World was available to the *Asomi* who did not make it to the United States and those who traveled to America became, consciously or unconsciously, the emissaries of Garvey in their homeland.

HISTORICAL CONTRIBUTION

This study seeks to provide insights into the crucial historical linkages between Africans in the continent, in this case Kenyans, and those of

African descent in America at the time when Kenya was surging ahead to shed the yoke of colonialism. Goaded by Pan-Africanism, Black Nationalism and liberation, and by the fear that Africa could be swept by the tide of communism, the African leadership in the United States joined hands with its Kenyan counterpart to extend the urgently needed assistance to help Kenya so that it successfully met the challenges of independence. Newly born Kenya needed skilled labor to wean and rear it to maturity, for under British rule, Kenya was left fatally short in skilled indigenous personnel to run and develop it for the Colonial system of education deliberately refused to extend advanced learning to the "natives." That Kenya urgently needed qualified personnel in the field of education, for example, was apparent even seven years after independence. The 1970 report of the Ministry of Education made clear that, at the time, Kenya was in need of 1,573 secondary school teachers. It pointed out that the East African Universities of Makerere, Nairobi, and Dar Es-Salaam would be able to provide over the following six years, which is by 1976, a total of 416 teachers at the most. Even present day Kenya continues to suffer from severe shortages in teaching staff at all levels of the school system. In October 2003, the Washington Post reported that although "Kenya (at present) has 175, 000 public primary school teachers (it) needs 60,000 more, according to the Kenyan National Teachers Union."[13] It was the will to confront this and other problems that African-American and Kenyan leaders worked hand-in-hand from the early decades of the twentieth century to promote their agendas on an international level. This undeniable collaboration refutes the contention by scholars, such as Martin Staniland, who argued that African-American activism towards Africa was a recent phenomenon. Staniland alleged that there was scarcity, even an absence of formidable ties between the Civil Rights Movement and the African Liberation Movements of the 1950s and 1960s. He considered the relations between African-Americans and Africans during the colonial period as one that lacked focus because African-Americans preoccupied themselves with domestic issues and thus could not identify with or come to the aid of Africa.[14] In contrast, this study shows clearly that the African-American presence in Kenya dates back to 1916 when Max Yergan, the African-American Secretary of the Colored Department of the YMCA, arrived in the country. Yergan was followed by the establishment in 1924 of the Jeanes School at Kabete by the Phelps-Stokes Commission.

Kenyans made their presence in black theological institutions and colleges in the United States from as early as 1908. As mentioned above, in that year, Molonkett Olokoinya Ole Sempele, a Maasai graduate of a white missionary school, came to the United States where he attended a trade school for Blacks in North Carolina before he joined the Boydton Academic and Bible Institute in Virginia. His experiences with African-Americans inspired him to secede from the white Church and found an Independent African Church in his homeland. These early contacts, limited as they may be, had however influenced Kenya and its *Asomi* in no small measure. Furthermore, extensive contact and collaboration between African-Americans and Kenyans took place from 1956 when the celebrated Kenyan nationalist, Tom Mboya, visited the United States at the invitation of the black leadership. The visit ushered in a new era of unprecedented partnership between Kenyan nationalists and the African-American leadership that resulted in hundreds of Kenyan students receiving higher education in colleges and universities in the United States. The overwhelming majority of these students returned home to participate in the rebuilding of their country, which had been devastated by the British colonial administration and white settlers. Hence, the thesis argues that the preoccupation of African-Americans with domestic issues did not preclude them from establishing solid, fruitful relations with Africans, and that collaboration between Africans in the Diaspora and those on the continent was not a recent phenomenon, as Martin Staniland wanted us to believe. Furthermore, the research shows that while the government of the United States was reluctant to assist Kenyans to reconstruct their country, African-Americans stepped forward to extend help to their brethren. Importantly, the study places the efforts spent by African-Americans to assist in the education of Kenyans within the context of Pan-Africanism, which viewed the struggle of blacks in the United States for justice and equality and that of Africans for liberation as the same fight against a common enemy, the white man.

The book, *Western-Educated Elites in Kenya, 1900–1963: The African-American Factor*, is divided into five chapters that consist of an examination of Traditional, Islamic, missionary and government education, and the subsequent higher education that Kenyan students received in the United States and then returned to their homeland. The first chapter provides the methodology and theoretical overview. It attempts to show the significant role that Pan-Africanism in the Diaspora and in Africa played in having Kenyans educated in American colleges and universities and that this gave birth to a highly qualified leadership and skilled labor personnel capable of governing the newly independent nation. Furthermore, the chapter gives a critical evaluation of the literature and details the primary sources on which the study depended.

Chapter Two examines the traditional and Islamic education in Kenya, both of which have been dismissed by western writers as "informal education." The chapter argues that far from being informal and irrelevant, the system of education in Kenya before the arrival of the European missionaries was well structured, methodical, and meaningful. The classrooms were found at home, in workshops, at mosques and Koranic schools. Traditional education was handled by parents and elders, and through apprenticeship, initiation, and age groups under the guidance of distinguished, skilled masters. Although the curricula differed at each institution and stage, traditional education equipped the youths, both male and female, with different skills and knowledge that nurtured them into useful members of the society. In other words, traditional education focused on social responsibility, the professions, political participation, and spiritual and moral values. In that sense, traditional education was at once liberal and vocational. This type of education, which was passed honestly from one generation to the next, made the society what it was. Islamic education, on the other hand, was received at the hands of the *mwalimou* (teacher). Young boys and girls at a very young age sat at the feet of their *mwalimou* who instructed them in the Koran and made them commit to memory a large number of its verses. Thereafter, students advanced to a higher level receiving their instruction in multifarious subjects including Islamic jurisprudence, history, mathematics, and Arabic grammar and literature at the *jamii* (mosque) or in the *madrasa* (school) that were mostly founded on the Swahili Coast and along the trade arteries into the interior. Islamic education could thus be defined as liberal in its curricula. The chapter concludes that Traditional and Islamic education were as formal and as relevant as western education.

    Chapter Three discusses the role of European missionaries in the development of western education, which has been referred to as "formal education," in Kenya. Initially, and upon their arrival in the region, the European missionaries extended learning the English language to Africans to enable them to read the Bible. They considered their effort in that regard as the essential instrument of their "civilizing mission," for it ultimately won them converts and produced indigenous catechists that converted their fellow citizens to Christianity. The chapter maintains that the subsequent expansion of western education in Kenya was the result of the close cooperation between the missionaries and the colonial government. That education aimed at the creation of a skilled low-level work force, rather than being a generous policy to provide educational opportunities for all Kenyans. The chapter attests that western education was expanded once the British succeeded in placing the region under their hegemony. The railroad from the coast to the interior was constructed, and Kenyan fertile lands were alienated to white settlers. These developments required a large army of semi-skilled local workers. Hence, vocational education to produce farm hands, craftsmen and junior clerical staff became the single dominant feature in the

Introduction 11

curricula of missionary and government schools. Incidentally, missionary and public education gave birth to the *Asomi,* some of whom reacted to the domination and racial discrimination of the colonial government and the paternalism of the missionaries by establishing political organizations and Independent African churches and schools.

Furthermore, the chapter argues that the African American factor in these developments was very significant indeed. It shows clearly that the first Independent African church was established by Molonkett Ole Sempele upon his return from America after having studied in a black trade school in North Carolina, a black theological institute in Virginia, lived among black communities and shared their experiences under segregation. Furthermore, the first nationalists, particularly Harry Thuku, the father of Kenyan Nationalism, were influenced by the ideas of DuBois and Marcus Garvey as copies of the Negro World found their way to East Africa. Again, the chapter sheds light on the fact that the first school, which was independent of missionary and government control, was the Kenyan Independent School and was established by Hon. Mbiyu Koinange who graduated from Lincoln University. These developments testify to the early connection between Africans in the Diaspora and Africans in the continent.

Chapter Four addresses the urgent need for holders of university degrees, that is, for a cadre empowered with liberal education so that it would successfully replace the ruling British personnel now that Kenya was marching steadily towards independence. The chapter argues that the colonial authorities were not concerned in the least with offering Kenyans any form of education beyond High School. It is true that the administration opened three institutions that they called Royal Colleges in Kenya, Uganda, and Tanganyika. However, these so-called colleges were no different from High Schools. They admitted a very small number of students to whom they offered A level certificates in vocational subjects. Cognizant of that critical problem, the African-American trade union and Civil Rights leadership and activists came to the help of their brethren in Kenya. Their first personal contact with Kenyan nationalists materialized when Tom Mboya, the renowned Kenyan political and trade union leader, visited the United States at the invitation the American Committee on Africa (ACOA). The African-American leadership heard from him about the concerns of his country and explored with him the different avenues for assisting Kenya. The chapter attempts to unveil the unmatched commitment of African-Americans to secure scholarships in institutions of higher learning and to find travel funds to airlift Kenyan students to the United States at the time when the Department of State was reluctant to extend a helping hand. In addition, the chapter seeks to identify the African-American leaders and organizations, explore their role in the "Kenya Education Drive," and the forces that inspired them, namely, Pan-Africanism and the Mau Mau Revolution.

Chapter Five will examine the need for university-educated elites to fill critical manpower positions following the departure of the British. Independent Kenya must now depend on its sons and daughters for reconstruction and development. The British left behind an extremely small number of highly qualified Kenyans. Thus, the chapter discusses the continued effort by Kenyan nationalists, African-American leadership and organizations, such as ACOA, as well as the Department of State in helping Kenya. Furthermore, the chapter focuses on the return journey of the American-educated *Asomi* and sheds light on their contributions to their motherland. By way of illustration, the chapter will look closely at some selected profiles of Kenyan students who returned home and those who, for one reason or another, chose to live permanently in the United States and contribute to the so-called Africa "brain drain."

REVIEW OF THE LITERATURE

There are a number of works that address education in Kenya. Daniel Sifuna's *Development of Education in Africa: The Kenyan Experience* and James Sheffield's *Education in Kenya: An Historical Study* provide a broad analysis of the contributions of both the British and the French in their African colonies in general with emphasis on Kenya.[15] Although their works help our understanding of the historical forces that led to the establishment of government schools, neither of them, however, discusses in any detail the educational experiences of Kenyans in the United States. In fact, the works carry no more than a mere paragraph on the significant role that Tom Mboya played in securing scholarships and placing trade union officers and students in colleges and universities overseas. In addition, the works make no mention whatsoever of the African-American contributions to the education of the Kenyan *Asomi*.

David Giuri's article, "The Education System as a Response to Inequality in Tanzania and Kenya," and George E. Urich, "Education and Colonialism in Kenya," are helpful in shedding light on the recommendations of the various education commissions that the administration formed and how the authorities acted on them.[16] However, they do not extend the discussion to cover the rise of the university educated *Asomi*, nor do they mention the nationalist Associations and the independent schools that sprouted in Kenya. Magnus O. Bassey's book, *Western Education and Political Domination in Africa: A Study in Critcal and Dialogical Pedagogy*, focuses on the rise of the western-educated elites in Africa.

However, Bassey focuses mainly on West Africa, particularly Nigeria.[17] Moreover, he does not include any useful discussion of education that Africans gained overseas.

The role of missionaries in Africa has been treated by a number of researchers. M.G. Copon's *Towards Unity in Kenya: The Story of Co-operation between Missions and Churches in Kenya: 1913–1947,* provides a good examination of the development and subsequent expansion of missions in Kenya and their cooperation with the colonial government.[18] It also offers a terse discussion of the reaction of African converts to missionary education and the subsequent development of independent churches and schools. The author, however, does not include the role of missionaries in the creation of the western-educated elites. The edited work of Sylvia M. Jacobs, *Black Americans and the Missionary Movements in Africa,* consists of twelve essays that mainly address the contributions of African-American missionaries in West and South Africa.[19] Although the essays underline the absence of black missionary work in Kenya, they are nevertheless informative concerning the significant task that African-American missionaries undertook in other regions of Africa. Likewise, the work of Leroy Fitts, *The Lott Carey Legacy of African American Missions,* broadens our understanding of African-American missionaries' service in Africa, particularly Liberia.[20]

Kenneth King has written two excellent pieces on African-American missionaries in East Africa. These are "The American Negro As Missionary to East Africa: A Critical Aspect of African Evangelism" and *Pan Africanism and Education: A Study of Race Philanthropy and Education in the Southern States of America and East Africa.*[21] King provided a brief but good examination of the factors that led to the lack of African-American missionaries in the region. He touches on the role of Max Yergan, Secretary of the Colored Work Department of the YMCA in Kenya. King devotes much of the discussion to the efforts of the Philip-Stokes Commission in importing industrial education in East Africa. He draws attention to Mohammad Juma, the Kenyan from the Coast, who rejected vocational education at Tuskegee as an example of Africans reaction to the exclusive vocational education that the missionaries offered in the region. King's studies help greatly in our understanding of the early connections between East Africans and both black and white Americans.

There are three excellent biographical studies on Tom Mboya, the man behind the drive to send Kenyan trade unionists and students to study in the United States. Amongst these are David Goldsworthy's *Tom Mboya: The Man Kenya Wanted to Forget, Tom Mboya's Freedom and After,* and Alan Rake, *Tom Mboya: A Young Man of New Africa.*[22] The works, however, touch briefly on the role that Tom Mboya played in securing scholarships for Kenyan students. On the other hand, Mansfield I. Smith Ph. D. dissertation, "The East Africa Airlifts of 1959, 1960 and 1961," Syracuse University, 1966, focuses mainly on the problem of transporting African students from East and Central Africa and the confrontation between Vice-President Nixon and Senator John F. Kennedy in regard to that issue. It pays insignificant attention to the African-American factor from the beginning of the century to 1963. Moreover, the dissertation does not discuss the significant role that the American-educated *Asomi* such as Hon. Mbiyu Kioinange, Dr. Julius Kiano, Hon. Kariuki Njiiri and others have played in inspiring and helping Kenyan students seek high education in the United States. Again, it does not address the contribution of the American-educated Kenyans to the liberation of their homeland, to the Africanization of the Church, the Civil Service and education or to their general role in the development of the country and securing its independence. Moreover, Mansfield does not pay attention to Traditional and Islamic education. Nonetheless, the dissertation is excellent in reconstructing the events surrounding the airlifts.

Repashy's Ph.D. dissertation, "The Reactions of Kenyan Returnees to their Educational Experiences Abroad," UCLA, 1966, is a collection of statistical data of East African students who studied in the United Kingdom, the United States, India, Canada, the Soviet Union and Ireland. Although the title of the study promises a thorough investigation of the reaction of students who returned to their homes, the dissertation, unfortunately, does not live up to its promise. No profiles were given and no examples of reaction were offered. Furthermore, as far as East African students who attended colleges and universities in the United States are concerned, the data was collected from those who participated in the airlifts only. There is no analysis of how and from whom the students secured their scholarships, nor is there any information about their contributions once they returned to their countries of origin. Moreover, there is no mention whatsoever of the involvement of the African-American leadership in the education of Kenyans in the United States. Yet, the dissertation is informative, though non-specific, about the orientation, academic, and financial problems that students faced in the host countries.

DESCRIPTION OF RESEARCH METHODS

The book brings together a wide range of materials from such fields as African history, African-American history, Kenyan history, Pan-African history, the history of United States foreign policy, and African Diaspora history. The primary materials utilized in the writing of the text were obtained

Introduction 15

from a variety of sources in Kenya and the United States that included archival collections, newspapers, publications, and records of governmental agencies, and personal interviews and correspondence. It was in the summer of 1999 that I conducted field research in Kenya where I collected substantial information from the National Archives, university publications, newspapers, magazines, and personal interviews.

In the United States, the Moorland-Spingarn Research Center at Howard University holds the manuscript collections of Congressman Charles Diggs, Max Yergan, and the American Society of African Culture (ASAC). These collections are a few of the valuable primary sources for this study. The papers of Congressman Charles Diggs contain correspondence, congressional reports, conference papers, and newspaper clippings. Diggs' support for African liberation movements and contacts with African leaders, including Tom Mboya, are documented throughout the collection. Box 25, Folder 1, contains newspaper clippings from the American Free Press for the Bureau of African Affairs regarding liberation movements in Africa, while Folder 10 contains pamphlets of the Charter of the Organization of African Unity. Box 110, Folder 1, comprises a report entitled "U.S. Policy Toward Africa," written by the Caucus of Black Democrats, and Box 194, Folder 10, contains a booklet entitled "Refugee Students from Southern Africa and African Students in the United States" as well as correspondence between Diggs and James Robinson, Director of Crossroads Africa, regarding the itinerary of African students coming to the United States.

Box 194 Folder 15 contains a 1959 letter from William B. Macomber Jr., Assistant Secretary in the Department of State, to Diggs regarding difficulties in transporting Kenyan students to the United States by the Military Air Transport Service. In addition, there is a letter from William X. Scheinman to Diggs about the airlift of Kenyan students to the United States. Attached to the letter is a list of seventy-five Kenyan students with confirmed scholarships and financial aid along with the names of the colleges the students would attend. Also, this folder contains a telegram from Tom Mboya to Diggs regarding efforts to assist Kenyan students in 1959 and a letter from Diggs to Dr. Robert G. Storey, Chairman of the Board of Foreign Scholarships, concerning Diggs interest in expanding the international educational exchange program. Box 194, Folder 16, contains a report by the African-American Student's Foundation (AASF) regarding criticism of the 1960 African Students Airlift that a number of Kenyan leaders had raised. There is information on the arrival of Kenyan students in 1960 as well as several letters concerning the reversal of the decision of the Department of State not to support the students airlift. Moreover, the Folder contains correspondence from Jackie Robinson of the African American Students

Foundation to Congressman Diggs concerning higher education in East Africa. Folder 30 in the same Box has a memo from June Nigh, Senior Staff Assistant of the Committee on Foreign Affairs, regarding the institutions and states participating in the African Scholarship Program of American Universities in 1961, while Folder 36 contains newspaper clippings from the *New York Times* and *Washington Post* on Pan-Africanism.

Box 201 has a letter to Diggs from David M. Abshire, assistant director of Congressional Relations, regarding the 1961 Mutual Education and Cultural Exchange Act. Box 207, Folder 19, carries remarks by Diggs in the House of Representatives entitled "The American Negro's Key Role in Africa," and "United States-African Relations." In Box 208, Folder 1 is found correspondence from African students requesting financial assistance in order to continue their education in the United States. Although most of this correspondence concerned African students in general, it certainly helps our understanding of the condition of Kenyan students in the United States. Box 208, Folder 34, and Box 220, Folder 13, contains correspondence that sheds light on the operatives of the American Committee on Africa (ACOA), and the policy of the United States Agency for International Development toward supporting African students. Furthermore, correspondence from the Tom Mboya Memorial Fund, as well as an article by Mboya in the *New York Times* entitled "The American Negro Cannot Look To Africa for an Escape" are found in Box 307, Folder 22.

On the other hand, Box 206, Folder 2, at Moorland-Spingarn Research Center holds the papers of Max Yergan. The papers show clearly that Max Yergan, Secretary of the Colored Work Department of the Young Men's Christian Association (Y.M.C.A.), was the first African-American to arrive in Kenya. Moreover, they contain brief but valuable information on his services in Kenya and South Africa. Again, they detail his visit to India prior to his work in Africa.

Another important source if primary material is the records of Department of State, which are preserved in the National Archives II in College Park, Maryland, under Decimal Files 1940 to 1973, RG 59, Boxes 365, 403, 1058, 2141, and 6245. The Archives also hold the Political, Defense, and Cultural and Educational files for the years 1940 until 1973. All these collections are most valuable to our understanding of the American foreign policy toward Africa during the Cold War era, the role that the Department of State played in the "African Students Airlifts," and the subsequent development of scholarship programs under the umbrella of the United States Agency for International Development. Additionally, Box 2141 contains notes on the Cultural Society of New Africa, which was founded by Dr. Julius Gikonyo Kiano and Kariuiki Niiri, as well as correspondence from

Tom Mboya to Reverend Martin Luther King Jr. requesting financial assistance for Kenyan students. Furthermore, Box 1058 holds the letter that Hon. Kariuki Njiiri dispatched to President John F. Kennedy requesting his assistance in helping thirty Kenyan students to be trained in the United States in various professions.

Invaluable primary information that sheds light on the connection and cooperation between the black trade union leadership in the United States and that in Kenya is found in the records of the Brotherhood of the Sleeping Car Porters, which are kept in the Library of Congress, Manuscript Division, under Box 97, Folder 1 Africa, and Box 98, Folder 1 Africa. The collections contain documents that reveal the development and subsequent collapse of the training program that was organized by the black leadership for Kenyan trade union officers in the United States. These records also provide a telling insight into the personal relationship between the two Pan-Africanist icons, Tom Mboya and Asa Phillip Randolph, and detail the vigorous effort that both leaders had made toward the Kenyan overseas "Education Drive." Likewise, they contain information about the experiences of a few Kenyan students in the United States. Importantly, the collections preserve the invaluable letters that Tom Mboya, Asa Phillip Randolph, and Dr. Julius Kiano exchanged concerning securing scholarships in colleges and universities in America.

Further original information was collected from Duke University where the papers of Horace Mann Bond, President of Lincoln University, and the records of the American Committee on Africa (ACOA) are preserved on microfilm. The original records are kept at the Armistad Research Center at Tulane University and W.E.B. DuBois Library, University of Massachusetts in Amherst, MA, respectively. The papers of Bond reveal the great number of scholarships that Lincoln offered to African students. They also show Bond's continued assistance, while he was a member of the AMSAC, in providing higher education to African students in the United States and his support for the liberation movements in Africa. The records of the American Committee on Africa (ACOA), on the other hand, have been most useful in detailing its extensive involvement in the "Kenya Education Drive" and the gigantic support of the black leadership in America for the decolonization of Africa.

The *"Open Doors"* reports that were compiled by the Institute of International Education provide statistical data of foreign students, including Kenyans, studying in the United States. The information was complied over a fifty-year period from various colleges and universities across the country. The data is divided into the following categories: nationalities, fields of study, academic levels, and financial support.

During my visit to Kenya in the summer of 1999, I conducted on the spot research at the National Archives in Nairobi where government reports from various ministries during the colonial period and independence are deposited. For example, reports of the Ministry of Economic Planning and Development provided me with information on the urgency of educating Kenyans in overseas universities and colleges to fill critical, highly skilled manpower positions as independence approached. Reports from the Colony and Protectorate of Kenya contain information concerning the educational system in the region prior to independence and the demand for higher educational opportunities. In addition, the documents provided information on the roles that some of the American-educated elites had played upon their return to Kenya. However, access to information from some ministries as well as that relating to various individuals, particularly those still living, is restricted. Furthermore, I looked at the archival collections of local newspapers and magazines including the *Daily Nation, East African Standard,* and *Weekly Review.* I had the opportunity of visiting the *Daily Nation* and meeting its Editor in Chief. Likewise, I consulted the publications of the University of Nairobi and Kenyatta University. Again, I looked into foreign newspapers that carried information about the "Education Drive" and Kenyan students in the United States. Such newspapers included the *Ghanian Chronicle, Uganda Times, New York Times, Chicago Tribune, Time Magazine,* and the *Washington Post.*

While in Kenya, I also conducted interviews with "willing" prominent Kenyan politicians and university professors including Dr. Julius Gikonyo Kiano, Dr. Godfrey Muriuki, Dean of the College of Arts and Science at the University of Nairobi, Dr. Macharia Munene, Chairperson of the Department of History at the United State International University, and Michael Kamau, a former Provincial Commissioner in the Mombasa district who serves as a "Foreign Service Nationalist" at the United States Embassy in Kenya. These individuals provided me with names of western-educated elites in Kenya and a general synopsis of the development of this elite class during the period of decolonization. Dr. Kiano was not hesitant to be interviewed and he provided me with a lengthy interview about his educational experience in the United States and his subsequent involvement with organizing scholarships for Kenyan students.

One of the limitations of this study is the reluctance, indeed the refusal of American-educated elites in Kenya to be interviewed. Despite exhaustive efforts to contact many of them by phone and letters, the response was disappointingly very low. Some did not even respond to my requests, while others politely declined to be interviewed. On the other hand, the excessive pouring of rains made travel to regions outside Nairobi dangerous if not impossible. Besides, many of the American-educated elites had already passed away and their relatives and close friends were not prepared to give information about them. Further still, ongoing political tensions between various ethnic groups at the time of my visit made travel around the country ill advised, so I was warned by the American embassy. Hence, for example, I was unable to interview Mrs. Pamela Mboya, who, at this time, made her base in distant Rusinga Island in Lake Victoria. Moreover, the heightened tensions that resulted from the bombing of the United States Embassy in Nairobi was also a factor in the reluctance of Kenyans to give information to "outsiders."

However, I gained much information through my correspondence with Professor Mugo Gatheru and Mr. George Houser. Both men provided first hand information about the campaign to bring Kenyan students to the United States as well the connections between African Americans and Kenyan trade union leaders. Professor Mugo Gatheru, the renowned Kenyan political scientist and novelist who is now an American citizen living in Sacramento, California, provided me with valuable information regarding the African "brain drain" and why he personally did not return to Kenya after he had completed his education in the United States. He provided eyewitness accounts regarding both the traditional and missionary education that he experienced in his homeland. George Houser, one of the founders of ACOA and its foremost white activist, explained the crucial role that his organization together with Tom Mboya played not only in training Kenyan trade union officers but also in securing scholarships for students to study in the United States. I also tried without success to contact Jane Saffarine, an African American woman who worked directly with Tom Mboya and the Kenyan trade unions. Locally, I interviewed Dr. Langley, citizen of the Gambia, who serves in the Department of African Studies at Howard University, Dr. Mutisya, a Kenyan professor in the Department of Education at North Carolina Central University, and Dr. Batran, a Sudanese, who serves in the Department of History at Howard University to get their views on why some African students did not return to their countries upon graduating from American universities.

I also looked at the registers and records of colleges and universities in the United States, particularly Tuskegee, Hampton, Lincoln, Howard, and Fisk as well as Theological Seminary records at Boydton in Virginia. The records provided me with the names of some of the African students who attended these institutions.

Chapter Two
Traditional and Islamic Education in Kenya

Kenyans, like all other African people, had an educational system prior to the arrival of the Europeans. Students of Kenyan history and society have referred to it as either traditional education, pre-colonial, indigenous, or informal education to distinguish it from western education which is called formal education.[1] Yet, European scholars of the colonial period denied that Africa had any type of education. Indeed, the German philosopher, Hegel, lashed out that Africans were naturally capable of "neither development nor education."[2] That statement was elaborated on by Professor A.P. Newton of the University of London who said before the Royal African Society in 1923 that Africa had no knowledge of writing and therefore had no history before the coming of the Europeans. It is true that scholars of the colonial period discovered that many societies in Africa did not develop the art of reading and writing. Hence, they arrived at the hasty conclusion that Africa as a whole had no history and that Africans had no "education" that could be passed to the succeeding generations. Yet, it is apparent that in reference to Africa and Africans, these "colonial" scholars deliberately ignored the simple fact that education is a method by which culture is transmitted from one generation to the next irrespective of whether or not societies possessed the knowledge of literacy. Education, we are reminded by Daniel Sifuna, is "a process by which people are prepared to live effectively and efficiently in their environment."[3] Traditional African education, though lacking in the knowledge of reading and writing, is indeed as effective, tangible, and definite as education in literate societies in the Western world and elsewhere. Besides, these scholars were quick to dismiss the fact that many African societies had been literate in Arabic ever since the advent of Islam on the continent in the course of the seventh century. The mosques and *madrasas* (*Koranic* schools) that Muslim scholars established throughout Muslim Africa provided solid, advanced education in multifarious subjects using the local vernacular, *Kiswahili,* and particularly Arabic. Indeed, the primary sources for the early history of North Africa, West Africa and East Africa, that is, chronicles and books, have been written in the Arabic language.

There were therefore two types of education in Africa before the arrival of the Europeans, the denial, indeed the ignorance of Western scholars notwithstanding. These were traditional education and Islamic education.

TRADITIONAL EDUCATION IN KENYA

The primary goal of traditional African education was to train the individual to become a productive and useful member of society. It equipped young people with the knowledge, skills, and behavior of their respective groups or societies.[4] Hence, African education was used as an instrument of "survival" whereby members of the society could pass from one generation to the next the means of creating useful citizens and preparing the youth for the lives they must lead in adult society. Speaking from personal experience, Dr. Mugo Gatheru asserts that traditional education "was very, very useful. It encouraged discipline, self-help, responsibility, the importance of survival, courage, awareness of your neighbors, and do's and don'ts."[5] In other words, education in Africa was a continuous, never-ending process. According to Jomo Kenyatta, the late President of Kenya (See Figure 4), African education "begins at the time of birth and ends with death."[6]

Transmitting their culture from one generation to the next proved to be very significant especially since the people could not control totally the natural environment. This made education even more valuable as it allowed the society to adapt to their ever-changing surroundings. The best defense against the often-unforeseen natural disasters such as droughts or floods was group cohesiveness and community responsibility. Therefore, traditional education was set up to foster and to preserve group values, not to simply impart knowledge and skills oriented toward individual advancement. Understandably, there were elements within the system that encouraged competitiveness in intellectual and practical matters, but these were controlled and subordinated to normative and expressive aims. Education, then, was concerned with the systematic molding of the younger generation into norms, beliefs, and collective opinions of the wider society. It also placed a strong emphasis on learning practical skills and the acquisition of knowledge that was useful to the individual and society as a whole. Nonetheless, individual merit and achievement were considered significant criteria for leadership. No individual seeking to become a leader could ignore or surpass any of the phases of traditional education. This was an important incentive to learning. Consequently, indigenous education focused on social responsibility, job orientation, political participation, and spiritual and moral values. Hence, scholars were able to identify three methods of traditional education: by parents and elders, apprenticeship to craftsmen; and by initiation rites.[7]

EDUCATION BY PARENTS AND ELDERS

Early education started in and around the home. Parents taught the children games, riddles, and stories, and gave them specific instructions regarding how to govern their behavior in the presence of relatives and elders. Knowledge of kinship was of absolute importance as it provided an understanding of a person's status and privilege in society. In simpler terms, parents and elders taught children, from birth, that they were part of an extended family network, which they were to love, respect, and honor. Thus, education by parents and elders emphasized a set of specific concerns: acceptable standards and beliefs governing correct behavior as well as unity and consensus.[8] Children were to understand if they misbehaved, they would dishonor their family. If the negative behavior continued, disgrace would be brought to the entire community. Being well acquainted with traditional education was indeed essential. Any departure from the accepted norms and deportment was considered a serious offence.

A division of labor marked the role of the mother and father. Upon birth, the mother took up the responsibility of educating all the children. Once the children reached adolescence, the father became responsible for the education of the boys, while the mother continued with the education of the girls. The elders also participated in the process. Education of children proceeded in various forms. One such form was through activities. The children would draw upon roles relative to their gender under the guidance of parents and elders. Young men would take up the responsibility of architects by constructing huts using grass and mud as well as hunting. Young women performed domestic duties that included cooking, grinding, and gathering wood and water.

Legends, folk tales, and myths, were also used as a method of instruction. Elders used myths to explain religious beliefs, and natural phenomena, such as drought etc. Legends, which were more realistic then myths, were used to explain the origin of the group and historical events that actually occurred. Folk tales, on the other hand, were recanted to recall ancient customs and traditions. Folk tales reiterated the necessity for communal unity, hard work, conformity, honesty, harmony, and responsibility. The folk tales, legends, and myths allowed the children to develop reasoning and sound judgment. They constituted the oldest African art forms that provided the foundation for the wisdom, strength, and values of people.⁹

It is to be mentioned that in contrast to classrooms, that is, formal method of modern or western educational systems, there was no "formal setting" in African education. The only exception, in this respect, occurred during initiation. Parents taught their children by allowing them to perform hands on duties. Children engaged in participatory educational activities through ceremonies, rituals, imitation, recitation, demonstration, farming, fishing, weaving, cooking, carving, knitting, wrestling, dancing, drumming, and storytelling. Children acquired their intellectual training through observation, listening, imitation and participation. Parents taught their children local geography, history, plant and animal behavior, and family genealogy for protective, cultivation, and rearing purposes. Special attention was always given to agriculture as it was and remains the main stay of many African economies. As agriculturalists, the Kikuyu of Kenya, for example, provided their children with knowledge of the land and the seasons. This information was useful as a survival mechanism since Kikuyu society was so dependent on weather conditions and on the suitable of land for cultivation. In this way indigenous education in Africa combined physical training with character-building and manual activity with intellectual training.

APPRENTICESHIP

The education of children through apprenticeship was direct. It was through apprenticeship that children obtained specialized skills to become wood-carvers, tanners, blacksmiths, basket-makers, potters, hunters, beekeepers, or medicine men. Training to enter into one of these craftsmen positions was generally hereditary. In any case, traditional education with regard to specialized skills emphasized learning by practical application.¹⁰ Apprenticeship began with an introductory period under the tutelage of skilled masters, during which time the fresh recruit was taught how to perform menial tasks such as watching, cleaning, and running errands. That was his initial introduction to the tools and materials of the trade. Thereafter, the tasks became increasingly more complex as learning through trial and error, and observation proceeded. In the final stages of the apprenticeship, the recruit was given responsibility for finishing pieces of work, dealing directly with customers and supervising junior apprentices. Training through apprenticeship was more than simply learning the technical skills. In fact, the recruits learned how to manage workshops in order to provide valuable services to the community to the satisfaction of the trainers. The skills acquired benefited both the apprentice and the community.[11] The methodology of learning through apprenticeship was by direct instruction, by example, and doing. In many cases, children, particularly boys, served their apprenticeships away from their parents. To specialize as skilled blacksmiths, or to obtain a high degree of knowledge in weaving or woodcarving required intensive training that, in most cases, could not be provided at home.[12] This would often be the first experience children would have away from their parents.

Unlike their male counterparts, who were trained on farms and in workshops, young women were mainly trained to perform domestic duties at home. They learned to prepare food, make clothing, rear children, and clean homes under the strict and stern guidance of their mothers. At times, these young women could be apprenticed to housewives other than their mothers to obtain the skills in such trades as dying materials, weaving, and plaiting. Thus, the indigenous educational apprenticeship system allowed each person to have the opportunity to be educated and become a productive and useful member of the society.

INITIATION/AGE SETS/AGE GROUPS

The initiation system was also formal and direct. It is often referred to as the rites of passage from childhood to maturity and adulthood. Initiation offered the initiates the opportunity of higher social status in the society. It involved, among the Kikuyu nation, circumcision of boys and girls, as well as training them in group solidarity, values, beliefs, and social responsibility. The council of elders, the highest level of social and political authority, supervised the initiations during elaborate ceremonies.[13] Boys and girls who had undergone circumcision in the same year formed a *riika* (initiation set), viewed one another as biological brothers and sisters, and behaved accordingly.[14]

At any rate, once initiated, the neophytes had to prove themselves worthy in order to be placed in important roles with various responsibilities and privileges in the society. The Kenyan historian, Godfrey Muriuki, himself a Kikuyu, noted one important example of the responsibilities of male initiates, that is, their role as warrior groups defending their territory and preserving their traditions. We learn from him that the warrior class consisted of junior and senior warriors. The senior warriors often acted as advisors because of their experience and knowledge. They did not however relinquish their responsibility of defending the territory or retire from active service until they were satisfied that the junior warriors were experienced enough to take over effectively.[15] Initially, the responsibility of the junior warriors included acting as executive officers to the elders, policing the markets and festivals, arresting habitual criminals, and arranging public gatherings during which rules and prohibitions were disseminated and important announcements were made. Thus, the function of the warrior class was to carry out administrative and military operations on behalf of the entire community. Their duties also included clearing virgin land, herding livestock planting specified crops such as bananas and yams, providing building materials, and building houses and cattle kraals. The warrior class was generally viewed as a privileged elite. It was indeed an armed force not only to defend people and territory but also to enforce law and order in the society.[16]

Upon reaching an appropriate age, senior warriors were expected to terminate their military service and marry. They were now eligible for the next phase of their lives, that is, joining the *kiama* (council of elders), whose main responsibility was the dispensation of justice. In this respect, the *kiama* acted as custodian and guardian of the values and heritage of the society.[17] Perhaps the example of Nandi resistance to British colonialism may provide an insight into the operatives of warrior groups in Kenya. Nandi homeland extends along the North West corridor of Kenya, close to Uganda. Their society was divided into *pororiet* or districts, and each district had its warrior group. However, the groups did not act independently; rather, they acted as one unit at times of war in defense of the homeland or raids on other territories. Hence, defense of the entire homeland, rather than the individual clan, was the collective concern of all warrior groups. All warrior groups were under the command of the *orgoiyoy,* leader. When the British began building the railways through their homeland, the Nandi warrior groups fought them as one man, unlike other groups whose clans resisted the British separately. The cohesion and solidarity of the Nandi, and absence of clan rivalry among them gave the Nandi a strong feeling of pride to such an extent that they considered themselves the superior of the white man. Their resistance began in the 1890s and ended with the cowardly murder of their *orgoiyoy* by colonial forces while on his way to begin negotiations with the British.[18] Henceforth, the colonial authorities banned this highly important warrior group institution throughout the land. They had thus dismantled one of the most essential cornerstones of education and cohesion in East Africa.

Young women initiates did not however form regiments. Nonetheless, they were divided into junior and senior groups. The senior women were charged with the responsibility of instructing the junior groups. This was done to ensure that the junior women conducted themselves in an honorable manner and would not disgrace their group. They were instructed on how to perform tasks specifically entrusted to women such as domestic chores. Women who failed to follow the rigid rules were fined and in extreme cases, they were ostracized from the group.[19]

There is no doubt that the initiation system of education provided the conditions for the transmission of values, beliefs, customs, and religion that were passed to succeeding generations.[20] It remains to be one of the most important vehicles of education in Africa generally, and Kenya in particular.

ISLAMIC EDUCATION IN KENYA

Early in 610 A.D., Muhammad ibn Abdallah, who was then forty years old, announced from his birthplace, the city of Mecca in Western Arabia, that he was chosen by the Almighty God to bring humanity to Islam. The first basic tenet of this religion was the *shahada,* or the pronunciation that "there is no god but Allah and Muhammad is His Prophet." The *shahada* carries the principle that Muhammad was simply a man chosen by the Almighty to deliver a divine mission to humanity. The other principles are: *salat* (ritual prayer), *zakat* (providing to the poor and needy), *saoum* (fasting during the month of *Ramadan*), and *hajj* (pilgrimage to Mecca once in a lifetime). But Islam is not simply a religion of rituals. It also offers "a complete way of life, catering for all the fields of human existence . . . individual and social, material and moral, economic and political, legal and cultural, national and international."[21] In that regard, the Muslims were to form an *umma,* that is, a community of believers guided by the principle of complete equality regardless of social status or wealth. It is therefore not surprising that the teachings of Muhammad threatened the privileged position that the ruling aristocracy of Mecca, that is, its wealthy financiers and merchants, had traditionally held. Hence, the Meccan oligarchy unleashed a wave of persecution against Muhammad and particularly the converts in an attempt to nip this "devastating revolution" in the bud. To escape persecution of his vulnerable followers, Muhammad sent a group of them to take refuge in Africa, in the court of the Ethiopian *Najashi* (King of Kings/Emperor) of the Kingdom of Axum. That flight, which took place in 615 A.D., is referred to in the Muslim annals as the first *hijra* (migration). The second *hijra,* which marks the beginning of the Muslim lunar calendar, took place in 622 A.D. when Muhammad himself migrated with all his followers from Mecca to Medina.

The *hijra* to Africa undoubtedly marks the advent of Islam in the continent even though the Muslim migrants were not known to have preached Islam to the people of the Horn of Africa to any degree. However, it was not until nearly two decades after the death of Muhammad in 632 A.D. that Islam planted a firm footing in the continent. Sometime between 639 and 640 A.D., Arab Muslim armies succeeded in wresting Egypt from the Byzantines. Egypt was thus the first African land to become part of the *umma*. It was however, under the first Muslim dynasty, the *Umayyads* (661–750) that Muslim armies from Arabia marched determinedly into the *Maghrib* (North Africa west of Egypt). By the end of the seventh century, the *Umayyads* succeeded in extending Arab/Muslim hegemony over the entire *Maghrib*. Throughout the period of 681 to 710, the *Umayyads* governed the region with an iron fist. Their main interest was not the dissemination of Islam but the exploitation of the native population, the *Imazigh* (known as Berbers to Western scholars) and the resources of the *Maghrib* to the benefit of their seat of government in Damascus. They did not bring the *Imazihg* into the brotherhood of the *umma*. Rather, they treated them as second-class citizens, inferior to the Arab overlords.[22] In essence, the Umayyad's did not create an environment that would nurture the conversion of North Africans en mass from their traditional religious beliefs to Islam. Nonetheless, the conquest opened the gates for scores of Muslim scholars, particularly the *Kharijites* who sought refuge in these distant lands far away from the center of power.[23] The *Kharijites* preached the return to the full equality and brotherhood of the *umma* of Muhammad and all that it entailed. Little wonder that the *Kharijites* found receptive ears among the disgruntled *Imazigh*. Henceforth, *Kharijite* Islam slowly and steadily won over the hearts of the *Imazigh*. In due time, North Africa became Islamized.

The relationship between North Africa and West Africa from ancient times is well documented by numerous scholars who referred to it as the Trans-Saharan trade in gold and salt.[24] *Imazigh* entrepreneurs organized huge camel caravans, loaded them with salt from the Saharan salt mines (*Taghaza* and later *Taodeni*) and dispatched them to *Bilad El-Sudan* (Land of the Blacks of West Africa). Salt was then exchanged for gold that the *Djula* (Mande traders) brought to the commercial centers in the *Sahel* from gold mines in the south (Bambuk, Bure, Ashanti). This trade peaked during the time of the Empires of Ghana, Mali, and Songhay. However, the *Imazigh* traders, now converted to Islam, brought with them their adopted faith accompanied by a written language, Arabic. They slowly and through a long time succeeded in converting the bulk of the *Djula* to Islam. These West African traders took up the task of converting their fellow men. Many of the *Djula* became scholars (*marabouts*) of Islam on their own right. They opened schools in which Islamic studies and Arabic language were taught. Islam therefore spread in West Africa slowly by West Africans themselves who blended it into their traditional beliefs. In other words, Islam was Africanized in West Africa. Islam found a fertile ground in West Africa, particularly in the *Bilad El-Sudan*, from as early as the beginning of tenth century. Abdal-Rahman Al-Saadi, the author of *Tarikh El-Sudan*, informs us that there was a large Muslim community in the capital city of Ghana and that there were Muslim officials in the imperial court.[25] However, it was during the time of the Empires of Mali and Songhay that the influence of Islam became all pervading. Mansa Musa, the celebrated Emperor of Mali, boosted in Cairo while en route to Mecca in 1325 AD, that Mali was the largest Muslim Empire in the world. Under his leadership, and the leadership of his successors, and the *askias* of Songhay, Islamic learning and literacy in Arabic spread throughout *Bilad El-Sudan*. The Sankoure University of Timbuktu stood shoulder to shoulder with the Institutions of Higher Learning in Tunisia, Egypt and Arabia. Islam and Islamic learning continued to flourish in West Africa in the eighteenth and nineteenth century cultivated by the *Qadiryya* and *Tijanyya* Bortherhoods and by *jihad* leaders such as Uthman dan Fodio, Al-Hajj Umar Tall, Sekou Ahmadu, Maba Diakou and Mahmadu Lamin.[26]

As in West Africa, the primary agents of Islamization in East Africa were Muslim traders, in this case, from southern Arabia and the Persian Gulf. It is to be noted that trading along the basin of the Indian Ocean predated the emergence of Islam. For many centuries, Arab merchants from the southern part of the Arabian peninsula as well as Persian (Iranian) traders from Shiraz (in Western Persia/Iran) regularly visited the East African Coast stretching from Somalia in the north to Mozambique in the south. Driven by the monsoon winds, Arabian and Persian ships arrived at the towns of *Bar Al-Zanj* (East Africa Coast of the Zanj/Bantu) to trade in varied items, most important of which were gold, ivory, iron, tortoiseshell, spices, incense, ostrich feathers and slaves. It appears that, at first, small numbers of these traders came to settle permanently as individuals, not families, on the coastal ports. The expansion of the Muslim Empire in Asia and North Africa in the seventh and eighth centuries led to a tremendous increase in the trade of the Indian Ocean, which in turn contributed to the founding of numerous towns on *Bar Al-Zanj*, of which Mombasa on the Kenyan coast stands out. The growth of trade and the development of ports along the East Africa Coast were accompanied by increased migrations of Muslim Arab and Persian traders who arrived as individuals as well as families.[27] Other Muslims from Arabia and Persia who fled political persecution vented on them by the *Umayyads* and the *Abbasids* augmented the number of the trading immigrant community. Many of the newly arrivals intermarried with the native Bantu population. The result the intermarriages was the birth of a Muslim community (*taifa*) on the *Sahel* (Coast) of East Africa known as the *Waswahili*. The *Waswahili* had a distinct Islamic/Bantu culture (the *Swahili* culture) and an Arab/Persian/Bantu language known as *Kiswahili*.

It seems that Islam was for a long time confined to the immigrants. However, with the rise of the *Swahili taifa* and the acceptance of Islam by the neighboring Bantu, Islam and Islamic education spread widely along the East African Coast. From there, Islam and Muslim culture gradually penetrated into the hinterland. It was a slow process of Islamization in which Islam married into the traditional African beliefs. Muslim scholars (*mwalimou*) of the coast, supported by merchants, opened *Koranic* schools, known as *madrasa*, for the education of the children, and ran mosques for the faithful in the commercial ports and along the trade routes leading to the interior. In fact, the mosque served, at the same time, as a school. In their class- rooms, students studied the Holy *Koran*, the *hadith* (traditions of Prophet Muhammad), the *sharia* (Islamic law), Arabic grammar and literature, mathematics, and history. So pervasive was Arabic, the language of the *Koran*, that the *Pate Chronicle* and the *Chronicle* of *Kilwa*, collections of the history of the coastal people in Kenya, were written originally in that language after writing in Arabic was introduced in the regions of Mombasa, Malindi, Lamu, Vanga, and Kilwa. These ports were the centers of learning in Kenya before missionary and government schools were established. It was from these centers that scores of scholars, *sheikhs, mualimous,* poets, and politicians graduated.[28]

Finally, one would say that in the pre-colonial traditional and Islamic educational experience, the child was the responsibility of the entire community, particularly the family, which helped him/her to develop a sense of social solidarity, ethical values, harmony and commitment to the society. The African family consists of the entire community or village. This kind of communal participation brings to life the African proverb that "it takes a whole village to raise a child." Consequently, the individual is considered to be part of the group (*taifa*), and the interest of the group takes precedence over the interest of the individual. This helped to perpetuate the idea of cooperation and unity (*asabyya*) in order to maintain responsible relationships between the group and the environment.

African education covered all aspects of life—religion, medicine, music, language, mathematics, trade, and commerce. It was at once vocational and liberal. It was community oriented requiring total involvement and active participation so that relevant skills, knowledge, values, and attitudes were smoothly and authentically transmitted for the development of the individual and the society. In this sense, it was a democratic system of education oriented towards an egalitarian society.²⁹ African education, therefore, was as complete and significant as education in western cultures.³⁰

As long as traditional African societies were not imposed upon by western influence, traditional and Islamic education flourished as a means of handing down the culture and value systems to future generations of Africans. However, the advent of colonialism signaled the progressive breakdown of the traditional African but not Islamic system of education, which was left untouched. Western education that the white missionaries pioneered was essentially geared towards the creation of Christianized Africans that disseminated the Faith among their people, and provided the labor force for the newly imposed colonial rule with its economic system and infrastructure. While it is generally argued that western education had led to the deterioration of traditional African belief and value systems, the "spirit of traditional education" has nonetheless remained strong, particularly in the Independent African Churches, the Independent African Schools, and in Islamic *madrasas*. That spirit has surly influenced the content of western education by preserving the vital elements of the old society.

Islamic education undoubtedly continued to be vibrant along the coastal areas of Kenya throughout the colonial period and beyond. Because of the highly charged sensitivities, the authorities, Christian in their beliefs, did not interfere in any way with Islamic education during the entire period of colonial rule. Hence, the local communities without government assistance or patronage ran the *madrasas*. The impact of Islamic education in the interior was confined to localities along the major commercial arteries. Islamic education provided the coastal *Waswahili* people in particular with formal instruction in reading and writing, and in Islamic subjects including history, geography, mathematics, medicine, astronomy, and literature. It was without doubt instrumental in the development of formally educated members of east African societies. Among those who attended the Islamic *madrasa*, are great academicians such as Professor Ali Mazrui and Professor Ahmad Idhra Salim, now Kenyan Ambassador to the Sultanate of Oman. These professors and others who were educated in the *madrasa* found their way to western education in Kenya and overseas.

Moreover, indigenous and Islamic education, as well as the Independent Churches and Schools provided an educational environment for living. They ensured that members of the society were united and responsible in accordance with traditional values and beliefs or governed by the principles and practices of their Africanized Islam. As a result, Kenyan societies maintained governance over themselves and passed their cultural belief systems from one generation to the next.

Chapter Three
The Rise of the *Asomi*

MISSIONARY AND GOVERNMENT EDUCATION

The term formal education, that is, modern or western education has been used in reference to the systems of education that came to Africa first with the Christian missionaries and afterwards with the colonial governments.[1] There is no doubt that the Christian faith had a long and continuous presence in the continent. We have always been reminded that "Jesus himself went to Egypt (as) asserted by St. Mathew in recounting the story of the flight of Joseph, Mary and the child from the wrath of Herod."[2] Indeed, Christianity entered Africa in the first century of our era. It was introduced, so it is claimed, by St. Mark, writer of the second Gospel, who founded in Alexandria, Egypt, the first Church in Africa. The beacon of Christianity showed brightly from the Alexandria church over the Nile Valley, Ethiopia and westwards into the *Maghrib*. Besides St. Mark, Christianity produced super African Christian leaders including Simon of Cyrene, said to have carried the cross of Jesus, Tertulian of Carthage who was the first to use the word Trinity, Antony of Nubia who is claimed to have founded hermit life, and St. Augustine, Bishop of Hippo.[3]

However, this ancient Christianity in Africa lost ground to Islam, which began its advance into the continent from the middle of the seventh century. By the fifteenth century, the entire Nile Valley was Islamized except for a minority Christian group in Egypt that came to be known as the Copts. It also survived in Ethiopia among large segments of the population and remained as a state religion until the fall of Emperor Haile Selassie in 1974.

Yet, another phase of Christianity began with the arrival of the Portuguese Jesuits in the wake of the Atlantic slave trade. In fact, by 1494 Portugal took the responsibility of conversion and commerce in the "newly discovered lands east of a meridian 100 leagues (one league is 3 miles or 4.8 km) west of the Cape Verde Islands," said to have been granted to it by the Papal Bulls that Pope Alexander VI.[4] Prince Henry was then the governor of Ceuta on the Northwestern tip of Morocco. The Portuguese had captured this port city in 1415 and used it as a base for their "exploration" of the west coast of Africa. All the same, the work of the Jesuits was concentrated on the three West African Islands of Cape Verde, Sao Tome and Principe, as well as coastal enclaves, particularly Luanda in Angola. The islands, enclaves, the Highlands of Ethiopia and South Africa remained strong holds of Christianity for the entire period of the Atlantic slave trade. However, the nineteenth century witnessed intensive pressure by humanitarian and evangelical forces in Europe aimed at the abolition of the Atlantic slave trade. It was this anti-slavery campaign that brought a new crop of missionaries to the African scene. But it was not until the 1840s that these forces turned their attention to East Africa as a result of the travels in the region of David Livingston of the London Missionary Society.[5] Livingston's writings and speeches inspired the European evangelical and humanitarian forces. He drew attention to the inhumane Arab slave trade in East Africa and the poverty and humiliation it caused African people. His cry that "for every slave exported, ten other Africans lost their lives" horrified his listeners and readers and inspired them to "redeem" the Africans. Livingston demanded the opening of a "path for commerce and Christianity" in the continent that would, he so believed, bring the continent closer to Europe and to Christianity.[6]

The British government with an eye on India and the commerce of the Indian Ocean, made unsuccessful attempts with the Sultans of the Omani Empire at their headquarters in Zanzibar, off the coast of East Africa, to limit the size of the Indian Ocean slave trade. For that purpose, the British appointed Colonel Atkins Hamerton as Consul to Zanzibar. Although Hamerton managed to persuade Sultan Sayyed Said (d. 1865) to sign the "Hamerton Treaty" in 1845, which sought to limit slavery within the Sultanate, neither the Sultan nor his successors were willing to enforce it.[7] Abolition of slavery was detrimental to the Zanzibar economy, which depended on slave labor on its clove plantations on the Island and grain plantations along the Coast. The British however applied both diplomatic pressure and threats on the third Sultan, Sayyed Bargash, forcing him in 1873 to ban maritime slave trading.

At the mean time, white missionaries stepped up their presence on the coast of East Africa, while the explorers traversed the interior. The first missionaries to arrive in 1844 at Mombasa on the Kenyan coast were three German evangelists dispatched by the Church Missionary Society (CMS). These

The Rise of the Asomi   35

were Johann Ludwig Krapf, Johann Rebmann, and J.J. Erhardt. Krapf, who served in Ethiopia. Two years later, in 1846, Krapf was joined by his countryman, Rev. Johann Rebmann, and in 1849 by Rev. J.J. Erhardt. The latter, however, died soon after arrival. Krapf and Rebmann established in 1847 the first white mission station in East Africa among the *mijikenda* (nine groups) at Rabai village (Freretown), about 25 km North West of Mombasa.[8] Rabai served several purposes: proselytism, a haven for freed slaves, and a platform from which missionaries launched their evangelical mission into the interior. About forty-five years later, in 1891, the Holy Ghost Fathers established their first missionary station in Mombasa itself.

Rabai community drew scores of coastal Bantu Africans, particularly from the *mijikenda,* who remained untouched by Islam. Most of the recruits, during this early phase, so Asare Opoku asserts,

> would appear to be those who were regarded by the Africans as social outcasts, and the downtrodden such as lepers and others who suffered various forms of social disabilities in traditional African societies. Included in this category were those who had broken certain traditional taboos and were fleeing from persecution.[9]

The flocking of such people to the mission centers was yet another reason behind the racist attitude of Europeans toward Africans. It added to the belief that Africans were culturally backward, miserable human beings and that the white man was justified in his efforts to uplift and transform the continent and its people through conversion and education into a modern Christianized/westernized society. In fact, the first Kenyan convert to be baptized by the CMS evangelists was, Mringe, a dying cripple of Giriama ethnic background.

In addition, Rabai, together with its sister station at Bagamoyo in Tanganyika, became the most important colonies for freed slaves.[10] Some of the slaves came from Bombay, India, while others were rescued by the British from slave ships that had originated in Southern or Central Africa. The first batch of the so-called "Bombay Africans," 150 of them, arrived at Rabai in 1875. In time, Rabai became the largest freed slave compound in East Africa. It teamed with coastal Africans and freed slaves. The resettlement of the "Bombay Africans" was an attempt by the British government and missionaries to establish communities for freed Africans in East Africa comparable to the settlement of the "Atlantic freed slaves" in Liberia and Sierra Leone.[11]

The Rabai community received instruction in reading and writing in English, Bible studies, and various skills and crafts such as carpentry and gardening. Nevertheless, the teaching of Christianity and conversion remained the prime goal of the missionaries. The graduates were fully expected to become religious teachers, "Christian Soldiers," to bring the Gospel to their kinsmen and rescue Africa from fetishism, animism, superstition, ancestor and idol worship, polytheism, and polygamy. They were to stamp out the "despicable" practices, such as, rites of passage, drumming and dancing, birth and death rituals, pouring of libations and all customs and traditions that the European missionaries deemed pagan. In other words, their responsibility was to bring Africans to Christ, imbibe them with European values, and train them in vocational crafts. Hence, education in Rabai and other missionary centers that sprang up at a later date could be described as practical and aimed at production. It was correctly noted that both lines of educational thinking, ranging from advocacy of abstract training of the mind to a commitment to training in agriculture and craftsmanship were firmly rooted in the formal mission education since its inception in Kenya.[12] Undoubtedly, the elements of individualism, competition, and elitism that were often not a critical factor in traditional African societies were strongly expressed ever since the establishment of the early missionary schools. At any rate, the graduates of Rabai, that is, the "Bombay Slaves" and coastal Africans constituted the first crop of the *Asomi*, that is, the western-educated elites.

It must be noted that the attitude of the missionaries at Rabai and other evangelical centers toward all their African disciples was marred by racial prejudice. The missionaries considered the African a primitive human being who could never fully be Europeanized, his conversion to Christianity notwithstanding. On the other hand, they consciously discriminated between their students from the free Bantu of the coast and the rescued "Bombay Africans." Unlike the Bantu, most of the "Bombay Africans" mastered different languages, including English, and possessed various skills in trade, carpentry and farming. Accordingly, they received better treatment from the Europeans than the indigenous coastal Africans. This discriminatory treatment fostered resentment and strained the relationship between the two groups. Albeit, the "Bombay Africans" appreciated the freedom vouchsafed upon them by the Europeans and made good of their skills. Furthermore, since the Europeans offered them a home and lifted them from slavery, they became closer to them than to their coastal colleagues. Missionary education thus offered the "Bombay Africans," and of course other students, the opportunity to become ministers, journalists, trade unionists, craftsmen, and junior civil servants particularly during the colonial period. It has been noted that European accounts on the social conditions and geography of East Africa were based primarily on reports and journals of "Bombay Africans" such as William Jones. Other significant Bombay graduates of Rabai were David George, Jacob Wainwright, and Matthew Wellington. All of these men helped in the establishment of missions in East Africa. In other words, missionary education in East Africa, and in the whole of Africa for that matter, produced western-educated African elites that eventually became the intellectual and spiritual equals to the Europeans.[13]

One cannot but note at this juncture the similarities between the fortunes of the "Bombay Africans" and their counterparts in West Africa, that is, the freed Atlantic slave communities that the British and Americans established in Sierra Leone and Liberia. Both the Americo-Liberians and Sierra Leone Creoles received preferential treatment from the missionaries and the British administration vis-à-vis indigenous Africans because of their susceptibility and readiness to accept the patronage of the missionaries and the colonial administration. They were educated by the church and enjoyed the protection of their "liberators," the British.[14]

Evangelists of the Church Missionary Society were joined in due time by other colleagues deployed by the University Mission to Central Africa, the Holy Ghost Fathers, the London Missionary Society, the Anglican Church, the Scottish Free Church, the Gospel Missionary Society, and the African Inland Mission. In fact, the last decades of the nineteenth century witnessed the tremendous flow of missionaries from the coast into the interior of the continent. The thrust was made possible by the opening up of the hinterland by explorers and geographers, the discovery of new medicine to combat tropical diseases that killed Europeans and the establishment of European rule. For sure, once the Europeans dug in, their colonial governments considered the missions true partners sharing the same values, culture and aspirations in transforming Africa through establishing European hegemony and extending Christian education to the natives.[15] Hence, the colonial authorities provided the missionaries with protection and offered them huge subsidies. Consequently, numerous churches and missionary schools sprang up in Kenya and the whole of Africa. In fact, the church also served as a school. Thus, with the relative increase of schools, missionary education became available to a section of Kenyans.[16]

Missionary education in Africa, from the point of view of its European bearers, was a great success ever since its inception. Hence, the Anglican Church newsletters in 1876 proudly described the "African Christian Soldiers" as "the best examples of what black men may become." But a few years later, that is, by 1881, the same men were dismissed as being "idle and slovenly in their habits and their women spend most of their time gossiping and sleeping." This change in attitude is reflective of the growing menace caused by African men of the cloth to the privileged position that the European missionaries had enjoyed. African evangelists aspired to positions higher than that of priesthood—positions that were exclusive to European missionaries. No European missionary was prepared to concede this to Africans for it implied subordination to a "lesser" human being. Furthermore, African missionaries demanded the Africanization of the Church in worship, theology, and understanding. According to them, Christianity ought not to be presented to Africans as it was understood and interpreted by Europeans. Such were certainly revolutionary demands that shocked European evangelism to the core for they entailed the blending of Christianity with what the missionaries described as "pagan" practices of Africans, and subordination of Whites to Blacks. Further still, African priests resented the fact that European missionaries were paid three times as much as African ministers and demanded equal pay. They decried the audacity of the British missionaries who appointed themselves as legal magistrates in order to administer civil and criminal law on Africans. In reality, African ministers aspired to reconstitute the environment that made the superiority and authority of the European missionaries absolute.[17]

The response of the European missionaries was dramatic. They stopped teaching English to their African disciples, decreased the school day to a half-day, and forced students to spend all their time on the farms. At any rate, the retaliation of African ministers to the refusal of the European missionaries to Africanize the church and offer them higher positions arrived in the form of the birth of Independent African Churches (*Akurinu* in Kukuyu language) under African leadership. At the same time, missionary education led to the rise of western-educated elites, the *Asomi* that carried the torch of nationalism.

A number of independent African churches rose in Kenya, some of which cut across ethnic boundaries such as *Dini ya Nsambwa* (Church of the Ancestors). Other churches included the *Nomiya Luo Mission,* which was founded in 1910 by John Owallo among the Luo. The *Nomiya Luo Mission* adopted biblical circumcision for men as a necessary tool of salvation, a previously unknown tradition among the Luo.[18] One may also note the following independent churches: the *Dini ya Roho* (Holy Ghost Church), founded in 1927 among the Abaluyia by Jakobo Buluko and Daniel Sande, the *Joroho* (Holy Ghost) that was founded by Alfa Odongo among the Luo, and the Independent African Church, founded in 1929 among the Maasai in Narok by Ole Sempele.[19]

The rise of the Independent Maasai African Church (IMAC) under the leadership of its founder, Molonkett Olokorinya Ole Sempele of the Maasai, provides an early Kenyan "feel" toward the plight of African-Americans in

America and an insight into the disenchantment of African missionary educated elites with racist, white dominated Christian societies in Kenya and the United States. It is also a reflection of the fear of its leadership that the same horrifying fate experienced by African-Americans in the United States would eventually reach them at their own home in Kenya, which was now steadily being dominated by racist white settlers, white colonialists, and white missionaries. It must be remembered that the Maasai were the very first group in Kenya whose land was taken by European settlers. Importantly, the birth of the IMAC shows clearly the influence of black institutions of learning and black communities in the United States on church leaders in the continent, a testimony to the emerging Pan-African movement and sentiment.

Ole Sempele was one of the first Maasai that missionaries of the African Inland Mission (now the African Inland Church) converted to Christianity and educated at Thogoto School. In 1908, he accompanied his (AIM) friends, the Stauffachers, to America where he attended a trade school for Blacks in North Carolina. Also, he joined the Boydton Academic and Bible Institute, which was established in 1878 in Boydton, Virginia, for "area blacks."[20] Throughout his studies in Kenya, North Carolina, and Virginia, Ole Sempele held favorable opinion about the positive role that Christianity played in America. However, his attitude toward "white Christianity" changed dramatically when he heard of the lynching of 230 African-American Christians by white supremacists. He instantly resented, not the Faith itself, but the hypocritical, racist attitude of its white bearers. Upon his return to Kenya, he immediately broke away from the AIM to found his Independent Maasai African Church.[21]

It must be said that it was not until Kenya attained independence that a number of African priests rose to the highest level in the white established church. Amongst them was Archbishop Festo Olang (b. 1914) who hailed from the Abaluyia nation. Rev. Festo Olang was educated in the CMS School in Maseno and at Alliance High. Thereafter, he attended St. Paul's Theological College in Limuru (1944–45), and was subsequently ordained as a Deacon in Nairobi. In 1948, he received a British Council scholarship that helped him attend Wycliffe Hall, Oxford, and Holy Trinity Parish in Bristol. In 1951, he became Dean for Central Nyanza and in 1955 was consecrated as Assistant Bishop of Kampala, Uganda. Thereafter, he became Bishop of Maseno Diocese, and in 1970 was elected as the first African Archbishop of the Anglican Church in Kenya.[22] Another Abaluyia, His Eminence Maurice Michael Otunga (b. 1923), likewise rose to the high post of Cardinal ten years after Kenya gained her independence. Otunga's father was a traditional paramount chief of the Bakhone who never converted to

Christianity. His mother, Rosa Namisi, was a renowned diviner. Nonetheless, Otunga was baptized at the age of twelve. He studied at Mangu High, one of the oldest Catholic institutions in Kenya before he attended St. Mary's Seminary in Kakamega and St. Mary's Seminary in Gbaga, Uganda. Thereafter, he joined the Pontifical College in Rome. Cardinal Otunga completed his major seminary training in Italy and was ordained priest on October 3, 1950. He went on to finish his studies at the College of Propaganda Fide before he returned to Kenya to join the Kakamega Seminary where he taught Theology from 1951 to 1956.[23] During the same period, he became diocesan chancellor and staff member of apostolic delegation in Anglophone Africa. On November 17, 1956, Pope Pius XII nominated him Titular Bishop of Tacape (1957–1960) and Auxiliary Bishop of Kisumu. Three years later, on May 21, 1960, Pope John XXIII elevated him to Bishop of Kisii and on November 15, 1969, Pope John Paul VI appointed him Titular Archbishop of Bomarzo and Coadjutor of Nairobi, with the right of succession.[24] On October 24, 1971, Otunga replaced Rev. John Joseph McCarthy as Archbishop of Nairobi. Two years later, on March 5 1973, Pope John Paul VI enthroned him Cardinal, receiving the red biretta and title of St. Gregorio Barbarigo *"alle Tre Fontane."* Cardinal Otunga, Kenya's first black Bishop, Archbishop and Cardinal, passed away on Saturday, September 7, 2003, of renal failure.[25]

A number of highly ranked Kenyan evangelists received advanced theological education in black seminaries in the United States. Amongst these were Henry John Okullu and Reverend Thomas Johnson Kalume. Both men climbed to the supreme level of Bishop after independence. Okullu, a Luo from Kisumu, was born to Ong'go Adero and Ms. Ngore Nyar in 1929 in Ramba village, Nyanza Province. He was baptized at the age of 18 and was given the name John Henry. He attended Kima Primary but soon abandoned his studies because of the harsh treatment and discriminatory attitude of his white instructors. Okullu then left for Uganda and worked with the East African Railways and Harbors while continuing missionary training at Bishop Tucker Theological College (1956–1958). He was ordained Deacon in 1957 and priest in 1958. Okullu then traveled to the United States and gained a degree of Bachelor of Divinity at the then "all-Negro" institute, Virginia Theological Seminary, in Lynchburg in 1965. He returned to Uganda to become editor of *New Day,* a Christian newspaper owned by the Church of Uganda. His firebrand editorials in which he opposed one-party political systems as being "tyrannical and unworkable . . . made life uncomfortable for President Milton Obote (of Uganda) who largely favored single party politics."[26] Okullo finally returned to Kenya in 1969 to serve as editor of *Target* (in English) and *Lengo* (in *Kisawhili*) that was published by the National Council of Churches of Kenya. Once again, his editorials pronounced his call for truly democratic multi-party political systems and his objection to monolithic politics. In 1971, Okullu was consecrated the first Kenyan Provost of All Saints Cathedral in Nairobi, and from 1974 occupied the post of Bishop of Maseno South Diocese. Throughout his life, Bishop Okullu used the pulpit effectively "to poke barbs at public institutions, including the Church, which did not live up to the people's expectations." He was accused by the Kenyan political establishment of being a "leftist," a charge that he simply dismissed by saying, "I do not know what it means to be a leftist, I just preach the truth."[27] In 1973, Bishop Okullu received an honorary Doctor of Divinity degree from is alma mater, Virginia Theological Seminary, for his "restless concern for freedom in Christ." Dauti Kahura of the *East Africa Standard* says of him, "Bishop John Henry Okullu was every inch the church minister—preaching to his flock the virtues of truth, social justice, honesty and, above all, Christian values."[28] Henry John Okullu, the "leftist" Bishop who graduated from the black Theological institution, Virginia Theological Seminary, passed away in March 1999.

A second Kenyan minister, Reverend Thomas Johnson Kalume from the Kamba nation received his advanced missionary education in the United States. He attended Jilore Primary, Bate Sector School and Katoleni Boarding School in Kenya. In 1950, he joined Kagumo Teachers College and the United Theological College in Lamuru (1962–1964). Thereafter, he went to the United States where he received a Masters degree in Religious Education from Union Theological College in 1967. He was ordained as the first Kamba Bishop in 1967.

The collective drive of the independent African churches, sometimes referred to as Breakaway Churches, of Kenya and other sister churches in Africa, brought Christianity home where African ministers interpreted the Bible in accordance with their own independent reading of it. Ironically, by rendering the Bible into African languages, the European missionaries, without realizing it, helped break down their monopoly over Christian spirituality in Africa by their own hands.

On the other hand, it was from the womb of Missionary education, in conjunction with colonial education, that western-educated African elites, the *Asomi,* emerged. Missionary schools provided the vehicle through which Kenyans not only converted to Christianity but also learned the languages, customs, and methods of the Europeans. In addition, government schools provided a somewhat broader learning in arithmetic, geography, and history.[29] Thus, besides religious leaders, both systems, which Kenyans call "enabling education," produced African elites who filled all kinds of subordinate positions in the colonial administration. Importantly, it was from the midst of this group of westernized African elites that colossal figures sprang up to challenge European presence, domination, and rule in Africa. A crop of missionary school graduates not only spearheaded the radical nationalist movements in Africa but also inherited power from the Europeans. These *Asomi* included Harry Thuku, father of Kenyan nationalism, the super Kenyan politician, Tom Mboya, *Mzee* Jomo Kenyatta, the first Prime Minister of Kenya, Hon. Mbiyu Koinange, Dr. Julius Kiano, Hon. K.K. Njiiri, Jaramogi Oginga Odinga, Daniel Toroitich arap Moi, the second President, Jones Beauttah, Jonathan Okiwiri, Jeremiah Awori, Reuben Omulo, Simon Nyendi, Jesse Kariuki, John Machuchu, Joseph Kang´ethe, to name a few.

There is no doubt that the missionaries and the colonial government were bedfellows. In fact, the march of the European powers into Africa owes greatly to the incessant appeals by the missionaries. Civilizing the natives and promoting commerce and agriculture were beliefs shared by both the missionaries and European policy makers. The missionaries were of the opinion that the task, "the White Man's Burden," could be successfully accomplished under the protection of European governments, preferably their home governments, in territories in which they operated. Hence, British missionaries in East Africa called upon their Imperial Government to intervene in the region. It is thus correctly stated, "on the whole it may be said that Christian missions in Africa were the ally and adjunct of European imperialism and the activity of missionaries were part and parcel of the advance and penetration of the West into the non-Western World."[30] Indeed, the immediate educational policy of the British administration in Kenya did not differ from that of the missionaries for both systems sought to produce religious converts, teachers, laborers for white farms and junior civil service positions.

The initial presence of the British along the coast of East Africa starting in the last years of the eighteenth century was an addition to their greater interests in India and the Indian Ocean trade.[31] It was consolidated further by the ambition to limit the scope of the Arab slave trade of the Indian Ocean, which was controlled by Sultan Sayyed Said in Zanzibar and substitute it with legitimate commerce. To this end, the British Consul General in Zanzibar, Colonel Hamerton, exerted intensive diplomatic pressure on the Sultan and later resorted to an outright threat. British commercial interests along the coast at that time were mainly in the hands of William Mackinnon, a member of the Scottish Free Church (SFC). Mackinnon and his partner, Robert MacKenzie, conducted business under the name Mackinnon, MacKenzie & Company. By 1862, the company, which rapidly became one of the largest shipping companies in the world, was renamed the British India Steamship Navigation Company. It conducted trading activities around the coast of India and Burma, the Persian Gulf, and the East Africa Coast.

In 1873, the company established a mail service between Aden in Southern Arabia and Zanzibar. Mackinnon established a good relationship with Sultan Barghash, and in 1878 succeeded in winning a lease for a territory extending 1,150 miles from the coast to the eastern province of the Congo Free State. On April 18, 1888, Mackinnon requested and was granted a charter for his company by the British government. The newly chartered company came to be known as the Imperial British East Africa Company (IBEAC). However, on July 1, 1895, the British government officially took over control of the company and the region. From this point forward, the region came to be known as British East Africa Protectorate. Thus, an effective British presence in the region was established.[32] Furthermore, the association of Mackinnon of the Scottish Free Church with the British colonial authorities shows clearly the partnership between the white church and the forces of colonialism in Africa.

However, the British were, for the time being, content with establishing company control over the Kenyan coast. This provided a strategic ground to safeguard their interests in India and East Africa as the Germans and French steadily penetrated the region. Yet, the British showed little interest in establishing a colony. However, the appearance of the Germans and the French in the region forced them to seek effective means to protect their interests. Consequently, they dispatched Fredrick Lugard to Buganda in 1890 to place it under the Company's protection. Although Lugard was able to gain the cooperation of the *Kabaka* (King) of Buganda, the British government quickly intervened to establish a protectorate over the entire region, which by 1895 came to be known as the British East Africa Protectorate.[33] At that time, Kenya was simply considered a supply route to Uganda whose societies were recognized as being highly developed and centralized. Kenyan societies, on the other hand, were seen to be defiant and wild.[34]

Late in the nineteenth century, the British developed the Ugandan Railway that connected Lake Victoria with the coast.[35] The primary objective for its construction was to promote the exploitation of East Africa's economic resources. Additionally, the railway strengthened British control in East Africa and laid the foundation for the colonization of the region by white settlers, from Britain, Australia, and New Zealand. A group of Afrikaners also came from South Africa, in the hope of establishing a colony modeled after the South African colony.[36] The appeal of Kenya to white settlers was obvious. The climate in the Kenyan Highlands was congenial and there existed huge tracts of fertile land and in the eyes of white settlers, this land was underused and under populated. Again, the railroad brought major changes to the demography of the region. Thousands of immigrants came from India and other regions of Asia to construct the railway. A huge Asian community subsequently rose in Kenya and Uganda that continued, after independence, to play a significant role in commerce and urban real estate supported by a considerable amount of lobbying influence from the Indian High Commissioner Office in London.[37]

Once British rule was established in East Africa with the blessings and support, and quite often at the behest of the missionaries, and the Highlands were firmly in the hands of white settlers, a new money economy based on plantations emerged in Kenya, the foundation having been laid down for decades in missionary schools. It was Saint Austin's missionary school, which was established in Nairobi in 1898, that pioneered the growing of Arabica coffee on the volcanic slopes of Nairobi. Subsequently, the cultivation of coffee expanded at an astonishingly rapid pace as coffee farms owned and run by white settlers as well as the missions that sprang up throughout the Highlands. By 1920, coffee, the black gold, turned out to be the leading cash crop of Kenya. The other cash crops were tea, pyrethrum, and sisal. Hence, the emerging money economy, the colonial administration, the efficient communication systems—railway, ports, and mail and telegraph services, that were subsequently developed, and the emergence of urban centers, such as Nairobi and Machakos, required a huge cadre of trained Africans to run them. A skilled and semiskilled African labor force became necessary and urgent particularly as British colonial policy demanded that each colony maintained itself.[38]

For that purpose, the colonial administration subsidized missionary schools to provide the needed workforce. However, it soon became clear that missionary education, because of its heavy concentration on religious subjects and the relatively modest number of mission schools, was unable to produce the huge army of African workers the colony required. In fact, by 1910 there were only thirty-five missionary schools in the whole colony. To solve the problem, the British established a commission headed by J. Nelson Frazer who was brought from India in 1909 to serve as advisor to the colonial authorities. The Frazer Commission recommended a dual-educational system: academic for Europeans and vocational for Africans, notwithstanding that the colonial government had been all along solely concerned with the educational provisions for the children of European settlers. In fact, the first schools for European students, the Prince of Wales and the Duke of York for boys, and the Duchess of York for girls, were opened in 1902 to prepare white students for administrative and professional positions. The Asian community opened its first school, the Duke of Gloucester, in 1910 where students received both academic and commerce oriented instruction that prepared them for positions as accountants, businessmen, and technicians.

The Frazer Commission, in other words, recommended that education be racially segregated. Accordingly, the colonial authorities established the first government school exclusively for Africans in Machakos town in 1913. The school provided technical and industrial education based on the model of African-American schools in the United States. At any rate, the Frazer Commission set the standard for education policy in Kenya for the colonial era and provided guidelines that the 1924 Phelps-Stokes Commission and the 1949 Beecher Commission followed faithfully.[39] The Phelps-Stokes Commission emphasized the need to train African youths in agriculture and craftsmanship for the benefit of Africans in the rural areas. The Beecher Commission stressed a curriculum for Africans that prepared them to work efficiently in settler farms and to fill clerical positions in the colonial administration.

Furthermore, upon the recommendation of the Frazer Commission, the authorities established in 1911 the first Department of Education in Kenya. James R. Orr was brought from India and appointed as its Director. The Department was charged with establishing and overseeing government schools, and by extension, keep missionary education in check. During his tenure in office (1911–1927), James Orr, like the Phelps-Stokes Commission of 1924, advocated and worked diligently to promote "village" industries and craftsmanship to meet the needs of Africans rather than to feed settler plantations. It was under his supervision that the first government school was established in Machakos. Yet, it remained true to many African students that working on settler plantations brought them more immediate financial reward than serving in the small, subsistence "village" economy. Hence, the overwhelming majority of young Africans gravitated around white farms after leaving school.

In 1918, Orr formed the Education Commission to reexamine the system of education in the country. The Commission recommended that the government should play the major role in education in the territory, but at the same time, allow the missions to maintain some influence in educational activities. The missions' form of educational instruction, the Commission suggested, must henceforth focus on "character building," that is, vocational education must be the first priority. Furthermore, the missions were to be officially registered in order to receive subsidies. This step, according to the Commission, ensured close government control over missionary education in the country. Accordingly, the Department of Education introduced in

1922 a grants-in-aid program to assist missionary schools, particularly those that agreed to offer "acceptable" industrial education.

Missionary schools in Kenya were, with few exceptions, underfinanced. The need for funds forced many of them to accept the government grants-in-aid program with all the strings attached to it in spite of the fact that the church continued to express the view that its primary role was evangelization. Besides, there were some missionaries, who sincerely believed that vocational education was absolutely right for Africans. In their opinion, the primitiveness and innate depravity of Africans precluded them from benefiting from liberal education. In essence, the missionaries believed that technical education would make Africans more industrious and instill in them Christian virtues to offset the lack of morality in African societies.[40] On the other hand, there were some missions that refused to "sell out" and even expressed open hostility to the policy of the administration. At any rate, a good number of the missions that collaborated with the colonial administration had a stake in the development of a skilled African cadre. In fact, many missions considered plantations as one of the tools that, in their opinion, promoted legitimate trade and commerce that saved the natives from the misery vented on them by the Atlantic and Indian Ocean slave trade and by destitution. Henceforth, government and missionary schools became "factories" producing a labor force for settler's farms and clerical staff for the colonial administration. The cooperation between the administration and the missions was now complete, and industrial education proceeded in earnest. Mission stations in the interior became primary schools, schools for catechists became teacher-training centers, and mission boarding schools became secondary schools. Professor Mugo Gatheru recalls that education in the primary and secondary schools was very demanding and that "discipline was imposed very severely . . . the schools were run like military academies. Social life was discouraged. Corporal punishment and obedience were encouraged (and) the students were overworked."[41] Still, neither the missionaries nor the colonial authorities intended to extend mass education in the colony. They provided, so Professor Gatheru notes, an "education for the very, very few Africans who were then absorbed into the colonial administration and were paid very low wages." Speaking from personal experience, Gatheru relates that the system was, nonetheless, "a very solid foundation for those few who had opportunities to study abroad for further education."[42] It also "enabled" many Kenyans including Harry Thuku, *Mzee* Jomo Kenyatta, Tom Mboya, Jaramogi Oginga Odinga, Daniel Toroitich arap Moi, Mwai Kibaki, Dr. Julius Kiano, and Mbiyu Koinange to become icons in the nationalist movement and in independent Kenya.

Vocational education opened the gates for Kenyan elites to enter the arena of employment not only in the cash crop economy but also in the colonial Civil and Military Services. Africans were thus able to unveil the secrets of the power and influence of the man. Kenyans now served as clerks and junior administrators in the Civil Service and privately owned European companies, as well as policemen and soldiers in the colonial army. They staffed hospitals, the police department and the army, filled positions in ports and the railways, manned the telephone, telegraph and mail services, drove lorries, became school teachers and of course evangelists.

A small pool of western-educated Kenyan elites was to some extent in full bloom. It was this *Asomi* that would eventually aspire for higher education and in due time for the power that enabled them to run their country. At any rate, the colonial system of education fostered community development for the majority, technical training for a minority, and academic secondary education for a tiny fraction of the Kenyan population.[43] Thus, the 1926 Annual Report, which was directed by the 1925 Memorandum, divided Kenyan society into three broad categories: First, the great mass of village life in the Native Reserves; second, the artisans and craftsmen; and finally, the educated and semi-skilled professionals required by the State and commerce.

THE AFRICAN-AMERICAN FACTOR

The initial contribution of African-Americans to the emergence of the *Asomi,* very limited as it may be, started in 1924 when the Phelps-Stokes Commission, with a five-year financial assistance from the Carnegie Corporation in New York, established its Jeanes School in Kenya at Kabete. The school "was set up . . . for practical training of Africans as supervisors in rural education."[44] In fact, the Phelps Stokes Commission called upon the colonial authorities and the missionaries to cooperate in extending an education that preserved African culture and improved the quality of life. Hence, at Kabete, female students were instructed in domestic services (home crafts), while male students were taught agricultural techniques. Importantly, education at Kabete was oriented towards producing agricultural teachers that assisted in the development of their own communities rather than working in white plantations. Thus, the Jeanes School followed faithfully the education philosophy then current among African-Americans of "teaching the dignity of labor." It was from this school that the celebrated politician and leading trade unionist, Tom Mboya, and the second President of Kenya, Daniel Arap Moi, graduated. Mboya (1930–1969), would eventually become the main Kenyan actor in the drive that saw

Kenyan trade union officers and students receive advanced training and education in the United States under the umbrella of Pan-Africanism. That campaign points to the solidarity and fruitful cooperation between Africans in Africa and in the Diaspora. Mboya joined Jeanes School in 1948 to train as a health inspector.[45] Within a few days of his enrollment, he exhibited brilliant talent for leadership. No wonder that at the age of 18, he became the president of the 1,000 strong student body at Jeanes School. Mboya did not receive further education except for a one-year study tour at Ruskin College, Oxford in 1955. By then he was already the undisputed King of the trade union movement in Kenya. In 1953 Mboya not only founded the Kenya Federation of Labor, he became the General Secretary of the organization. It was, thus, at the Philips-Stokes institution that Mboya completed his studies and took his first step toward becoming a trade union leader, a Pan-Africanist giant, a political icon, and an achiever before he was shot dead on July 5, 1969.[46] At independence, the Jeanes School was transformed into the Kenya Institute of Administration.

The Phelps-Stokes Commission indirectly opened channels for the introduction of higher liberal education in Kenya. A handful of educated African and African-American elites arrived in Kenya with the Commission. Among them was Dr. James E.K. Aggrey, a native of Ghana, who was educated in America. Dr. Aggrey vehemently opposed the colonial view that technical education was better for Africans than liberal arts education. Additionally, Aggrey spearheaded the debate over the institution of higher education in the country. His positive opinion was shared and supported by both the educated Kenyans and missionary advocates of higher education. At the same time, Dr. Aggrey himself presented the example of an African who succeeded in life and was able to penetrate western society on the wagon of liberal education. He and his colleagues proudly pointed to Hampton and Tuskegee as examples of how vocational institutions of higher learning for Africans could be successful. The experience of Hampton and Tuskegee could be replicated in Africa. Thus, Dr. Aggrey and his colleagues transported the debate over liberal education versus vocational education for African-Americans that had been raging in America since the early twentieth century to Africa.[47]

The modest but significant contribution of the Phelps-Stokes Commission to education in Kenya was not however paralleled by the presence of substantial African-American missionary or secular activities in the region. In reality, there was, with very few significant exceptions, an almost complete absence of African-American missionary and civilian work in East Africa. In the first place, African-American missionaries were, in most cases deployed, not by black Christian organizations, but by white church denominations to the regions of West and Central Africa because of health and weather considerations. These areas had a climate considered unhealthy and were infested with diseases that were deadly to Europeans. For that reason, evangelical societies preferred to send white missionaries to areas like South Africa where the climate was hospitable for them while dispatching African-American missionaries to West and Central Africa. Consequently, there were rarely any white sponsored black missionaries in "healthy" Kenya and South Africa. It is thus true that white missionaries regarded the black missionaries as being useful in Africa when health issues did not allow the white clergy to enter certain areas.[48] W.E.B. DuBois noted this policy and condemned it as outright, blatant discrimination against black missionaries. In fact, both W.E.B. DuBois and Carter G. Woodson were said to have been of the opinion that opportunities for Negro mission work in East Africa had been deliberately frustrated by white missionary and philanthropic organizations.[49] Yet, it was pointed out that white missionaries in East Africa openly encouraged black ministers to involve themselves in missionary activities in the region. To this end, the Church of Scotland in Kenya is said to have sent representatives to America to persuade African-American evangelists to come to the country and engage in mission work.[50] There is however, no evidence that indicates whether or not any black ministers inquired about entering into missionary work in East Africa or whether or not any of them had ever applied to serve there and was turned down.

Albeit, there have been a few unsuccessful efforts by individuals including Harry Thuku and Dr. James Aggrey to recruit African-American missionaries. Indicative of his confidence in the usefulness of black mission services in Kenya, Thuku was reported to have sent massages to DuBois, Garvey, and Tuskegee pleading for help.[51] In 1921, Dr. James Aggrey toured Historically Black Colleges and Universities in the South encouraging students that "now was the time to make entry into East Africa." These passionate pleas went unheeded. At the time, African-American missionaries concentrated their work in West, Central and Southern Africa. The African Methodist Episcopal Church (AME), the African Methodist Episcopal Zion (AMEZ), and the National Baptist Convention (NBC) deployed some black missionaries to South Africa, Liberia, Sierra Leon, and the Gold Coast (Ghana).[52] They did not, as yet, sponsor any black missionaries to East Africa, notwithstanding their announced commitment to redeem the whole of the continent. In the words of Bishop Turner: "God brought the Negro to America and Christianized him so that he might go back to Africa and redeem that land." The 1893 conference held at Gammon Theological Seminary in Atlanta concurred with Turner that African-Americans were obligated to spread Christianity in Africa "from the Cape of Good Hope to Egypt . . . thence Sierra Leone and Liberia thence onward . . . to the Sudan and the Congo State."[53] African-American missionaries however remained enthusiastic toward South Africa, Liberia and Sierra Leone but not to East Africa. This is understandable, since a sizable number of Africans in these societies spoke English and had a seemingly close affinity to Blacks in America in contrast to East Africa where its population spoke a host of languages, and even their rescued slave population did not come from across the Atlantic but from Bombay across the Indian Ocean.

However, the major factor for the absence of African-American missionaries in East Africa seems to rest on the anti-African-American mission policy of the colonial administration in the region. British policy toward African-American missionaries in East Africa was simply "slam the door shut in their face." The Governor of the East Africa Protectorate, Sir Edward Northey, recommended that African-American missionaries be kept out of the region. His successor, Governor Coryndon, went further and enacted the recommendation as an official policy in the Protectorate. The Governors arrived at their decision in the wake of the anti-British activities of Reverend John Chilimbwe and his subsequent uprising in Nyasaland (now Malawi).[54] They considered Chilimbwe's movement a disease that he contracted at the all-black Virginia Theological Seminary, which he had attended, and through his personal contact with black "agitators." They therefore feared that this "disease" would contaminate East Africa if African-American missionaries, that is the "agitators," were permitted to enter the region. That was precisely the reason why the application of Marcus Garvey to enter East Africa in May 1923 was denied.[55]

Chilembwe began his missionary education at the Church of Scotland Mission in Nyasaland but was later converted to the National Baptist Convention by Joseph Boothe, a British Baptist missionary, and became his assistant from 1892–1895. Boothe's teachings of radical equality resonated with Chilembwe's own sense of pride and self-worth. In 1897, Boothe took Chilembwe to America and enrolled him in Virginia Theological College. While in America, Chilembwe was introduced to the educational philosophy of Booker T. Washington. Upon his return to his homeland, Chilembwe founded his own mission station, the Province Industrial Mission, in Shine Highlands where white settlers maintained plantations.

Chilembwe's three-year sojourn among African-Americans stressed in him the urgency to acquire political, social, and economic rights for his countrymen. In the same vein, he sought to develop African education along the technical lines of Tuskegee Institute. Chilembwe believed that his institute must advocate the following tenets: promote independent African activity in all economic fields; receive a just land settlement; move toward the encouragement of a pro-African press and literature; and support the growth of independent African Christianity. As a by-product of his missionary education, Chilembwe, like many African church leaders, took the teachings of the Bible much more literally. The stories in the Bible provided the doctrine for justice and equality for all humankind rather than oppression and injustice. Chilembwe articulated the grievances and aspirations of his people but to no avail. Consequently, he organized and led in 1915 an uprising against the conscription of Africans in World War I, the ill treatment of Africans on settler plantations, the burdensome taxation, and British rule.[56] He was captured and subsequently executed. Hence, the fear from Chilembwe and his like who had fallen victim to the "fanatic, seditious influences" of Blacks in America was real in the mind of the Governors of the East Africa Protectorate. Consequently, African-American "agitators" were banned from entering the region.

Ironically, the official embargo against African-American missionaries received the blessings of Dr. Jesse Jones of the Phelps-Stokes Commission and Joseph Houldsworth Oldham of the International Missionary Council. The two men feared that the newcomers would bring with them DuBois's philosophy of liberal arts education, which, they thought, would threaten their emphasis on vocational education, the hallmark of Jeanes School.[57] Therefore, their non-supportive position for bringing African-Americans to East Africa reflected their fear that leaving the door wide open for African-Americans would allow the bearers of the ideas of DuBois to inundate East Africa.

It remains to be said that there is little doubt that most African-Americans in America had been indoctrinated, indeed brainwashed, by white racism. They therefore carried notions such as the inferiority of their own race, and the wild "Dark Africa" and its primitive, poverty stricken and diseased inhabitants. Far away, Africa with its "jungles" and its depraved dwellers was not a place to visit let alone to sojourn in for sometime. Those stereotypes naturally scared away many of the hoped for black missionaries notwithstanding that some of them served in Central, West, and Southern Africa under the patronage of black churches but mostly under the auspices of white missionary organizations. Moreover, there is little doubt that African-American missionaries in Central, West, and Southern Africa, like their European counterparts, considered Africans as culturally backward and dubbed their mission in the continent the "Negro Burden." Hence, there was a reluctance of many black men of the church to leave home for Africa. It is to the credit of African-American evangelists who served in

Africa that their negative attitude toward Africans eventually changed once the African was Christianized in contrast to the European missionaries who continued to hold to their racist view that the African remained inferior no matter what. African-American religious teachers would now see the "civilized native" as their equal. By the end of the nineteenth century, it is so noted, African-American missionaries and the converted Africans worked hand in hand to dismantle the negative stereotypes that surrounded Africans and descendants of Africa in the Diaspora. Eventually, some African-American missionaries in Africa, particularly in South Africa, were able to develop affiliations with independent African churches. Their cooperation helped bring Christianity and western culture to Africans through the westernized African congregations.[58]

Several opportunities did however present themselves for African-Americans to work in East Africa and contribute to the advancement of its people but none came to fruition. For example, in 1907 Booker T. Washington, who had sent Tuskegee graduates who possessed skills in the cultivation of cotton to Africa, particularly to the Sudan, was asked by a prospective East African settler if he could furnish a number of black experts for cotton experimentation in the region. There is no clear reason as to why the venture never went further than a simple request. However, the reported failure of the experiment of cotton cultivation in Kenya in that year might have been the reason.[59]

However, it would not be until well into the twentieth century before a fistful of African-Americans was involved in East Africa. It was not, however, through the agency of missionary societies that these black individuals came for the first time to the region. It was through the agency of the International Committee of the Young Men's Christian Association (YMCA) that they affected a presence there. The YMCA came to East Africa to establish a link with the Native Carrier Corps, the transport system of the British Army in East Africa.[60] In 1916, the YMCA dispatched its African-American Secretary of the Colored Work Department, Max Yergan, to work with African troops in British East Africa. Yergan was born in Raleigh, North Carolina, and graduated from Shaw University in 1914. He entered East Africa in 1917.[61] As a devout Christian evangelist, Yergan stressed to his audience in Kenya strong Christian values, racial tolerance, and obedience to the authorities. It is of no surprise that the British military command in the colony was highly impressed by his work. Accordingly, it cabled the YMCA headquarters in New York requesting six additional Negro officers. In response, the YMCA sent two of its fresh African-American employees. These were Lloyed, a graduate of Howard University, and Ballou who received his diploma from Knoxville College. The two young men joined Yergan in East Africa. No further information on these men, even their full names, was found. However, Yergan stayed in Kenya for a few years after which he left for South Africa where he spent fourteen years as Senior Executive for the International Committee of the YMCA performing educational and social work. He eventually became a fighter for the liberation of South Africa.[62] Consequently, no African-American missionaries were granted entry to the region, even if they wanted to do so. As a result, Kenyans were left to the prerogative of the white missionaries.

REACTION OF THE *ASOMI*

Missionary and government schools in Kenya, and the whole of the East Africa Protectorate for that matter, had thus laid down the foundation for the development of the *Asomi,* western-educated elites that came to react radically in different ways to the realities of colonialism and racism, to European Christianity and its white bearers, and to white settlement. The first reaction of the *Asomi* was directed toward their mentors, the white missions, pioneers of western education in the region. The reaction involved, as discussed above, the formation of independent indigenous churches to provide "a place to feel at home for the many Africans who had accepted Christianity but found it intolerable to live under missionary patronage."[63] The independent Churches provided the spiritual inspiration to fight white missionary domination and blend Christianity with African spiritually and beliefs. In other words, the independent Churches were part and parcel of the larger resistance movement to British colonialism. Further still, the *Asomi* were credited with the founding of independent schools and the establishment of political organizations, known as the Young Associations, which articulated the grievances of the masses.

In 1929, the western-educated Kikuyu formed two organizations, the Kikuyu Independent School Organization (KISA) and the Kikuyu Karanja Education Association (KKEA), to look into the possibility of establishing their own schools free of missionary and government control. The Kikuyu elites were reacting to missions, particularly the Church of Scotland prohibition of the ancient custom of female circumcision, to the absence of Kikuyu voice in the administration of missionary and government schools, and to the curricula that these schools offered. Prohibition of female circumcision was viewed as being a western tradition rather than being Christian. In that way, KISA and KKEA endeavored to incorporate western culture into their traditional society and contribute mightily to the advancement of the people without destroying their basic values. Thus, the independent schools should be considered yet another expression of resistance to European supremacy. Consequently, the first independent school was founded at Kiambu, in the heart of Kikuyu homeland. The colonial authorities initially viewed the independent schools as a step toward promoting denominational schools rather than yet another tool in the nascent, radical African nationalist movement. However, the authorities soon realized the menace that these schools nurtured toward the colonial situation in the country. Thus, in 1931 the authorities drew up a plan to control the proliferation of independent schools and extend government stewardship over them.

The plan included granting greater representation to Africans in the Local Native Councils, whose duties included, among other things, overseeing education in their respective districts, and providing grants-in-aid to the schools.[64] However, the Great Depression of the 1930s brought with it financial constraints that made it rather impossible for the colonial government to finance and consequently control the independent schools movement. That gave the Africans almost complete freedom to open new schools and run them the way they wanted. The independent schools offered their students curricula that fostered the nationalist spirit and provided reasonable or free tuition to students who could not afford it. The development of independent schools therefore represented the rise of cultural nationalism in Kenya. Like missionary and government schools, the independent schools were thus a vehicle of change, different as it may be, and the platform that produced a cadre of elite that challenged the Europeans.

Furthermore, KISA and KKEA were instrumental in the founding of the independent Kikuyu African Orthodox Church with an African-American/Caribbean/South African influence. In 1930, the organizations invited Bishop Daniel William Alexander to visit Kenya for a period of sixteen months. Bishop Alexander (1882–1970) was born in Kimberly, South Africa, to an emigrant from Antigua and an African woman.[65] He traveled to America in 1927 to join the African Orthodox Church (AOC), which had been established in 1921 by the Antiguan George Alexander McGuire in close association with the Universal Negro Improvement Association (UNIA). Bishop Alexander knew about the AOC through his reading of the *Negro World*, published by Marcus Garvey, which was disseminated widely in the continent.[66] On September 11 of the same year, Alexander was consecrated by McGuire. He promptly returned to South Africa to establish his church, St. Augustine of Hippo, in Kimberly. While in Kenya, Bishop Alexander trained and ordained four priests that KISA and KKEA assigned to him. Thus, Alexander laid down the foundation for the African Orthodox Church in Kenya. Consequently, three independent, indigenous AOC churches rose immediately in Muranga, Kiambu, and Nyiri in Kikuyuland.

The independent schools movement received a big boost with the arrival of Peter Mbiyu Koinange (See Figure 1) son of the great Chief Koinange of the Kikuyu nation, from the United States in 1938.[67] Mbiyu, who attended Baxton School and Alliance High School in Kenya, had a long academic sojourn in America, where he studied at Hampton Institute (1927–1931); Ohio Wesleyan University (1931–1933), and received his Masters of Arts degree in political science from Columbia in 1936. Mbiyu was the first Kenyan student to complete a postgraduate degree in liberal arts in America. Moreover, Mbiyu joined St. Johns College in Britain in 1936–1937, during which time he met and had discourses with Jomo Kenyatta over the colonial condition in their homeland. His academic pursuits in America and, most importantly, his close association with Mr. and Mrs. Ralph Bunche, and the atrocities committed by Whites against Blacks, which he had witnessed in America, ignited in him the flames of fighting European injustices in his homeland. Hence, upon his return to Kenya in 1938, he embraced the independent schools movement and shortly thereafter he single handedly founded the Kenya Teachers College at Githunguri as an independent institution under the umbrella of KISA.[68] To demonstrate that the independent schools were a true reflection of the sprit of *uhuru* (freedom) and *harambee* (self-reliance), Kenyans proudly recall the story of Njeri, the illiterate market woman who helped organize the construction of a dormitory for girls at Githunguri. Njeri heard of the college from other market women. She then went to see it. She found the boys housed in a stone building while the girls lived in a mud hut. She returned three weeks later with five women, each one representing a different district. They informed Mbiyu Koinange of their intent to build a suitable dormitory for girls. Hundreds of women joined the campaign. They collected money to buy building materials and pay the workers. As a result, a modern dormitory, a dining hall, and a reception hall were built.[69]

Mbiyu was so impressed with his academic experiences in America and with his relations with Ralph Bunche and other African-American leaders that he turned into one of the strongest advocates of the "great benefit" of American education. He therefore encouraged and assisted students, such as Julius Gikonyo Kiano, to seek higher education in American institutes of higher learning.[70] Mbiyu participated in the founding of the Kenya African Union (KAU) and thus became one of the dominant figures in the nationalist movement, as well as in the Cabinet of *Mzee* Jomo Kenyatta.

With the small expansion in secondary schools (Middle Schools) in the middle of the 1930s, the British colonial government recognized the need for higher education in their African dominions. Accordingly, a commission, the de la Warr Commission, was appointed in 1937 to determine the necessity for higher education in Kenya. The report of the Commission was criticized for being too focused on technical and vocational education. Nonetheless, the Commission recommended that Makerere institution in Kampala, Uganda, established in 1922 to promote skilled trades, be transformed into a college open to secondary school graduates in the Protectorate. Furthermore, the 1945 Asquith Commission recommended the formation of an Inter-University Council for Education in the colonies to establish colleges as satellites of the University of London. Makerere was accordingly raised to the status of a University College linked to the University of London. Finally, general academic "college" education was extended to a few East Africans. Consequently, a small crop of western-educated professionals—nurses, technocrats, journalists, and academicians—sprouted. They too stepped forward to raise the level of resistance and the nationalist movement in the region.

Likewise, western education fostered the emergence of political organizations, which were generally known as the Young Associations that addressed concerns and grievances of the masses, which hitherto had been addressed by chiefs appointed by the colonial authorities. Their founders in Kenya were a group of youths who graduated from missionary schools.[71] The mother of all the organizations that appeared in East Africa was the Young Baganda Association, founded in Uganda in 1919 by Z. K. Sentogo. Its secretary, Joseph Kamulegeya, who had a close relationship with W. E. B. DuBois, Marcus Garvey, and Tuskegee, introduced a young Kikuyu nationalist, Harry Thuku, to this leadership of Africans in the Diaspora. The Young Baganda Association was a protest movement against the authority that the colonial government vested in the appointed chiefs. It was this organization that inspired the rise of sister organizations in Kenya such as the Young Kikuyu Association, The Kikuyu Central Association, and the Young Kavirondo Association.

In June 11, 1921, Harry Thuku, a young Kikuyu graduate of the Gospel Missionary Society School who lived in Nairobi where he was employed as a telephone operator, launched the Young Kikuyu Association (YKA), with the assistance of Josse Kariuki, Job Muchuchu, and Abdulla Tarrar. The presence of African leaders from outside Kenya, such as Z. K. Sentongo, founder of the Young Baganda Association, at the inauguration ceremony, gave the Association an international flavor. In fact, within a couple of months, the founding members realized that the name, the Young Kikuyu Association, did not represent the all-encompassing philosophy they hoped to implement. That philosophy was delineated by Thuku who announced that "unless the people of this country form an Association, the Native in Kenya will always remain voiceless."[72] The change in the name became urgent as Thuku canvassed for membership in Nairobi not only amongst the Kikuyu but also the Kamba, the Luo, the Ganda, the Maasai, the Swahili, and the Asian community. Furthermore, Thuku's exposure to the thoughts of Du Bois and Garvey helped shape his political awareness and inspired him toward embracing all Kenyans irrespective of their ethnic background. It has been reported that Thuku had received copies of the *Negro World*. Accordingly, in July of the same year, the name of the YKA was changed to the suitable East African Association (EAA).[73] Thuku proceeded to attract support from sister associations, such as the Young Kavirondo Association (YKA) of the Luo and Abaluyia nations, the Indian community, and the Thogoto educated Maasai. Henceforth, the political manifesto of the East African Association addressed general issues that were the concern of the entire nation such as land alienation, the excessive hut and poll tax, the reduction of wages by the government and settlers, the registration system, and forced labor (*kipande*).[74]

Thuku cabled these issues directly to London. He persisted in bypassing the local colonial authorities, and raised complaints to the Colonial Office. On March 14, 1922, the authorities arrested and incarcerated him in the police station in Nairobi allegedly as a danger to peace and order. The arrest caused an uproar in the city. On March 16, the masses in Nairobi went on a general strike and surrounded the police station. The police intervened, opened fire, and left twenty-one Africans dead. Thuku was deported to distant Kisimayu where he was detained for nine years. That signaled the death of the first multi-ethnic, multi-racial organization in Kenya. However, a new factional organization rose from its ashes. One such organization was the ethnic focused Kikuyu Central Association (KCA). The Kikuyu elected Thuku as its head in absentia. A younger Kikuyu activist, Kamau wa Ngengi, better known as Johnston (Jomo) Kenyatta, who was educated at the Thogoto Missionary School, assumed its leadership. The political agenda of the newly founded Association was reclaim the land taken by the government, settlers, and missions and restore the land to the Kenyans.

Western Kenya likewise witnessed the emergence of its own Young Association in 1921, the Kavirondo Taxpayers Welfare Association (KTWA), as successor to the ill-fated Young Kavirondo Association. The KTWA was founded in Nyanza among the Luo and Abaluyia farmers. Its founders were Jonathan Okiwiri, Reuben Omulo and Simon Nyende, all of whom graduated from Maseno mission school. The goals of the Association were the abolition of the *kipande,* the reduction of both hut and poll tax, the introduction of land title and deeds, and increases in wages. The Association also strongly opposed the change of the status of Kenya from a Protectorate to a

Crown Colony for fear that all land in the country would be at the mercy of European settlers. The association cultivated a close relationship with Thuku's organization. But in 1931, the Association split up on ethnic lines, with the Luo and Abaluyia developing their separate organizations.

Consequently, the establishment of the mission school of the Church Missionary Society in 1846 at Rabai, near Mombasa, led to the development of formal western education in Kenya. More sister schools were subsequently opened by other denominations. The initial purpose of these mission schools was evangelism, or transforming Kenya into a Christianized-Westernized compound. However, with the colonization of the country now complete and the influx of settlers underway, the railway into the interior constructed, a cash crop economy developed, and the country received thousands of immigrants from Asia, the whole fabric of the Kenyan society was transformed. This necessitated a change in the track of the education system for Africans. Hence, mission schools shifted toward the production of laborers for the farms of the European settler population, and clerical staff for the colonial administration. This "formal education" gave birth to educated elites that aspired for a high level in the new system and eventually for replacing it. Consequently, the western-educated elites, the *Asomi,* broke away from the established colonial and missionary organizations to develop independent churches that "Africanized" the Christianity of the white man, formed Associations that became the voice of the masses in place of the colonial chiefs and white pastors, and built national schools to instill in the young generation a sense of patriotism and pride. Yet, one cannot but notice the small, albeit significant presence of African-American influences in Kenya in the first thirty years or so of British control of the country. Although the colonial administration barred black 'agitators' in the Diaspora from entry, the Phelps-Stokes Commission was able to establish the Jeanes School, which contributed to the development of educated elites in Kenya. Besides, the views of DuBois and Garvey, and the inspiration of Tuskegee and Hampton had a great impact in shaping the political philosophy of some of the indomitable elites such as Harry Thuku, the father of Kenyan nationalism.

Chapter Four
The Quest for Higher Education in the United States, 1945–1963

THE QUEST FOR HIGHER EDUCATION

Between 1914 and 1940, Kenya's educational system was to a large extent under the control of the colonial authorities. During this period, there existed a variety of schools in Kenya: missionary and government schools; independent schools such as Jeanes School of the Phelps-Stokes Commission, Kabete Independent School, and the Independent Kenya Teachers College, as well as the exclusive schools run by the Asian communities and white settlers. Besides, in 1922 the government established the Makerere Government Institute in Uganda, as a trade school to train carpenters and mechanics for private and Government employment. A para-medical course was added to the curricula in 1923 and shortly thereafter, other courses in veterinary science, surveying, and agriculture.[1]

However, the idea for expanding higher education had its beginning after 1923 when the British Advisory Committee on Education in the colonies advanced the argument that:

> The first task of education, is to raise the standard alike of character and efficiency of the bulk of the people, but provision must also be made for those who are qualified to fill posts in the administrative and technical services, as well as of those who as chiefs will occupy positions of exceptional trust and responsibility. As resources permit, the door of advancement, through higher education, in Africa must be increasingly opened for those who by character, ability, and temperament show themselves fitted to profit by such education.[2]

Further reports were later submitted by a host of commissions. These were the Currie Report of 1933, the De La Warr Report of 1936, the Channon Report of 1941, the Asquith Commission Report of 1943, and the Elliot Commission Report of 1945. All these reports called for the establishment of universities in Africa as indigenous institutions that provided education relevant to the needs of Africans.[3] In fact, the reports recognized the urgent need for skilled and sophisticated graduates of higher institutes of learning to assist the authorities in the development and administration of the colonies now that they have become self supporting. Additionally, the reports insisted that modern development depended more on western-educated elites rather than the favored appointed African chiefs. Dr. James Aggrey echoed the same concerns when he visited Kenya with the Phelps-Stokes Commission in 1924. To him, higher education was needed, not to shore up the colonial situation but to uplift the condition of the African. His views found receptive ears among the educated elites in Kenya who realized that higher education was the sure way to move them up the social ladder and to penetrate colonial circle. Furthermore, the colonial authorities were weary, indeed fearful of the small number of Kenyan students who found their way to college education abroad, particularly to the Historically Black Colleges and Universities in America. These students, the authorities strongly believed, would import into the region the 'virus' of self-assertion and nationalism that contaminated them in Tuskegee, Hampton, Howard, and Lincoln as well as through their contact with the ideas and philosophy of Marcus Garvey, W.E.B DuBois and George Padmore. It was best they stayed at home and received higher education in local colleges. Of course, the 'insidious rebellion' of Chilembwe in Nyasaland was still fresh in the mind of the Colonial Office.

The few Kenyan men and hardly any women who studied in colleges, universities, and seminaries overseas benefited from nineteenth century liberalism by receiving financial assistance from philanthropic individuals and missionary organizations. The students were expected to train as highly qualified pastors and evangelists, lawyers, doctors and teachers. Among the first crop of Kenyan students who traveled to America and Europe were Molonket Olokorinya Ole Sempele, Muhammad Juma, Hon. Peter Mbiyu Koinange, Eliud Mathu (See Figure 11), Hon. Kariuki Karanja Njiiri, Akiiki Nyambongo, Dr. Julius Gikonyo Kiano, Tom Mboya, Professor Reuel Mogu Gatheru, Dr. Njorogi Mungai (See Figure 12), Dr. Mwai Kibaki, and *Mzee* Jomo Kenyatta. We have given in Chapter Two a short account of the career of Ole Sempele, the Maasai graduate of Thogoto Missionary School, who with the assistance of the African Inland Mission traveled to America in 1908 where he entered the Boydton Academic and Bible Institute in Boydton, Virginia. He was thus the first Kenyan to experience the condition of African-Americans on the ground. He returned to Kenya to secede from his white missionary mentors and their church to found his Independent African Church. Upon his return he joined with other Maasai elite and the East African Association of Harry Thuku. Throughout his eventful life, Ole Sempele, remained a colossal figure in Kenyan nationalism.

Yet another Kenyan arrived in America in 1915. That was Muhammad Juma. His father, Juma Yohari, a *Swahili* man, had served President Theodore Roosevelt and his son Kermit. It is said that in appreciation of Juma's services, the President promised to help his son, Muhammad, attend Tuskegee when Muhammad was able to travel to America. In October 24, 1915, Muhammad arrived at Cheechaw railway station in Alabama, presumably having received travel money from his family and community on the Coast. He enrolled in Tuskegee and became the first student from East Africa to join its 1,300 or so black students.[4] However, Muhammad soon realized that the strong emphasis on industrial courses at Tuskegee was not for him. Having been schooled in Islamic education at home with its emphasis on jurisprudence, Arabic language and literature, mathematics and history, Muhammad preferred liberal arts to vocational education, which was the focus of Christian missionary education in Kenya. He therefore suspended attending classes and delved instead into reading books with great enthusiasm and determination, notwithstanding that he was nearly illiterate in English.[5] When Roosevelt heard of Muhammad's obstinacy, he wrote to E.J. Scott, secretary of Tuskegee, to exhort the young Kenyan that industrial education was more important for him than literary education. The letter reads:

> Now will you read this to Muhammad Juma—What we are trying to make everybody in this country understand is that working with a man' hands, that is, industrial activity is even more important than a literary education. Muhammad can never be a clerk in this country; he will never know enough; but he can be a very good man with his hands doing industrial work.[6]

In effect, the Roosevelt letter dismissed as irrelevant the Islamic education that Muhammad had received on the *Swahili* Coast. At any rate, the exhortations of the President had no effect whatsoever on the *Swahili* young man. His firm intention to receive the education he desired led him to leave Tuskegee a few months after Roosevelt's letter was read to him. Unfortunately, no further information on Muhammad was found in Kenya or the United States. It was of course impossible to restrict Kenyan students forever to industrial and theological education exclusively. Indeed, the road to liberal arts education was paved when Kenyans themselves raised funds to support students in the United States thus breaking the monopoly of missionaries and philanthropists over funding, sponsoring and placement of students in American institutions. The "freedom of choice" had its beginning with Muhammad Juma, the Muslim young man from the Coast, and his steadfast rejection of vocational education, the hallmark of missionary education. Muhammad was indebted to no one but his own people, the *Swahili* community that funded his travel to America. Albeit, the focus on liberal arts education surged forward with Peter Mbiyu Koinange whose education in America was sponsored by his wealthy father, Chief Koinange, whom the colonial authorities had appointed as chief of the Kikuyu. Mbiyu needed no other sponsor, missionary or otherwise. Hence, he had the absolute freedom to choose whatever type of education he desired.[7] At first, Mbiyu joined Hampton Institute, where he received vocational and technical training. However, he left Hampton to enter Ohio Wesleyan College, where in 1935; he obtained a BA degree in sociology and political science. Thereafter, Mbiyu attended and graduated from Columbia University Teachers College with an MA degree in education. Mbiyu had thus made history as the first Kenyan ever to receive post-graduate studies in any discipline.

Upon his return to his homeland, Mbiyu became the champion of American education. He encouraged Kenyans from a younger generation to study in the United States of America. One of these students was Julius Gikonyo Kiano (See Figure 2), a promising young Kikuyu who in 1945 graduated from Alliance High School. Mbiyu offered Kiano a teaching position, junior instructor, at his Kenya Teachers College where he spent two years. Thereafter, in 1947, Mbiyu dispatched him to Makerere College in Kampala. Two years later, in 1949, Mbiyu, was instrumental in raising local funds that helped Kiano to travel and pay his tuition fees in America.[8] Kiano enrolled, first at the Pioneer Business Institute in Philadelphia. Thereafter, he attended Antioch College in Yellow Springs, Ohio. It was at Antioch that Dr. Kiano met and cultivated a close friendship with a classmate, Coretta Scott King, future wife of Reverend Martin Luther King, Jr. This friendship proved its worth in later years when Dr. Kiano, together with two Kenyan leaders, Tom Mboya and Kariuki Karanja Njiiri, launched the successful drive to have Kenyan students study at American colleges and universities.

Upon his graduation from Antioch in 1952, Kiano received a fellowship from Stanford University that helped him obtain a Master of Arts degree in public administration. He succeeded in 1956 in gaining a Ph.D. degree in political science from the University of California at Berkeley. Kiano was thus the first Kenyan to receive a doctoral degree, and the second (the first was Mbiyu Koinange) to complete non-vocational education in America. In September 1956, almost immediately after his graduation from Berkeley, Dr. Kiano returned to Kenya to begin his career as lecturer at the Royal Technical College in Nairobi teaching constitutional law and economics.[9] Dr. Kiano was thus the first Kenyan to join the faculty of this institution that later became the University of Nairobi. Importantly, like his patron, Mbiyu Koinange, Dr. Kiano became a staunch advocate of American education. In fact, he became so much pro-America that Walter White, the Executive Secretary of the National Association for the Advancement of Colored People (NAACP), said of him that if the United States really wished to prevent the expansion of communism in Africa, then it must educate future African leaders such as Julius Gikonyo Kiano.[10]

Once at home, Dr. Kiano cooperated with Kariuki Karanja Njiiri, yet another graduate of American universities in setting up the Cultural Society of New Africa (CSNA), to provide private financial support for Kenyan students to study in the United States of America. The money was collected at fund-raising events that were held in Nairobi, Muranga (Fort Hall), Nakuru, and Naivasha as well as in the Kikuyu villages. As a result, the Society succeeded in sending two male students to Smith College. The following year, Professor Gwen Carter of Smith College and his students visited Kenya. Professor Carter offered the Society a scholarship for one student to study at the college. A young Kikuyu female benefited from the scholarship. The sources however do not mention her name nor do they give an account of her fate.[11]

Dr. Kiano's greatest contribution to the rise of the *Asomi* in Kenya was his involvement with Tom Mboya and Kariuki Karanja Njiiri in what is commonly known as the "Student Airlifts" of 1959, 1960 and 1961. The three men worked in collaboration with private American organizations, particularly African-American organizations, with private and some state colleges, as well as with influential American figures to secure scholarships at American universities and colleges for hundreds of Kenyan students. These Kenyan students, the beneficiaries of American education, came to form the backbone of the highly educated work force that Africanized, that is, replaced the British elites that had dominated the country for decades. Dr. Kiano informed me that although Britain, the Soviet Union, France, India, and other countries offered scholarships to Kenyan students, the majority of scholarships were extended by the United States.[12] That was, in his judgment, the main reason why American-educated Kenyan *Asomi* occupied most of the top-level positions in independent Kenya. Dr. Kiano himself left his teaching position at the Royal Technical College to join the ranks of the nationalist politicians. He succeeded in 1958 in representing

Muranga in the Legislative Council. The following year, he was chosen as Secretary of the parliamentary delegation that traveled to Britain seeking to persuade the British government to lift the State of Emergency and release the detained politicians during the Mau Mau insurrection.

As Independence Day approached and the ban on countrywide African parties was still in effect, Dr. Kiano, together with Oginga Odinga and Tom Mboya, formed and led the Kenya Independence Movement (KIM), forerunner of KANU, the largest national party in Kenya that was founded on May 14, 1960.[13] The general elections of May 1963 witnessed the triumph of KANU, and the election of this American-educated former professor, to the National Parliament. When *Mzee* Jomo Kenyatta assumed the responsibility of forming a cabinet, he appointed Dr. Kiano as Minister of Commerce and Industry. Other appointments to the cabinet followed. Dr. Kiano was Minister of Labor from 1966 to 1968, Minister of Education for one year (1968), Minister of Local Government from 1969 to 1973, Minister of Commerce and Industry for the second time in 1973–76, and Minister of Water Development from 1976 to 1979.[14] Dr. Kiano was one of the founders the Gikuyu-Embu-Meru Association (GEMA) and its first national Chairman. GEMA was the most powerful ethnic lobby organisation in the country.[15] Furthermore, Dr. Kiano was editor of the Journal, *Bendera ya Uhuru* (The Banner of Freedom), Chairman of Kenya Film Corporation, Managing Director of Kenya Industrial Development Bank, member of the University of Nairobi Council, and Chairman of the University Grants Committee. His last public position before he passed away was Chairman of Kenya Broadcasting Corporation. It was in recognition of his unmatched service to his country that Dr. Kiano received in 1989 the prestigious Haas Award from his alma mater, the University of California at Berkeley. Likewise, in 1997 he was awarded D. Litt. (Doctor of Letters) by the University of Nairobi, and was inducted as Elder of the Golden Heart of Kenya (EGH).[16] Dr. Kiano died on August 8, 2003 of a massive cardiac arrest. He is survived by six children. Dr. Maathai Wangari, Assistant Minster for the Environment praised him "for spending a substantial part of his life opening doors for people, showing the way forward and being of service to others."[17] President Mwai Kibaki described him in a message of sympathy to the family as "a role model for Kenyans in education."[18]

Dr. Kiano's American-educated colleague, the late Hon. Kariuki Karanja Njiiri, who worked closely with him and Tom Mboya to send Kenyan students to study in the United States, was the son of Chief, Njiiri, of the Kikuyu stronghold of Muranga. He was born in 1930. It was his father, Chief Njiiri, who paid for his education in India. Njiiri attended, together with Dr. Reul John Mugo Gatheru and George Mbugua Kimani,

St. Joseph's Collegiate School, a Catholic institution in Allahabad, India. Dr. Gatheru recalls that two years after his arrival in the United States, he successfully pleaded with Dr. Horace Bond, President of Lincoln University, to offer Njiiri and Kimani full scholarship. He says, "Kariuki Njiiri and George Mbugua Kimani were my friends . . . I pleaded with Dr. Horace Mann Bond, then the President of Lincoln University in 1952, so that they could be offered full scholarships to attend Lincoln in the fall of 1952. I succeeded."[19] Subsequently, Njiiri and Kimani arrived at Lincoln in Fall of 1952. Njiiri majored in sociology while Gatheru majored in history and political Science. Gatheru completed his undergraduate studies on June 8, 1954, while Njiiri remained at Lincoln University where he received his Masters of Arts degree in 1958.

Following his graduation from Lincoln, Njiiri returned to Kenya where he was appointed as Education Officer. Soon thereafter, he founded, together with Dr. Julius Kiano, the Cultural Society of New Africa (CSNA), and at the same breath threw his weight behind the Kikuyu Independent School Association (KISA). In that respect, he founded the Kenya Education Trust to raise funds for the independent schools. Additionally, he used his influence and the wealth of his family to sponsor five *harambee* secondary schools and four Day Nurseries in Kikuyuland.[20] Furthermore, he became a member of the Board of Governors for Njiri High School, K.F. Shah High School, and Muthithi Day Secondary School, all of which were independent institutions. On the other hand, Njiiri worked in close association with Tom Mboya and Dr. Julius Kiano to raise funds, secure scholarships, and place Kenyan students in colleges and universities in America. It was because of the relentless campaign of these three men to send students to America and their reputed "soft stance" concerning the Mau Mau revolution that their detractors stigmatized their role in the nationalist movement as the "ambiguous policy of the new men." Nonetheless, the late Hon. Njiiri was an active nationalist, who served his country well as one of the founders of KANU and its Secretary of Education and Publicity, the negative opinion of his detractors of him notwithstanding.

At any rate, this American-educated nationalist, Kariuki Karanja Njiiri, entered the political arena in 1961 as a member of the Legislative Council representing his birthplace, Muranga. However, he soon vacated his seat to make way for *Mzee* Jomo Kenyatta to replace him in the Council. But in 1963, he was reelected to the newly established National Parliament representing Kigumo constituency. He then served as Parliamentary Secretary in the Ministry of Natural Resources and thereafter as Assistant Minister for Local Government.[21] Hon. Njiiri was thus one of the first batch of Kenyans to receive higher education in a historically black college in the United

States and who returned to their homeland to play significant role in the nationalist movement and in the development of their country. Undoubtedly, he was instrumental in that monumental task of building university educated manpower that Kenya sorely needed in the wake of independence. To that end, he wrote to President John F. Kennedy asking for the assistance of the American Administration.[22] As a graduate of a black university in the United States, Hon. Njiiri appreciated and made use of the educational opportunities that America offered. In turn, America was quick to respond favorably to his and his colleague's pleas for scholarships for Kenyan students.

Other Kenyans who studied in America will be mentioned below. But we must reiterate here that the perceived or real menace that those individuals, who had studied in America and befriended African-American pan-Africanists, had posed to European domination was one significant reason for the establishment of institutes of higher learning in the colonies. These institutions were to absorb Kenyans students who, the colonial administration so believed, would otherwise make their way to the black colleges in the United States. In fact, the Advisory Committee that was appointed by the Colonial Office stated bluntly that if more institutions of higher education were not established in Africa more students would be drawn to American and European universities.[23] African students had to stay at home. However, the only institute of higher learning in East Africa, that is, Makerere Government Institute in Kampala, which was established in 1922, was designed to accommodate only a very small number of students from Kenya, Uganda, Tanganyika and Zanzibar. Hence, Makerere had to be expanded and new campuses set up in the region. Both the De la Warr Commission and the Channon Report of 1937 and 1943 respectively recommended that Makerere be promoted to a university college "in the near future and of a university at no very distant date." Makerere was accordingly raised to the level of a University College in 1949 with the name of the University College of East Africa so that students studied for "A" level certificates that qualified them for admission to diplomas of the University of London. Makerere was however preceded by Egerton College, which was set up in 1939 on land donated by Lord Egerton. This institution was established for the exclusive use of white soldiers who had recently been settled in Kenya. It was to train them in agriculture and veterinary science. Egerton was followed in the 1940s by the establishment of a Veterinary Training College (High School) for the local population at Ngong in the midst of Maasai homeland. At the same time, another High School, Kagumu Teachers College, was established to produce local teachers. Furthermore, plans to establish a technical and commercial institute in Nairobi were in the air since 1947. However, it was not until 1954 that the Nairobi campus of the Royal Technical College of East Africa was inaugurated. It admitted students for the first time in 1956. However, following the recommendation of the "Working Party" that was chaired by Sir John Lockwood, Vice-Chancellor of the University of London, the Nairobi campus was elevated in 1961 to the same level of Makerere and renamed the Royal College Nairobi. A third campus was opened in Dar Es-Salam in 1961. The Indian community, on the other hand, drew up a plan to build an independent academy, the Mahatama Ghandi Academy, in Nairobi. However, to avoid duplication, the community opted to incorporate the Academy into the Royal Technical College Nairobi.

Each of the three East African campuses offered specialized courses: Nairobi focused on arts, science and engineering; Dar Es-Salam on arts, social studies and law; and Makerere on arts, sciences and medicine. All three campuses were linked as satellites of the University of London. Following independence in 1963, the three colleges terminated their relationship with London and joined together to constitute the University of East Africa. But in the 1970s, the three colleges separated and each was raised to the level of a fully-fledged university.[24] As a result, the University of Nairobi began in that same year the huge project of expansion, that is, of creating new faculties (schools) and departments, and building new facilities. However, until 1963, the highest degree that the three campuses of Makerere, Nairobi, and Dar Es-Salam offered was a general certificate of Education (A Level). In effect, these colleges were similar to high schools in the United States. Consequently, students in Kenya, Uganda, and Tanganyika who aspired after university degrees were obliged to seek admission in American, European, Indian, as well as in the African universities of Addis Ababa and Cairo. Kenyan students continued to flow to universities and colleges in America, Europe, and Asia at a staggering pace and in unprecedented numbers despite the opening of these university colleges in East Africa. Our focus however is not on Kenyan students in Great Britain, the Soviet Union, or India. It is on Kenyan students who attended colleges and universities in the United States in the period before independence.

THE TRICKLE TO AMERICA TURNS INTO A FLOOD

Political events in Kenya in the 1950s quickened the pace of the development of the *Asomi*, particularly those who studied in black institutes of higher learning in the United States. It was due to the efforts of trade unionists like Tom Mboya, Asa Philip Randolph and George Houser, to politicians like Congressman Charles Diggs, Senator John F. Kennedy and

Martin Luther King, to white wealthy activists like William X. Scheinman, to black entertainers and sportsmen such as Harry Belafonte, Sidney Poitier and Jackie Robinson, as well as to the government of the United states that Kenyan students flooded in their hundreds to black and white universities and colleges in America. Pan-Africanism and the Mau Mau insurrection were the major catalysts behind the Kenyan students pilgrimage to the United States.

Kenya of the early 1950s was dominated by the Mau Mau revolution that erupted in October 1952. Mau Mau is generally considered the water shed in the nationalist movement in Kenya. With it, Kenyan nationalism reached its peak. Nationalism in Kenya could be traced back to the forces of the early 1920s, that is, the *Asomi* graduates of missionary schools, who established independent churches and Young Associations that challenged white rule as well as missionary and settler domination. These forces compelled the colonial authorities to make some concessions to appease the Kenyans. Consequently, in 1944, the colonial administration appointed Eliud Wambu Mathu, a Kikuyu former teacher who graduated from Fort Hare College in South Africa and Oxford University in Britain, to the Legislative Council (Legco). In 1947, the authorities added yet another Kenyan to Legco. That was Beneah Apolo Obanga, a former teacher of Luo extraction. It is to the credit of these two appointees that during their tenure as legislators, they pressed hard but unsuccessfully for the expansion of education in Kenya.[25]

At any rate, Kenyan nationalists immediately followed the appointment of Eliud Mathu to the Legislative Council with the formation of the Kenya African Union (KAU) as an extra-parliamentary support group for him. Two years later, in 1946, Jomo Kenyatta returned from Europe (Britain and briefly the Soviet Union), having been sent by the Kikuyu Central Association (KCA) to press for an end to the discriminatory policies of the colonial authorities and for self-government. A year later, he assumed the presidency of KAU (1947). Kenyatta electrified the masses with his rhetoric and militant call that "the tree of freedom must be watered with blood."[26] Consequently, the authorities, suspicious and fearful of him, placed him under constant surveillance. The inevitable confrontation between Kenyatta's organization, KAU, and the colonial administration ensued with the rise of Mau Mau and the declaration of the State of Emergency in October 1952 when KAU sent what appeared to be a pro-Mau Mau statement to the Colonial Office. The statement reads:

> Much of the present trouble is due to the fact that Africans are not adequately associated with the machinery of Government to make them

feel that they are a real part or partners in the Government of their country. This has the two-fold effect of denying to the Government the benefit of considered African opinion in the making of Government policy, and on the other hand of creating an impression in the mind of the people that the Government because of its composition, does not work in the interests of Africans. During the last thirty years, while the requests of the European community have been conceded, the requests of the African community has been consistently ignored. This has led the ordinary African to believe that only if he has a government of his own can he benefit and not otherwise.[27]

That was the straw that broke the back of the camel. The authorities considered KAU as collaborator, even the mother, of Mau Mau. They immediately proscribed the organization. Its leadership, including Jomo Kenyatta, Paul Ngai, Achieng Oneku, Bildad Kaggia, Fred Kubai, and Kung'u Karumba, to be arrested under Operation Jock Scot, and placed in detention. A total of 128 leaders were incarcerated with Kenyatta receiving a sentence of seven years in prison with hard labor. The charge was complicity in helping organize Mau Mau. From that moment, Kenyatta came to be seen as the embodiment of the aspirations of the populace and the voice of discontent. People in towns, the countryside, and the forest sang his praise and considered him their deliverer.

Mau Mau was the expression of the people's rejection of British rule and their dissatisfaction with non-participation of Africans in the governance of the country, the expropriation of land by white settlers, white racism and discrimination, unemployment, forced labor, low wages, burdensome taxation, overcrowding and miserable living conditions in the slums of urban centers, particularly Nairobi. Above all, Mau Mau demanded the return of the 'stolen land' to its rightful owners and freedom from the shackles of colonialism. Although the young men of Mau Mau held membership in KAU, this organization had no hand in the founding of the movement. On the other hand, Mau Mau won the support of organized labor, that is, the East African Trade Union led by Makhan Singh and Fred Kubai, the Transport and Allied Workers' Union, led by John Mungai, and the Labor Trade Union, led by Bildad Kaggia. However, under the threat of being outlawed, Tom Mboya's Kenya Federation of Labor as well as the Kenya Federation of Registered Trade Unions led by Aggrey Minya, distanced themselves from Mau Mau.

Mau Mau was undoubtedly an alliance of peasants, workers, the unemployed, as well as the return soldiers.[28] Militant *Asomi,* independent of KAU, such as Ngunjiri, Washira Rugi and Dedan Kimathi (captured and executed in 1965) led the movement. At any rate, the backbone of Mau Mau was mostly squatters (over 250, 000 of them in 1946), and Kikuyu farmers who, most than others, were highly affected by land alienation. The thousands of young African squatters, half of them Kikuyu, who lived and worked on European farms in the White Highlands found themselves without work when the settlers introduced modern technology, that is mechanization. What followed was massive expulsion of these young men from the farms. Consequently, some squatters settled around urban centers such as Nakuru and Nairobi while others headed for the forest. The farmers whose land was 'stolen' by white settlers were herded into reserves. By 1948, members of the Mau Mau movement began taking secret oaths of solidarity and struggle on the "Goat" rather than on the "Bible."[29] According to the *East African Standard* ,"one of the most chilling oaths stated: When the reed-buck horn (*coro*) is blown, if I leave a European farm before killing the European owner, may this oath kill me."[30] That most of the Mau Mau were in their twenties, that is to say of the same age group, coupled with the taking of a secret oath, is undoubtedly a return to the ancient tradition of the warrior groups that the colonial government had banned. Again, since many in the leadership of Mau Mau had received missionary education, the "Goat Oath" signified their strong attachment to their roots and heritage.

In late October 1952, Mau Mau erupted. White farmers were attacked and some Africans loyal to the colonial government, such as Chief Waruhiu, were put to death. The authorities and settlers reacted quickly in a number of ways. First, under pressure from the settlers, the government declared a State of Emergency in the country. Secondly, the authorities banned KAU and incarcerated most of its leaders. Thirdly, at the behest of the government, the appointed chiefs and some of the western-educated elites who were known for their loyalty to the administration founded the Torchbearers Association. The Association condemned Mau Mau as an evil force against Christ. The western-educated loyalist elites cried out that "black and white need each other in the task of building a prosperous and peaceful Kenya."[31] Eliud Wambu Mathu, the first Kenyan appointed by the administration to the Legislative Council in 1944, supported the Torchbearers and acted as a liaison between them and the authorities. Mathu "opposed any compromise with any Mau Mau leaders such as General China who, he advocated, should be shot on sight." Mathu summed up the sentiment of the group of loyalists in these words: "We must go into the forest whole hog and get these fellows shot dead, bring their bodies and then burn them in Nairobi."[32] Fourthly, the government formed the Home Guard, which was composed of over 100, 000 Kikuyu recruits to take the fight into Mau Mau hideouts in the forest. Fifthly, the settlers formed the Capricorn African Society that advocated the transformation of Kenya into a multi-racial society. That agenda signified the first crack in the absolute domination of the white settlers.

Mau Mau gained international attention. It became 'breaking news' in the *New York Times* as well as in other respected newspapers from London to India. Most importantly, Mau Mau caught the imagination of black people around the globe, particularly African-Americans, Afro-Caribbeans, and South Africans, all of whom were burdened by white racism and colonial domination. According to Bethwell Ogot:

> As an experience of black people (Mau Mau) commanded the early attention of African American intellectuals, such as Martin Kilson and Bill Cayton, the editor of the black newspaper, the Courier. As a cultural event, it attracted the attention of the urban youth of Harlem, who took to 'Mau Mau-ling' and to calling themselves 'Jomo X. Kenyatta,' as well as the rural poor in Jamaica, who devised a Mau Mau dance step and expressed an interest in the *panga* as a weapon of liberation. The South African government banned the purchase of the *panga* by Africans.[33]

Although the flames of Mau Mau were extinguished in 1955, the movement succeeded in forcing the colonial authorities to reexamine their policies in Kenya in order to appease the disgruntled public. Consequently, Africans were permitted to form political associations at the district level only in preparation for the 1957 elections of eight Africans to the Legislative Council. No national parties were allowed and political associations were prohibited in the Central Province, the bedrock of Mau Mau. Hence, as a national movement, Mau Mau was never able, or more precisely not allowed, to transform itself into a political party. It simply vanished from the open political arena but remained as an inspiration to Kenyan nationalists and black people throughout the world.

The concessions however had a negative side to them. They deepened ethnic divisions in the country as each group hurried to form a party that represented its particular interests.[34] Nairobi was however different. In that cosmopolitan city, the celebrated lawyer, Argwings-Kodhek, tried, in December 1955, to circumvent the directives by his attempt to register his Kenya African National Congress (KANC) with the slogan "Africa for the Africans." Argwings-Kodhek, a graduate of Makerere, Lincoln Inn (Barrister at Law, 1951), and the University of Wales (BA 1955), had in the years between 1952 and 1955, gained the reputation of the 'Mau Mau

Lawyer.' The man, his party and its political agenda posed a real threat to the foreign communities in the country, white settlers and Asians alike. Accordingly, the government refused to register the KANC, whereupon Argwings-Kodhek, together with Tom Mboya, founded the Nairobi District African Congress (NDAC). Shortly before the 1957 elections took place, Mboya left the Congress to form the Nairobi People's Convention Party (NPCP). From that moment, this charismatic leader, Tom Mboya, Secretary-General of the Kenya Federation of Labor, founder of the highly organized and popular NPCP, who graduated from the Phelps-Stokes Jeanes School and the Holy Ghost College, and who spent some time studying industrial relations at Ruskin, Oxford, a British trade union institution, became the dominant force in the political stage in Kenya. In fact, Mboya's star began to shine brightly once the authorities banned KAU and detained its leaders in 1952 leaving his Kenya Federation of Labor as the strongest body representing the masses. It was Tom Mboya who led the campaign to send Kenyan trade unionists and students to train and study in the United States, not in Britain.

The 1957 elections gave Africans eight seats in the Legislative Council, one seat for each of the eight districts.[35] All thirty-three candidates were from the *Asomi* who had, at minimum, secondary school education. In fact, a small number of them had college or university degrees. Moreover, the overwhelming majority of them were teachers. Again, the eight winners, beneficiaries of Mau Mau rebellion that opened the door for "meaningful African participation in running the country," were western-educated of the same age (warrior) group. It was they, together with other *Asomi*, who steered the country to independence. It is interesting to note that voting in the 1957 elections was generally referred to as "qualitative franchise." It was so called because depending on education, income, and public service; a voter could be allowed up to three votes. At any rate, the eight *Asomi* who won the election presented programs that advocated nationalism and rejected the multi-racial society that loyalists and settlers hoped to emerge in self-ruled Kenya. Tom Mboya for example raised the slogan "To Hell with European Domination." Mboya defeated his close associate, Argwings-Kodhek in Nairobi. Oginga Odinga, graduate of Makerere, former teacher, president of Luo Union, and founder of Luo Thrift and Trade Corporation, won in Central Nyanza; Daniel arap Moi, former teacher, won in Rift Valley; Ronald Gideon Ngala, graduate of Makerere and Redland College, Bristol, England, won his Coast Constituency; Masinde Muliro, former teacher who graduated from St Mary's Yala in Kenya (1946), St. Peter's College in Uganda (1948), and University of Cape Town (1954), won in Nyanza North; L. G. Oguda, former teacher, won in Nyanza South; and Bernard Mati, former Meru teacher who attended Alliance High (1939–1942), Makerere (1945), the University of Bangor in Wales (BA degree in 1953), and the University of Edinburgh (Dip. in Education, 1954), won in Central Province.

Mboya, Oginga Odinga, Moi, Masinde, and Ngala formed a parliamentary pressure group that came to be known as the African Elected Members Organization (AEMO). The organization demanded that Africans be given fourteen seats equal to the seats assigned to the Europeans. The Colonial Office conceded to the demands and even gave the Africans two ministerial posts. More Kenyans, including Dr. Julius Kiano, occupied seats in the Legislative Council. At the same time, events toward independence moved at a rapid pace. In January 1959, a delegation representing the elected Africans and Asians joined by one European formed a parliamentary pressure group, the Constituency Elected Members Organization (CEMO). They elected Dr. Julius Kiano, one of the first American-educated *Asomi,* to serve as its Secretary, and dispatched him with a delegation to London to demand the lifting of the State of Emergency and the release of all political prisoners.

Sovereignty was now in sight. Prime Minster Harold Macmillan made his famous statement in South Africa in February 1960 that 'the wind of change is blowing through this continent.' The elected African members in the Legislative Council and the *Asomi* in general began to prepare themselves for the inevitable with the formation of countrywide political parties. In May 1960, the Kenya African National Union (KANU) was formed with James Gicheru holding its presidency until Kenyatta was released. Oginga Odinga became the Vice-President, while Mboya held the office of Secretary-General. The coastal representatives and those from smaller ethnic groups in the interior formed the Kenya African Democratic Union (KADU) with Moi as Chairman, Ronald Gideon Ngala as President and Masinde Muliro as Vice-President. The State of Emergency was lifted and Kenyatta was released in August 1961 to assume the presidency of KANU. The general elections of May 1963 witnessed the landslide triumph of KANU. Jomo Kenyatta became Prime Minister of independent Kenya. The victory of the *Asomi* was now complete. June 1, 1963 marked *Madaraka* Day or Day of Responsibility/Self Rule/Independence.

The ranks of the *Asomi* swelled in the period following Mau Mau, that is, beginning from 1956, with Kenyan students flooding colleges and universities in the United States, England, the Soviet Union, India, the Middle East, Ethiopia and even China. Many actors participated in assisting Kenyans to receive education in America. They included Kenyan *Asomi* such as Tom Mboya, Mbiyu Koinange, Hon. Kariuki Njiiri, and Dr. Julius

Kiano, African-American leaders of Trade Unions, African-American Civil Rights leaders and notables, Congressmen, as well as the Department of State. Each of these actors sought to serve his particular agenda. The Kenyan actors admired the American education system and were politically attuned to western democracy. The African-American Labor and Civil Rights leadership was inspired by the spirit of Pan-Africanism, the struggle against racial discrimination, the fight against European domination, rejection of communism, and the experience of Mau Mau. The American government and politicians, caught up in the Cold War, were guided by the Eisenhower doctrine of combating the spread of Marxism around the globe, particularly in Africa, which was now moving steadily and surly toward independence. Hence, all the American actors extended a helping hand to Kenyan students to study in the United States of America.[36]

In August 1956, one year after Mau Mau exited the political scene, Tom Mboya, Secretary-General of Kenya Federation of labor, arrived in the United States at the invitation of the American Committee on Africa (ACOA). The Committee was formed in 1953 by a group of African-American leaders and white activists to publicize and lobby for African independence and liberation movements.[37] In fact, ACOA became the largest and most effective private organization devoted to African-American relations and American assistance to Africa. Importantly, it offered educational opportunities in America for future African leaders to have them prepared for the task of nation-building, and at the same time to win them over to capitalism and democracy before they fell "victim" to the dictatorship of communism. Noted members of ACOA included Asa Philip Randolph, George Houser, a white activist and one of the founders of the Congress of Racial Equality (CORE), who served as its executive Director, William X Sceinman, Charles Diggs Jr., Hubert Humphrey, Martin Luther King, Jr., Rayford Logan, Adam Clayton Powell, Jackie Robinson, Mrs. Franklin D. Roosevelt, Ms Cora Weiss, Bayard Rustin, Roger Baldwin, Sidney Poitier, and Roy Wilkins. The voice of ACOA was the journal, *Africa Today*.

The trip of Tom Mboya to the United States took place at the recommendation of Rev. Michael Scott, a white minister who has been since the 1920s lobbying for Africans in South Africa and South West Africa. Rev. Scott lived and worked for many years in South Africa before he was "kicked out of (the country) because of his activities in supporting the African liberation struggle."[38] Thereupon, he went to England where he set up the Africa Bureau to support the nationalist and liberation movements in the continent. George Houser, then President of ACOA, recalls that Rev. Scott wrote to them about Tom Mboya who was then (1956) attending a one year course at Ruskin College in Oxford, the foremost British trade union institution, suggesting that ACOA invite Mboya for a speaking tour in the United States. Apparently, Mboya had met with Rev. Scott in London and informed him of his interest in contacting trade unionists in the United States. Houser continued to say, "At first, ACOA hesitated at bringing Mboya to the United States because the months of August and September are notoriously known for not being good times for having speaking tours and we did not have the necessary funding for Mboya to travel throughout the United States . . . We were also hesitant because Mboya was a virtual unknown personality and we were not sure how Americans at various American labor unions, colleges, universities, and churches would respond to him."[39] Nevertheless, the strong recommendation by Rev. Scott convinced ACOA that inviting Mboya was worthwhile. To cover the expenses of the strip and engagements, ACOA raised the necessary funds by charging fees at the venues where Mboya spoke. Furthermore, Kenyan students in the United States including, Mugo Gatheru, Julius Gikonyo Kiano and Mungai Njorogi, gathered in New York to support Mboya and help the ACOA with coordinating the tour. On August 8, 1956, Mboya arrived in New York. He was thus, according to Houser, "the first African leader invited to the United States for a speaking tour."[40]

The two-month visit of Tom Mboya to the United States was, by all accounts, a tremendous success. He met and held discourses with trade union leaders including, "George Meany, of the American Federation of Labor and Congress of Industrial Organization (AFL-CIO), Walter Reuther of the United Auto Workers, Asa Philip Randolph of the Brotherhood of Sleeping Car Porters, David Dubinsky of the International Ladies Garment Workers' Union, Philip Murray of the United Steelworkers, Sidney Hillman of the Amalgamated Clothing Workers, and Ralph Helstein of the United Packinghouse Workers . . . in Detroit, Chicago, New York, Washington, Boston, Los Angeles, Atlanta, and Pittsburgh."[41] According to Houser, it did not take long for Mboya to capture the attention of the rank and file of trade unionists in the United States. He charmed and captivated his listeners by his "charismatic personality and ability to speak without notes in front of him, (and by) his accent (which) was more British than Luo."[42] Above all, Houser said, "Mboya articulated the atrocities that were occurring to Kenyan workers at forums, on television, and at radio appearances."[43]

Mboya asked the AFL-CIO to help with training Kenyan trade union personnel in the United States, with the construction of a building in Nairobi to serve as headquarters for his Kenya Federation of Labor, and with scholarships for Kenyan students. The AFL-CIO immediately contributed $35,000 from its William Green Fund toward the construction of the building. However, C.H. Millard, Director of the International Confederation of Free Trade Unions (ICFTU), objected to the donation on the grounds that his union was not consulted in the first place and that although the contribution was generous, it was nonetheless insufficient.[44] Asa Philip Randolph personally presented the check to the Kenya Federation of Labor. The building was constructed. Anyhow, both the AFL-CIO and the ICFTU were said to have continued to heavily subside the Kenya Federation of Labor. It is further claimed that "the CIA, through the ICTFU, gave the KFL $1,000 a month, a huge sum of money those days."[45]

Moreover, the AFL-CIO formed a committee of three—Asa Philip Randolph, George Meany, and Walter Ruther—to set up and administer training programs for the Kenyan trade unionists. A sub-committee, the Workers Education Committee, composed of George Brown, John Connors, and Theodore Brown was established to select schools and colleges that offered courses in workers' education. The AFL-CIO also chose Maida Springer to oversee and dispense the scholarships. Once the institutions were identified, Kenyans were duly enrolled for three to four months and took courses in organization, administration, public relations, rules of agreement, rules of negotiation, operation of grievances, development and conduct of strikes, and observation of democratic trade unionism.[46] The training program was the brain child of the shared belief of the AFL-CIO and Mboya, Secretary-General of the Kenya Federation of Labor, that since Africa was a primary target of communist ideology, African trade union leaders ought not only learn the general history of organized labor and the mechanism of trade union organizations in America, but also gain a broad perspective of the difference between the forces of democracy and those of communism.[47] The American Administration was quick to endorse that relationship. Vice-President, Richard Nixon, praised the collaboration of African-American and Kenyan trade unions as an effective method of preventing the penetration of communism into Africa.[48] According to the *Sunday Nation,* the United States considered Kenya the gateway to the landlocked East and Central African countries, "a strategic point in (its) push for capitalism in Africa—becoming communist was unsettling."[49]

The training program did not however last long. It folded up in its second year because of inadequate funding.[50] Tom Mboya, the leaders of the AFL-CIO, and those of the ICFTU, searched for an alternative when they met at the All Africa People's Conference held in Accra in December 1958. Mboya was the chairperson of the conference. They agreed that a trade union school be established jointly by the ICFTU and the AFL-CIO in East Africa. Tom Mboya hoped that the school would be built in Nairobi. Mr. Hammerton, the ICFTU representative in Africa, managed the project. He decided on his own volition to construct the school in Kampala, Uganda, to the disappointment of Mboya who was never consulted about this move.[51] At any rate, the school, the African Labor College, was established in Kampala with George McCaray as its Principal. It opened its doors to students in November 1959. Henceforth, trade union officers from East Africa were trained at home. Admission to the college was open to students who had a command of the English language, a minimum of five-year service in the unions, and some secondary school education. In that way, the College restricted admission to the top trade union officers not to the rank-and-file personnel. That is why many of its graduates elected to join more remunerative jobs in the Civil Service and private enterprises.[52]

Although the training program in the United States came to an end, it nevertheless sponsored several Kenyan trainees. Amongst them were Arthur Ochwada, William Kiwanuka, and Patrick Mandawa. These trainees took classes at Harvard University from February 17 to May 16, 1957. The AFL-CIO provided full tuition, room and board, as well as medical expenses. In addition, each of the trainees received $10.00 per day for food, personal expenses and textbooks. Their families were given $67.00 per month to sustain them until the trainees returned home.[53] Furthermore, the three trainees completed their practical training in Detroit, Michigan, home of the strong automobile unions. Their performance at Harvard received high commendation from Joseph P. O'Donnell, Executive Director of Harvard Trade Union Program. So pleased was he to see one of the trainees tutoring an American classmate in Kiswahili.

One African-American among the leadership of the AFL-CIO stands out for his tireless efforts to bring Kenyan trade unionists to America. That was Asa Philip Randolph (1889–1979), President of the Brotherhood of Sleeping Car Porters.[54] Randolph was captivated by the charismatic personality, dedication to the black cause, Pan-Africanist spirit, and pro-American stance of Tom Mboya, and by the 'fragrance' of Mau Mau that filled the air. Mboya was the first Kenyan leader of note to visit America in the wake of Mau Mau. Although Mboya took no part in the movement, and in reality distanced his trade union from it, he nevertheless hailed from Mau Mau soil. Randolph and the other African-American leaders embraced this 'hero' from the motherland whose sons carried arms and thousands of them lost their lives as martyrs fighting white racism and domination. They therefore cultivated a close personal friendship with him. Mboya also shared that sentiment toward them. Randolph often spoke of Mboya as "one of the great leaders of Africa who gives force, reality, and integrity to the avant-grade of the great laboring masses for the achievement of independence and human dignity." On his part, Mboya often referred to Randolph as "the grand old man of world Negro labor."[55] According to George Houser, "Mboya and Randolph maintained a close relationship."[56]

Be that as it may, whenever Randolph was questioned about his genuine concerns and his unqualified, tireless endeavor in helping Kenyan workers to come to America to receive trade union training, he answered: "I am glad to do what I can to help the African cause not only because it is right, but also because I am of African descent." These words testify to Randolph's absolute commitment to Pan-Africanism. Hence, he gave his all to the training program. In 1957, he personally offered financial assistance to at least four non-trade union students: Evanson Gichuhi to study at Lincoln University, Paul Mwena to attend Central State College in Wilberforce, Ohio, James Denis Akumu to attend Grambling College, and a fourth student, a relative of Mbiyu Koinange whose name was not mentioned, to join the Teachers' College in Missouri.[57] News of Randolph's assistance to students rang throughout Africa whereupon Randolph's office received a torrent of inquiries and pleas for assistance from perspective students, particularly from Kenya. Some students called on him to assist them with scholarships. Others asked for travel money. Yet others who had both tuition and travel money but were unable to secure entry visas to the United States asked his permission to use his name as their sponsor.[58] Furthermore, Kenyans students who were already in America, such as Arthur P. Osanya-Nyyneque, asked Randolph to find summer employment for them. However, practically, Randolph could in no way meet all these requests. In such instances, he referred the students to other organizations such as ACOA. The keen interest of Randolph in Africa and his contributions to the scholarship and training programs for Kenyan students and trade union officers were so outstanding that he was selected to join the delegation that accompanied Vice-President Richard Nixon to attend the independence celebrations of Ghana. Other African-American leaders in the delegation included Governor Walter A. Gordon of the Virgin Islands, Fredrick Morrow, the first black administrator to serve on the White House staff, Dr. Ralph Bunch, and Rev. Martin Luther King and his wife, Coretta King. Nixon's tour of Africa took him through eight independent countries: Ghana, Morocco, Liberia, Uganda, Ethiopia, Sudan, Libya, and Tunisia.

Mboya also appealed to and charmed the private and public sectors in America. He contacted black and white individuals, as well as universities and colleges who quickly furnished him with scholarships. Dr. Horace Bond, President of Lincoln University, stepped forward and offered several scholarships and promised to admit any number of qualified students from Kenya. Throughout his tenure at Lincoln, Dr. Bond earned the reputation of never turning away a qualified African student. In fact, Lincoln University was the home of great African leaders, such as Dr. Nnamadi Azikiwe of Nigeria, Dr. Kwame Nkrumah of Ghana, and Kariuki Njiiri of Kenya.[59] Again, several individuals offered to take Kenyan students who attended High Schools or Junior Colleges to live in their homes, as no boarding facilities were available in these institutions.[60] Furthermore, Mboya addressed the members of the Southern Christian Leadership Conference. He also met and corresponded with Rev. Martin Luther King requesting him to assist a Kenyan student, Nicholas Wandia Rabala, who attended Tuskegee Institute. King and his Church sponsored the student.[61]

At the conclusion of his visit, Mboya succeeded in securing over eighty scholarships. But one critical problem remained to be addressed. That was transporting the students from Kenya to the United States. Funds must somehow be raised to cover the airfare. At this juncture, William X. Scheinman, a wealthy white activist who was a member of the executive board of ACOA, and owner of Arnav Aircraft Associates Inc., came forward and offered his assistance.[62] As a result, fifty-three Kenyan students arrived in the United States in 1957. Thirty-six of them were airlifted at the expense of William X. Scheinman. The remaining seventeen students were provided with travel funds by their own families, their communities, or Mboya's Scholarship Program, which he set up in Nairobi following his return to the country. The following year another batch of thirty-six students arrived in the United States.

George Houser credits himself for introducing William X. Scheinman to Tom Mboya. The *New York Times* described Scheinman as "a self taught Wall Street analyst ? an enthusiastic supporter of the independence movement in Africa."[63] Born in 1927, Scheinman attended college for two years upon which he left to circulate among the band of professional poker players in the Midwest. Thereafter, he went to New York and drifted into the Jazz world of Harlem. That appears to be his first, real encounter with African-Americans. He became a publicist for Count Basie and other black musicians. At the same time, he served as a salesman for a company that sold aircraft parts. Shortly after leaving the aircraft parts company, Scheinman started his own prosperous company, Arnav Aircraft Associates Inc. in Little Ferry, New Jersey. Ironically, Scheinman's company dealt in aircraft parts. In the mid 1950s, he entered Wall Street, obtained a license as a broker, and joined a number of brokerage houses specializing in technical analysis. His book "Why Most Investors are Mostly Wrong Most of the Time" has received favorable reviews.[64]

Scheinman's involvement with black entertainers in Harlem threw him into the milieu of the black world in America and Africa and its concerns. He become fascinated with Kenya and the Kikuyu people when he read Jomo Kenyatta's magnum opus, *Facing Mount Kenya*. Dr. Mugo Gatheru maintains that Scheinman "was impressed by the Kikuyu and their own institutions. We used to call each other Brother Mugo and Brother Bill. He also met my real (Kikuyu) mother in Kenya in 1963 during the Independence Celebration." Furthermore, Dr. Mugo described Scheinman as "a staunch supporter of African causes (and also Negro causes in New York), especially education for African students. He was particularly interested in Kenya—and he later on became financial supporter for Mr. Tom Mboya."[65] Scheinman was co-founder of the American Committee on Africa and served on its executive board. It was in that capacity that ACOA dispatched him to Kenya in the wake of Mboya's visit to investigate the educational system of the country and explore ways by which the Committee could help Kenya in the field of education. That visit solidified an everlasting close relationship between him and Tom Mboya. The two men, both of nearly the same age, became very close family friends. Scheinman's friendship with Mboya's family continued even after the assassination of Mboya in 1969. It is reported that Tom Mboya was best man at the second marriage of Scheinman. Scheinman attended the wedding of one of the daughters of Mboya in Kampala, Uganda, in January 1999. Four months later, on May 24, Scheinman died of kidney failure at his home in Reno, Nevada. His ashes were flown to Kenya to be buried next to the grave of his friend, Tom Mboya, on Rusinga Island in Lake Victoria.[66]

Scheinman was the person who introduced Mboya to Senator John F. Kennedy. Mboya invited Scheinman together with Thurgood Marshall, then the noted Civil Rights Attorney, to attend the Lancaster House Constitutional Conference of 1960 that laid the ground work for African rule in Kenya. Marshall traveled to Nairobi at the expense of ACOA and accompanied the African delegation to London. He acted as the main constitutional advisor for the Kenyan negotiators.[67] Marshall insisted at the conference on including a Bill of Rights in the constitution. Scheinman also worked from behind the scenes with Mboya to win tacit approval for the release of Jomo Kenyatta from detention. Other Pan-Africanists, including Felix Houphët-Boigny, President of the Ivory Coast (Côte d'Ivoire), were at hand in London to lend support and advice to the Kenyan delegates. Dr. Julius Kiano and Joseph Murumbe (Minister of State in the *Madaraka* cabinet) went to see President Houphët-Boigny immediately upon their arrival in England. The two Kenyan colleagues entered at the President's room "suffering from jetlag and exhaustion and Houphët-Boigny (spoke) to them while still in his dressing gown."[68] In any case, Scheinman attended *Madaraka Day* celebrations with George Houser and a huge African-American delegation that included St. Clair Drake, Thurgood Marshall, and Asa Philip Randolph.

George Houser recalls, "this was the first opportunity that I was able to obtain a passport to go to Kenya because I was banned from coming to British East Africa because of my affiliation with supporting African liberation struggles."[69]

In April 1959, Mboya visited the United States for the second time, again at the invitation of ACOA. He came to America in search of travel funds for at least seventy-five students who had already received scholarships to colleges and universities, as well as to secure more scholarships and travel money for the hundreds of other eligible students on the waiting list. To coordinate this drive, Mboya, Scheinman, Frank Montero, and Dr. Julius Kiano, established the African American Students Foundation (AASF) Inc. in New York, with Montero as President and Scheinman as Vice-President. The Foundation inaugurated its services with organizing a fund raising event. A host of powerful black and white individuals with keen interest in Africa attended. Among the speakers at the function were Senator John F. Kennedy and Congressman Charles Diggs.[70] In the following years, Kennedy and Diggs would play a significant role in what came to be known as the "Africa Students Airlift."

The AASF was responsible for seeking scholarships and travel funds, as well as placing students, preferably in black colleges and universities in the United States. This organization, more so than any other organization, was the major fund-raiser and scholarship seeker, and indeed the driving force behind the "African Students Airlifts" of 1959, 1960, and 1961. Its energetic President and Vice-President combed a large number of the 2500 or so colleges and universities across the United States appealing for scholarships. They contacted the Department of State, and lobbied Congress and the White House for financial assistance, organized fund raising functions to which thousands of notable Americans were invited, asked for assistance and support from philanthropic and other organizations, and canvassed private companies and enterprises to extend a helping hand.

Once scholarships and funds were secured, the AASF informed Mboya's Scholarship Program in Nairobi to select the eligible students. Priority was given to students who through their own initiative had already applied and were accepted by American colleges and universities, as well as to those who had collected travel expenses by working or fund raising in their communities.[71] The names of the selected students were then forwarded to the colleges and universities and the campaign to transport them to the United States would now begin. However, before passports were issued, the Department of Education in Nairobi made sure that the colleges and universities that admitted the students were accredited. Thereafter, the United States Cultural Officer in Nairobi interviewed the students. The "cleared" students were then issued entry visas. There are however reports that a few family and community funded students who had no sponsors in America were denied entry visas. Some of these students wrote to Asa Philip Randolph to sponsor them. There are no reports that the American Embassy turned any student in Mboya's Scholarship Program away.

Furthermore, during his 1959 visit, Mboya received extensive publicity as he made appearances in major cities: New York, Washington D.C., Detroit, Chicago, Minneapolis, San Francisco, and Los Angeles. The superstar of Baseball, Jackie Robinson, and the superstars of entertainment, Harry Belafonte and Sidney Poitier, joined his fund raising campaign. Some African-American leaders that Mboya had spoken to approached the Department of State on behalf of Kenyan students. For example, Charles Diggs wrote to James K. Penfield of the Department of State asking for a scholarship for Abraham Waka Wabuti to be trained in trade union organization.[72] Wabuti was a graduate of Witwatersrand University, Johannesburg, and Exeter University, Great Britain, from which universities he earned a Bachelor degree in commerce and a post-graduate diploma in public administration. In addition, he served in the Economic Research Division in Kenya Government. Charles Diggs embraced the case of Wabuti at the request of Arthur Ochwada, Secretary-General of Kenya Federation of Labor, who had attended a training course at Harvard University. J.C. Satterswaite of the Department of State responded to Diggs by saying that the request was under review and that the Department was likewise interested in promoting an exchange program with Africa through which the best qualified individuals in both the United States and Africa worked together to develop the continent.[73] In fact, in 1957, the year when the first group of Mboya's students arrived in America, the Department of State offered scholarships to only seven of the thirty-four Kenyan students who had been studying in America. That was followed by nine scholarships in 1958. By 1959, the Department offered a total of only twenty-four scholarships.[74]

A host of powerful Americans offered assistance to the visiting Kenyan icon. One of these African Americans, as mentioned earlier, was Congressman Charles Diggs who had just been appointed to serve in the House Foreign Affairs Committee. Scheinman communicated to Diggs the strong desire of Mboya that a United States Air Force aircraft rather than a commercial plane provide transportation for the seventy-five students who had been accepted at various colleges and universities. Mboya argued, "A United States Air Force plane would constitute just the sort of publicity needed, (which) would cause the United States foreign policy to undergo a change."[75]

Diggs forwarded the request to William B. Macomber Jr., Assistant Secretary of the Department of State. Macomber responded that Executive Order 9492 of October 24, 1944, entitled "Regulations Governing Non-military, and Non-naval Transportation on Army and Navy Air Transports," did not permit the Military Transport Service to airlift the students.[76] Undaunted, Congressman Diggs, together with Jackie Robinson, contacted the office of Vice-President, Richard Nixon. They received the same response that the law did not allow for shipping students on military planes. Thereupon, Diggs wrote to Robert G. Storey, chairman of the Board of Foreign Scholarships, requesting an explanation as to why there was a limited number of African participants in the International Educational Exchange Program. He asked why in that year, 1959, seven out of twenty Latin American countries participated in the program while only one African country participated. Why did the Board ever since it was established provide funding for only 140 scholarships to students from the entire continent? Diggs brought to the attention of the Board the fact that the Soviet Union and China were feverishly recruiting African students, "even those already attending colleges and universities in France and other European countries." The Soviet Union and China, he warned the Board, recognized African young students as prospective leaders and therefore wished to embrace them before they were swept by the capitalist tide of the West. The Board, he advised, must change its policies and emphasis toward Africa.[77]

The appeals of Diggs went unheeded. Scheinman and his African-American Students Foundation had to rely on a charter plane to transport the students. The Foundation raised the majority of the funds by appealing to eight thousand individuals. A total of approximately $50,000 was collected locally by Mboya's Scholarship Program in Nairobi to meet supplementary needs. Eighty-one students arrived in New York on September 9, 1959, by chartered plane. During the reception at the airport, a banner with the colors red, gold, and green was displayed with nine black stars representing the African states that had by then gained their independence. Also displayed on the banner were two outlined maps of Africa with the word, *uhuru*, inscribed across the central gold stripe of the banner.[78] Furthermore, by the end of his visit to the United States, Mboya received more than fifty scholarships from both Historically Black Colleges and Universities and majority institutions.

Kenyan students who arrived in the United States were graduates of missionary, government and independent schools. They hailed from institutions that included Makerere, Kiambu, Kabete High School, C.M.S. Maseno, Coast Secondary School, Alliance High School, Kakamega Secondary School,

Kisumu, Nyri, Kisii, Limuru, Machakos, Mombasa, Karima, Mangu, Kagumu, Kitui, Pumwani, Kangaru, Nabamali, Kapsabet, Cheowyet, Karura, Shima la Teasa and Lorets High Schools, AIM Schools, the Church of Scotland Mission Schools, Arab Secondary School, Nairobi Girls High School, G.A.S. Kangundu, R.C.M. Chepteril School, Holy Ghost College (Meng'u), Nyabururu Secondary, Baxton High, Government African School, Kenya Teachers College, Jeanes School, and St. Joseph's High School (India). They were placed in both majority and minority institutions such as Tuskegee, Columbia, Stanford, Cornell, Howard, Lincoln, Spelman, Clark, Hampton, Harvard, Purdue, Fisk, University of Nebraska, Philadelphia South, and U.C. Berkeley. They majored in multifarious disciplines: political science, history, economics, education, communication, mathematics, agriculture, engineering, medicine, applied science, and anthropology.

By the close of 1959, the number of Kenyan students in the United States on Mboya and the Department of State scholarships rose to four hundred fifty-one compared to the total of forty-five in Britain, the colonial power in Kenya.[79] That the number of Kenyan students in the United States in the late 1950s surpassed by far the number of those in Britain was not surprising in the least. First, scholarships that were offered to British colonial subjects to study in Britain were mainly administered by the governmental agency, the British Council. These scholarships were of course extremely limited in number because if Britain did not promote higher education in its African colonies, including Kenya, in the first place, it would be absolutely unrealistic to expect the colonial authorities to send their subjects in large numbers to study in London. In contrast, scholarships for Kenyans to study in the United States were mainly in the hands of Pan-Africanist leadership and organizations rather than in the hands of the agencies of the government of the United States. The black Labor and Civil Rights leadership, Historically Black Colleges and some state colleges, as well as white activists and organizations committed and dedicated themselves to educating Kenyans in America. The British trade union leadership expressed no interest in helping train Kenyan trade union personnel. Mboya's appeals for scholarships to Kenyan trade unionists while he was at Ruskin College were turned down politely and firmly. The refusal of British trade unions to be involved stemmed from their strong attachment to the Colonial Labor Advisory Committee.[80] After all, the Kenyan Federation of Trade Unions, in the absence of the voice of the banned political parties, not only raised the concerns of labor but also agitated for political rights and the end of British colonialism. In contrast, the black and white leadership of the AFL-CIO welcomed and embraced Mboya and his Kenyan trade union and worked ceaselessly in collaboration with black organizations and leadership to secure scholarships and travel funds for hundreds of Kenyans to attend colleges and universities in the United States. Hence, the United States rather than Great Britain received the overwhelming majority of Kenyan students.

Early in 1960, Mboya's Scholarship Program Office in Nairobi received the good news from the African American Students Foundation that it succeeded in securing over 200 scholarships worth $1,000,000.00. Arrangements were now afoot to airlift the eligible students to the United States. The AASF approached the Department of State to provide $100,000 needed to transport the students. A response came from, Joseph Satterthwaite, Assistant Secretary for African Affairs, that the Department was not able to furnish the required amount. Immediately, Jackie Robinson wrote to Vice-President Nixon requesting assistance. The letter was forwarded to Satterthwaite who informed Robinson of Vice-President Nixon's interest but added that it was not possible for the United States government to finance the air transportation.[81] Undaunted, Frank Montero and Scheinman continued to press the case with the Department of State. They held a three-hour meeting with a number of officials from the Department but failed to win them over. In fact, the officials reiterated the position that the request of the AASF was reviewed at the "top" and was turned down.

The African-American Student Foundation cabled Mboya asking him to fly immediately to the United States to lead the campaign. On July 25, Mboya attended a conference in New York organized by the Phelps-Stokes Fund to discuss the problem of transportation for African students. Some fifty representatives of organizations concerned with higher education in East and Central Africa attended. Also present were representatives of the Institute of International Education, the Carnegie Foundation, the Foreign Policy Association, the African-American Institute, the American Society of African Culture, the American Council on Education, and the Rockefeller Foundation. Mr. Synder represented the Department of State during the meeting. He made the shocking statement that the United States government was limited in its endeavors in colonial territories such as East Africa.[82] Mboya and the participants were now certain that no assistance was coming from the Department of State. Other avenues must now be explored.

The following day, Senator John F. Kennedy, who was then Chairman of the Senate Foreign Relations Committee, invited Tom Mboya to visit with him at his residence in Hyannis Port. The two men discussed at length the urgent need for funds to transport the students. Practically, Senator Kennedy had no real power to force the Department of State to meet Mboya's request. He, therefore, offered to transport the students with a grant from the Joseph P. Kennedy Jr. Foundation. However, it was agreed that no public announcement be made so that the grant would be kept out of politics. Nonetheless, news of the grant soon found its way directly in the forefront of the political arena in Washington, D.C. once the AASF accepted the Kennedy grant.[83] At this point, the presidential elections in the United States were fast approaching. Kennedy and Nixon were campaigning for the votes. When news of the Kennedy grant was made public, James Shebley, an aide in the office of Vice-President Nixon, raised the issue of the airlift with the Department of State. In a matter of days, the Department reversed its decision and agreed to provide the required funds, of $100,000.[84] Senator Scott, a member of Vice-President Nixon's campaign strategy, announced the news. This reversal of policy was met by fiery criticism in the light of the constant refusal of the Department of State to act. Congressman Diggs led the charge. He accused the Department of State of being hypocritical and was playing politics with the grant. He charged that the Department was forced to act only when its inaction was about to prove embarrassing to the Republican Party.[85] Likewise, Senator Fulbright was quick to say that using the "African Student Airlift" as a political strategy to gain votes for the upcoming elections was not a politically sound strategy.[86] At any rate, the AASF declined the offer since it came a few days after it had received the grant from the Kennedy Foundation. The AASF advised the Department of State to allocate the money to the Government International Educational Exchange Program.

While the debate over the grant raged in the United States, Tom Mboya faced criticism at home. Some Kenyans, particularly from the Kikuyu, cried allowed that student selection was based on "tribalism," and funds from the United States were unequally distributed; and that qualified students were rejected while less qualified students were endorsed.[87] In other words, Mboya favored students from his own ethnic group, the Luo. Mboya fired back saying that the allegations were not only untrue but they had the potential effect of being destructive to the scholarship program as a whole. After all, the selection process was almost totally in the hands of the college or university the student wished to attend not in the hands of the Scholarship Program in Nairobi or the AASF in New York. Hence, students from all parts of Kenya were selected on merit. The seemingly inadequate number of Kikuyu students in the Airlift, Mboya argued, should not alarm anyone because the trend was also reflected in the number of Kikuyu students studying at Makerere, in India, and Great Britain. The number of Kikuyu students who received scholarships abroad was reflective of population ratios, of the availability of secondary schools in various areas and its influence on the number of candidates, as well as the ability to raise money by various organizations and ethnic groups. Mboya noted that there was neither effort to send inferior students to the United States nor one to hastily keep highly qualified students out of Makerere. Mboya dismissed the criticism as unfair stating, "We must urge all our people to strive to help themselves and this has nothing to do with politics, but with the moral duty and responsibility of every African leader. We should seek to improve rather than wreck what we already have."[88]

The 1960 "Students Airlift" arrived Monday, September 12 at Idlewild, New York. The students numbered two hundred and twenty-two from seven countries in East and Central Africa. The overwhelming majority came from Kenya. During the first week of orientation, Congressman Charles Diggs addressed the students on *"American Foreign Policy Toward Africa."* Representatives from the American Society of African Culture and the American Committee on Africa held informative sessions and receptions for the students. Also in attendance was Reverend James Robinson of Crossroads Africa.[89]

In January 1961, and at the entreaties of Tom Mboya, the Assistant Secretary of State for Educational and Cultural Affairs, Phillip H. Coombs, called a number of agencies to a meeting to discuss ways and means to provide scholarships to African students. These agencies included the African-American Institute, African-American Students Foundation, African Scholarship Program of American Universities, Institute of International Education, Phelps-Stokes Fund, and the United Negro College Fund. The delegates formed a new organization, the Council for Educational Cooperation with Africa (CECA). The primary responsibility of the Council was to help African students begin and complete their studies at American colleges and universities. However, the Council found itself at the center of the 1961 "African Students Airlift."[90]

The Council dispatched a two-man team to East and Central Africa. The team met Tom Mboya who informed them that financial assistance in an amount between $200,000 -250,000 was needed to provide transportation, services, and supplementary assistance for between 160 to 200 students from East and Central Africa. Consequently, the CECA offered 132 awards, while the Department of State sponsored 100 students. The first plane of the 1961 "Airlift" arrived on schedule on September 7 with 86 students on board. Eighty-three of them were CECA students. Another fifty-one CECA students departed East Africa on September 22, and nine students left on September 27. Twelve students paid their airfare on a non-CECA sponsored flight on September 30. The grand total was 148 students. One-hundred-sixteen were Kenyans, one student from Northern Rhodesia, one from Southern Rhodesia, eleven from Tanganyika, seventeen from Uganda, and two from Zanzibar.[91]

Mboya's connections with African-American leadership and black labor, with politicians and private organizations in the United States helped him build the urgently needed manpower that replaced the dominating British personnel. Americans saw Mboya as a friend and an ally, who not only represented progressive democratic African leadership, but also as the strongest rival of Oginga Odinga, the pro-Soviet Kenyan nationalist. Both Mboya and Odinga, it must be remembered, hailed from the same ethnic group, the Luo. For the United States government, helping Tom Mboya was part of that greater design of combating communism. Mboya's relationship with the United States and his friendship with President John Kennedy, as well as his colossal international stature won him the jealousy and enmity of many.[92] It is claimed that in 1968, hardly a year before his death, the then Attorney-General, Charles Muhane Njonjo, attacked him viciously at a private meeting of the KANU Parliamentary Group. "The center piece of Njonjo's diatribe was that Mboya was a stooge of America," so it was reported in the *East African Standard*.[93] For sure, to both his friends and foes, Mboya was a man of vision—the President who never was.

Ten years after he successfully initiated the first "East Africa Student Airlift," Mboya was assassinated in Nairobi in broad day light on July 5, 1969. He was stepping out of Chhanis Pharmacy on Government Road (now Moi Avenue) when Nahashon Njiguna Njenga, a Kikuyu, cut him down in a hail of bullets. It was whispered in Kenya that the culprits were no other than the henchmen of *Mzee* Jomo Kenyatta. Mboya was "clearly too intense, too focused, too brilliant a player ... (who) had his sight on the Presidency, a fact that alarmed and angered those close to President *Mzee* Jomo Kenyatta especially the so-called Kiambu Mafia or simply the Court."[94] Mboya, it is said, was "an achiever, an accolade not even Kenyatta could lay claim to ... He was a strategist and an unrelenting schemer and master hatchet." Removing him from the scene was a relief to the Kiambu Mafia whose acknowledged leader was Mbiyu Koinange.

Recently, the *East African Standard* disclosed a heart breaking, dramatic step-by-step recollection of the murder of this flamboyant, political icon. Shortly before 1:00 pm, on Saturday, July 5, 1969, says the *Standard*, Mboya left his office at the Ministry of the Treasury "told his driver to go home, got into his car, and drove off alone. A few minutes later, he pulled up on Government Road, outside Chhani' Pharmacy. The shop had just closed for the weekend, but Mboya was a regular at Chhani' and often called there at this hour on a Saturday. Indeed, the proprietors, Mr. and Mrs. Sehmi Chhani, were family friends of the Mboya. As Mboya got out of the car, a man he knew, a freelance photographer asked him casually what he was doing there at that time of day. "Just shopping," Mboya replied. He was well dressed as usual in a suede jacket and a red shirt. Mrs. Mohini Sehmi Chhami opened the shop door for Mboya, and closed it again behind him. He bought a small bottle of Alpha-Keri lotion, and then stayed at the counter for approximately 10 minutes chatting with Mrs. Sehmi and a pharmacist. When Mboya was ready to go, Mrs. Sehmi accompanied him to the door and opened it. They talked briefly; she was eager to know when he and Pamela would next be able to come to the Chhani home for dinner. Outside the shop, seven or eight feet from the door, stood a young, slightly built man in a dark suit, holding a briefcase in his left hand. His right hand was in his pocket. He appeared to be busy at window-shopping. Mboya said good-bye to Mrs. Sehmi and shook hands with her. He then stepped out. Then two gunshots rung out. "Tom, Tom, what is wrong?" cried out Mrs. Sehmi as Mboya slumped against her and they staggered back towards the shop. "I saw blood on his shirt, which was red anyway, and I realised [sic] what had happened. He never uttered a word. He fell into my arms and began to slump to the ground. I now had his blood on my hands and we managed more or less to break his fall and we helped him to the floor . . . I closed the door and called the pharmacist and said the police must be called in, as well as an ambulance."[95] On that fateful day Tom Mboya was pronounced dead. The following statement, which Tom Mboya made only a week before his murder, reflects his vision and hope for the new independent Africa:

> The new nations of Africa have passed through one stage–that of the movement to independence from colonial rule–and are now engaged in the post-independence stage of nation-building. The first stage was primarily political, our objective being to achieve the political goal of self-determination. The present period is that of development. It is less dramatic with fewer headlines and fewer heroes. Nationalist sentiment must remain powerful, but it can no longer be sustained by slogans and the excitement of independence. Rather, it must itself sustain the population during the long process of development. It is a process that requires time, planning, sacrifice, and work. Colonialism could be abolished by proclamation, but the abolition of poverty requires the establishment of new institutions and the development of a modern technology and an enormously *expanded education system*. We are engaged in an economic and social revolution that must take us far beyond the condition we had achieved when we won independence.[96]

Chapter Five

American-Educated *Asomi* Return Home, 1958–1963

AMERICAN GOVERNMENT SCHOLARSHIPS

Time Magazine designated the year 1960 as the year of Africa because seventeen African countries, more than one third of the continent, gained their independence. That same year saw the convening in London of the Lancaster House Constitutional Conference on Kenya. The Conference marked, for the first time, the British government concession of the principle of African majority rule in Kenya. Consequently, a Legislative Council of sixty-five members was announced. Thirty-three members were to be elected in open seats. Twenty seats were reserved for minority groups; ten for Europeans, eight for Asians, and two were allocated to Arabs. In spite of the refusal of European settlers to endorse this new measure of African majority rule, Kenya, like other sister nations in Africa, was well on its way to *"uhuru."* Henceforward, the present and the future of Kenya were firmly in the hands of its sons and daughters.

One of the major problems that Kenyans faced in the wake of independence was the Africanization of the civil service, the army, and the police force, and the filling of a huge assortment of high-level positions required university degrees. Kenya was in urgent need for a highly trained professional cadre in public administration, engineering, architecture, surveying, economics, political science, chemistry, biology, physics, education, medicine, pharmacology, and law.[1] Hon. Kariuki Karanja Njiiri, graduate of Lincoln University, who was then KANU Secretary of Education and Publicity, spelled out these needs in some detail in a letter that he dispatched to President John F. Kennedy through Richard B. Freund, the American Consul General in Nairobi. Njiiri requested that Kenyan students be trained in the United States in youth organization and leadership; twenty in public administration; six as interpreters; eighty for the Ministry of Internal Security and Defense; twenty for Radio and telecommunications; ten for geology and mine prospecting; twenty for power generation; ten for metallurgy; forty for mechanical engineering; fifteen for electrical engineering; ten for chemical technology; ten for cartography; ten for photography; fifty for communications in harbors and airports; fifty road transportation experts; fifty civil engineers and architects; 500 teachers; 500 agriculturists; twenty journalists; one hundred cooperative experts; one hundred trade unionists; and one hundred building contractors.[2] On his part, the first Kenyan Minister of Education, Joseph D. Otiende, stated that by 1970 Kenya would be in dire need of 1,573 new secondary school teachers. If Kenyan students were not able to be educated abroad, he argued, there would be severe shortage of qualified teachers because East African colleges could only produce approximately 416 teachers over the next six-year period.[3]

Moreover, in its 1964 survey, the Ministry of Economic Planning and Development under Tom Mboya estimated that approximately 5,611 highly qualified Kenyans were needed by 1971 to fill occupations that required university education. However, the estimate indicated that in the best-case scenario only 4,637 Kenyans would be prepared to fill these positions leaving a shortfall of 974.[4] Furthermore, the survey identified the most urgent and important professional and managerial occupations that must be increasingly Africanized. These were positions in the professions of town and physical planning, lawyers, physicians and surgeons, all engineering, surveyors, chemists, all university teachers, directors, managers, and working proprietors, secondary school teachers, agronomists, and agricultural graduates. In order to meet these necessary high-level manpower needs, the survey identified four avenues. First, utilization of the high-level Kenyan personnel, small as it were, already at work; second, up grading presently employed lower skilled workers; third, providing education and training in East African colleges as well as overseas colleges and universities; and finally, contracting foreign technicians when qualified Kenyan personnel were not available.[5]

In addition, the survey advised that more attention be steered towards the education of women, especially since there was a need for skilled office workers such as stenographers, secretaries, bookkeepers, cashiers, and speed typists, professions that were generally considered primarily the domain of women. It must however be said that women educated in Kenya, and the whole of Africa for that matter, had consistently lagged far behind that of men. Women were often the last members of the family to go to school. That was largely the result of economic consideration as well as conservative thinking. A large segment of the male population held the conviction that women must be confined to their traditional roles as wives and mothers, and work in the fields. In reality, these men did not want to loose women to schools for women constituted the backbone of the peasantry. Hence, the enrollment of women in secondary and high institutes of learning remained low. However, there were some 'enlightened' Kenyan parents who recognized the important role that educated women would play in enhancing the quality of life of their families and participate in the development of the country. Dr. Wangari Maathai (See Figure 3), graduate of American universities, world-wide renowned environmentalist, the first Kenyan female to hold a Ph.D. degree and recent Nobel prize winner, told the *Chicago Tribune,* that her parents must take all the credit for allowing and encouraging her to pursue her advanced education locally and particularly abroad at the time when very few women left the household to attend school. She recalls, "my parents were progressive people, and they decided that I should have a chance to go to school. If they had not done that, I would probably never have left the farm."[6] Progressive parents, together with the handful of women who had received higher education, continued to encourage and press for the advancement of women education. Consequently, women's education advanced steadily and at a fast pace after independence.

Highly educated manpower in Kenya was extremely low at independence. That was basically due to the deliberate policy of neglect that the colonial administration followed faithfully. Throughout the colonial period, Whites filled the top positions in the country while Kenyans were to a large extent kept out. Nonetheless, a handful of these positions were opened to Kenyans and only in the late 1950s. This "progress" took place with the assistance of overseas scholarship programs from the United States and to a far lesser extent from Great Britain. Hence, Kenyans' share of top occupations rose from 5.6% in 1961, the time when self-rule loomed in the horizon, to 22.7% in 1964, a year after independence. That was an increase of 40%. However, this increase amounted to less than 10% of all high-level manpower positions, particularly in the areas of physical planners, lawyers, physicians and surgeons, engineers, and surveyors. On the other hand, this negligible but significant increase was largely in the public rather than in the private sector.[7]

The deliberate colonial policy of neglect is seen in its fullest clarity when one investigates the educational opportunities that were available to Kenyans under colonial rule. In 1945, there were 718,000 Kenyan children of school age. Of that number, 134,185 attended school, and only seven held matriculation certificates, the equivalent to an American high school education with honors in five or more subjects.[8] Fifteen years later in 1958,

651,758 students were enrolled in primary schools, while 20,291 were enrolled in intermediate schools.[9] However, while the enrollment of students in primary and intermediate schools appears to be expanding, the existing two colleges in East Africa, that is, Makerere and Nairobi, could not accommodate as many students as one would have thought. In 1955, a total of 205 students from the entire region, including nine Asians and three Arabs, attended Makerere College. Makerere was up to that year the only college in East Africa. Of these students, approximately 10 were women. The total number increased to 222 in 1956, and increased further to 251 in 1957. These students pursued a two-year "A" level preliminary studies in science, arts, education, agriculture, veterinary science, and medicine. The table below shows the number of East African students attending Makerere in the years, 1955, 1956 and 1957.[10]

Degree Sought	1955	1956	1957
Preliminary Science	54	60	61
Preliminary Arts	54	50	58
Science Degree	9	10	8
Arts Degree	27	30	35
Education (two-year diploma)	22	26	18
Agriculture	8	11	14
Veterinary Science	3	9	11
Medicine	22	23	35
Post-Graduate Education	4	3	9
Fine Art Diploma	1	0	1
Art Teacher's Certificate	1	0	0
M.Sc	0	0	1
Totals	205	222	251

On the other hand, Tom Mboya estimated that 341 Kenyan males and 22 females passed the Cambridge Overseas Exams in 1957. Of these 363 students, 73 males and 1 female were admitted to Makerere, while 53 males and 4 females joined the Royal Technical College in Nairobi. In other words, both colleges accepted the total of 131 Kenyan students for the 1957 academic year. That was just a little more than one third of eligible students. In 1958, 491 students passed the Cambridge Examination. Of this total, 451 were males and 40 were females. Only 88 males were admitted to Makerere, while another 51 males were admitted to the Royal Technical College in Nairobi. The situation was even direr for female students. Out of the forty females only one was admitted to Makerere and two were admitted to the Royal Technical College.[11] Thus, the two colleges increased their enrolment to 142 students, an increase of 10 students from the previous year.

At any rate, in 1957 a total of 38 Kenyan students graduated from Makerere. Five students completed their studies in medicine; twenty-four in education; eight in agriculture; and one in veterinary science. However, none of them received further college education in the region. It must also be remembered that both Nairobi and Dar Es-Salam Colleges opened their doors for students in 1956 and 1961 respectively. Hence, no students graduated from these two establishments until the late 1950s and mid 1960s. At the time of Kenya's independence in 1963, the total of 478 students were enrolled in the University College in Nairobi, 749 students in the University College in Makerere, and 84 students at the University College of Dar Es-Salam.[12]

In general, the three East African "colleges" were unable to provide the large number of trained personnel needed for Africanization following independence. Hence, expansion in higher learning became very necessary and urgent. In due time, particularly in the late 1960s and into the 1970s, a number of new colleges were opened in the former British colonies, and the old colonial colleges were up-graded to universities. Consequently, the heads of African universities held several meetings to draw up a plan of cooperation between them. During a conference in Rabat, Morocco, in 1971, the heads of African universities formed an international non-governmental organization, the Association of African Universities (AAU) to encourage and enhance the exchange of information (research and curricula), and cooperation among universities in the continent. In the words of the Executive Vice-President of the AAU, the organization was formed:

> to create the type of students, of future leaders, who, through their assimilation in more than one African social scene, will develop an

awareness of the realities and aspirations, of the traditions and ideals of their peoples in Africa and hence a sense of belonging not to one tribe or nation but to Africa as a whole, and this is the unity of Africa which we like to see and are out to achieve.[13]

In reality, the inter-university cooperation remained ineffective due to an of absence governmental support. In other words, no substantial contribution particularly at the graduate level emanated from it. On the other hand, the universities were only able to admit a limited number of undergraduate students, and a far smaller number of post-graduates. Thus, it was not until buildings and facilities were constructed, sizeable faculty and administrative staff were hired, and libraries expanded that students in their hundreds were able to join the universities. One must note at this juncture that the United States helped some African colleges with the construction of new facilities, expansion of libraries, and furnishing faculty for short terms. The student body at most African universities during the two decades of independence cannot be considered large enough to meet the urgent needs of Africanization. In fact, as recently as 1972, Kenya had only one university, the University of Nairobi. This University, as stated above, began as the Royal Technical College of East Africa. It admitted students for the first time in 1956. It was renamed the Royal College Nairobi, and the University College of Nairobi in 1961 and 1963 respectively. Three years later, in 1966, it became the University of Nairobi, independent of the University of London. In 1973, a new campus of the University of Nairobi, that is, Kenyatta University College, was opened to prepare teachers for secondary schools.[14] However, Kenyatta University College and Egerton College, the latter of which was established exclusively for white students, were up-graded to full-fledged universities in 1985 and 1987 respectively. Two more public universities, Moi University in Eldoret with a Maseno Campus, and Jomo Kenyatta University at Juja, were opened in 1985. Recently, in 2002, the government inaugurated two universities, Kiriri Women's University of Science and Technology and Kabarak University. In 1969, a small private university, the United States International University, founded by Dr. William Rust, was inaugurated in Kasarani with three American students. However, students of USIU completed their studies at San Diego. It was not until 1979 that the first batch of 23 students graduated from USIU in Nairobi. Another private university, the Aga Khan University, was given a charter in 2002. There were also a host of missionary universities that sprang up in Kenya including the University of East Africa. Baraton, which was founded by the Seventh-day Adventists (1980), Africa Nazareine University (1988), the Catholic University of East Africa (1992), the Daystar University founded by Dr. Donald K. Smith, an American missionary, with strong ties with Messiah and Wheaton Colleges (1994), and Scott Theological University (1997) were all missionary universities. Moreover, the Phelps-Stokes school, Jeanes School at Kabete, was converted in 1961 into the Kenya Institute of Administration.

The student body in all of these universities, most of which were established almost two decades after independence, remained for sometime very small. For example, Kenyatta University College opened its doors with 200 students, while Moi University started with only 83 students. That is why at independence in 1963 there were less than 500 graduates in the country, all of whom received university degrees outside Kenya.[15] Hence, in the years before and following independence, higher education overseas became a welcome and necessary enterprise to train Kenyans to fill high-level manpower positions now being vacated by the Whites. The United States as well as other European and Asian countries opened the doors of their universities for Kenyan students. Even the USSR founded the Lumumba University, now Friendship University, in Moscow for African students. In fact, the U.S. government had been, for sometime, offering scholarships to African students under the Smith-Mundi Act of 1948 that authorized the interchange of persons, knowledge, and skills between the United States and foreign countries. However, for the whole period between 1948 and 1958 the number of scholarships that the Department of State provided was very low. Only two hundred and six scholarships were awarded to students from twenty African countries. Five countries received one scholarship each, while Morocco, Sudan, and Kenya received twenty-four scholarships each. Kenyan students and trade union personnel who arrived in the United States in the period between 1958 and 1961, as mentioned earlier, received financial assistance from private organizations, such as the AFL-CIO, the African-American Students Institute and the Joseph Kennedy Grant, and from colleges and universities as well as individuals and their own families and communities.

However, in the opening years of the 1960s, the United States, under the presidency of John F. Kennedy, played an effective role in providing scholarships to African students. In that respect, the Department of State joined hands through its Agency for International Development (USAID) and the Council for Educational Cooperation with Africa (CECAF) to develop two agencies, the African Scholarship Program (ASPAU) for undergraduates, and the African Graduate Fellowship Program (AFGRAD) for graduate students. Later, a newly established program, the Inter-African Scholarship Program (IASP), took the responsibility for undergraduates while the ASPAU focused on graduate students. One hundred forty-five colleges and universities participated in the programs.¹⁶ The two programs were placed under the administration of the African American Institute. Strict guidelines were drawn up for accepting students into the programs: First, the students must have been accepted by an accredited and appropriate American college or university; second, the student must have at least a partial scholarship or private assistance; third, the student must meet the required academic qualifications; and finally, the student must not be diverted from available spaces in African institutions of higher education.

The ASPAU and AFGRAD programs worked closely with government agencies, American colleges and universities, and private organizations. The member institutions dispersed the tuition and fees for each student. The home country of the student covered, as much as it could, the round trip transportation costs. On its part, the USAID paid for the students' maintenance expenses in addition to administrative costs incurred by the African American Institute. Private funding was also sought to cover transportation and maintenance expenses. As far as the government of Kenya is concerned, it offered some assistance to meet the transportation and tuition costs of very few students.

The ASPAU began its initial program in 1960. In that year, approximately twenty-four students from Nigeria were enrolled into nineteen American colleges. However, during the academic year 1960–1961, the two programs succeeded in enrolling the 1,823 African students in nearly 500 American colleges and universities. In the 1965–1966 academic year, the number of students rose to 6,880. These students came from forty-seven countries and were enrolled at 928 colleges and universities throughout the United States. Of the 6,880 African students, 6,046 were men and 834 were women.[17] In 1965 more students arrived in the United States from Africa than from other parts of the world. In that academic year, Kenyan students in the United States numbered 983, of whom 855 were men and 128 were women.[18] The Institute of International Education in Washington D.C. provided a list containing a year-by-year estimate by gender and academic status of Kenyan students studying in the United States in the period between 1955 and 1974. However, the list focused on students on ASPU, AFGRAD and IASP only. Most importantly, the list shows that the undergraduate students had by far outnumbered the graduate students.[19] At present, there are more Kenyan students studying in the United States than from any other African country. During the 2000–2001 academic years, Kenyan students numbered 7,097, while Nigeria had 4,499 students followed by Ghana with 2,672 students.

By 1967, approximately 63% of the African students attending colleges and universities in the United States were undergraduates. Nearly

50% of them majored in courses in the humanities or social sciences. Only 18% studied engineering and less than 10% majored in agriculture or medical science. However, the expansion in undergraduate programs coupled by the extremely limited nature of the graduate programs in the local universities in Africa led to the thinking that scholarships overseas should be increasingly directed toward graduate studies. In addition, by 1967, more and more African students, particularly undergraduates, began to remain in the United States upon graduation rather than return to their home countries. This failure to go back to Africa resulted in the loss of many young and talented people whose minds and skills were needed for the development of their homelands. During the period from 1962 to 1966, the number of African students who changed their student visa status to permanent residency in the United States increased from ninety to two hundred-six. In 1965, five hundred and five students, who were trained in professional and technical fields, were granted immigrant status. This was the beginning of the African "brain drain." The United Nations Educational, Scientific, and Cultural Organization (UNESCO) addressed this problem at its 1962 conference. The consensus was that the focus of overseas scholarships must be directed more and more to graduate studies. After all, students with graduate degrees, so it was argued, would more likely return to their home countries after graduation. Consequently, Kenyan students were encouraged to seek higher educational opportunities in the United States while undergraduates were advised to study at home in the East African universities.

Kenyan students who studied in the United States not only received high education in all branches of knowledge that equipped them to face the formidable challenge of developing their homeland, they also had first hand experience with American life and culture. In general, Kenyan students retained a favorable impression about their years in the United States and their experiences there. However, of course some students naturally had bad experiences. By way of elaborating on this point, we will relate the experiences of three Kenyan students, Joseph B.K. Ulayeneza, Peter Njogu, and Thaddeus Okatch.

Joseph B.K. Ulayeneza who attended Rutgers University explained his experiences in America in a letter that he addressed to the American Consulate in Nairobi on April 4, 1957. He described his experience at that university as being 'delightful.' The students and faculty, he wrote, were kind, friendly, helpful, and interested in learning about East Africa. He said that he had a number of American friends and was quite frequently asked to attend various events such as dinners, dances, parties, speeches, athletic and other social events. He traveled through a number of states and visited several College campuses in order to broaden his experience and to have a better understanding of American society. He visited Boston, New York, Newark, New Jersey, Philadelphia, Pittsburgh, Toledo, Cleveland, Detroit, and East Lansing. Ulayeneza, however, related that he was taken aback by the lack of knowledge that American students in particular and the American public in general had about the rest of the world. He thought that the citizens of the United States would have a broader understanding of the complex international issues and at least a general knowledge of geography with all of the modern technology, including radio and television, in hand. However, he was sad and amused to discover that in spite of all the advances in technology, his American colleagues would simply ask whether India was in Africa.[20]

Peter Njogu, on the other hand, was rather unlucky to have a first hand experience with police harassment as attested to by eyewitnesses. Njogu was a graduate student at Bemidji College, now Bemidji State University, in Minnesota. He was considered to be a promising student and was well respected and liked at the college and in the local community. However, he was arrested and charged with burglarizing a jewelry store. Njogu claimed that he walked past the jewelry store on the way to his apartment building when he heard the alarm sound off in the store. He entered the building to make sure that no one was hurt. After realizing that he might be suspected of burglarizing the store, he then ran to his apartment only to discover that his keys were missing. He returned to the store and climbed through the window to retrieve the keys. Those who saw what happened reported him to the police who duly arrested him. The owner of the store did not report any merchandise missing and did not sign a complaint against Njogu. However, the local judge did not drop the charges in spite of eyewitness accounts that supported him. A member of the community, Mrs. Young, wrote to the Department of State complaining about the injustice Njogu had received. She reported, "he was harassed, abused and called all kinds of nasty names by his accusers."[21] No further information, police records or otherwise, regarding this case were available. The violation of the Civil Rights of black people by local authorities was a common theme during the 1960s and 1970s. At times, students from African countries, in this case Kenya, were regularly swept into the injustices of American society.

The third Kenyan student, Thaddeus Okatch, was subjected to the worst faith of all, that is, death. Okatch was a graduate student at the University of Missouri. In November of 1968, he was shot to death in Kansas City, Missouri. Okatch, reportedly a friend of Tom Mboya, was married to a white American woman and had a son. He was robbed and murdered by two African-American males in the parking lot after leaving a bar with another white woman. The representative of the Kenyan government, who was responsible for the welfare of Kenyan students in the United States, suggested, "Okatch's murder was racially motivated because Okatch was married to a white woman, was in the company of another white woman at the time of the murder, and had many white friends."[22] However, these incidents, though not a common occurrence, are illustrative of the complex realities of racism and crime in urban areas in the United States. While the murder of Okatch could possibly have been because he was in the company of a white woman, the culprits might as well have been under the assumption that he had a large amount of money on him.

THE JOURNEY BACK HOME: AFRICANIZATION OF THE COLONIAL ADMINISTRATION

The overwhelming majority of American-educated Kenyan elites as well as those who studied in Western Europe and Asia returned home to embark on the enormous task of nation building. They began to fill the top positions vacated by the Europeans following the transition of power from the colonial authorities to the nationalists. Employment opportunities for them were readily available as educators, politicians, administrators, army and police officers, medical doctors, dentists, engineers, architects, magistrates and lawyers, community leaders, and businesspersons. In contrast, their colleagues who graduated from universities in the Soviet Union faced much difficulty in landing employment. The American Embassy in Nairobi estimated that about 700 Kenyan students were studying in the USSR in 1968. Most of them received training in engineering and natural science.[23] The Embassy claimed that in 1970 there were about 264 USSR-educated Kenyans who were still searching for employment. The Embassy named George King Makodollah, recipient of a degree in economics from the USSR, as the champion of the cause of his colleagues.[24] It appears that the stigma of communist indoctrination stood in the way of these students. Besides, there has been the tendency of graduates of the same education institutions to favor their colleagues. Hence, one may describe the graduates from colleges and universities in a particular country as a "tribe." Thus, it is not surprising for the American and West European-educated *Asomi* to favor their members vis-à-vis the Soviet Union-educated Kenyan elites.

However, even though the majority of Kenyan students who were educated overseas made their way home, many students stayed permanently in the host countries. Such a problem was not exclusive to Kenya. Other African nations were also affected by this "brain drain." As mentioned above, the seriousness and urgency of this problem prompted UNESCO to address it in its 1962 conference. The solution, it was so believed, rested on discouraging undergraduate students, rather than graduate students, from seeking studies overseas. It was argued that undergraduate students were more likely to be tempted and "fascinated" by the quality of life in the United States and Europe and would therefore prefer not to return to the homeland. Likewise, Professor Ali Mazrui was sure that the African "brain drain" was the result of two factors: "the pull-in force of the host countries welcoming migrating professionals and this involves better facilities, better pay, nicer working conditions and greater freedom; and the pull-out forces in our countries, such as lack of recognition, lack of adequate facilities, and very often governments that are intolerant and so on. "People who work very hard in our countries often feel that nobody gives a damn, which is what makes them want to go and work elsewhere, if only to feel that what they do is at least recognized."[25] Such reasoning was true concerning a number of Kenyan graduate students, as well as other Africans, who stayed in America after graduation.

One of these Kenyan students was Professor Reuel John Mugo Gatheru. This noted historian/political scientist and novelist was born in 1925 into a large Kikuyu family. He maintains that his father had two wives. "My mother had eight children: four boys and four girls. I was the first-born. The other wife of my father had fourteen children: five boys and nine girls." Mugo's father, a squatter on a white settler farm, was a reputed "medicine man." He sent his young son to Kanuti-Weithyaga Sector School of the Church Missionary Society, from which Mugo graduated in 1941. Thereafter, Mugo attended Kambui School for three years. Although he passed the school certificate examination that permitted him entry into Makerere College, the colonial authorities blocked his admission. He was branded as a "radical" who dared writing a "seditious" letter to a local newspaper in which he condemned racial discrimination in the country. Mugo objected to being called a radical. He insists that "the adjective 'radical' in reference to an African who was fighting for his people did not have any meaning." To him, the words "agitators, subversives, and troublemakers who were only talking hotheaded nonsense to the Africans" that the colonial establishment hurled at the nationalists were no more than "foolish" adjectives aimed at discrediting an honorable and just cause."[26]

Mugo relates a situation that he experienced at Bethune-Cookman College in fall of 1950 to show that such statements were simply bosh to hide the truth and turn listeners against those who demanded justice and fought for liberation and dignity:

here was a football match between Bethune-Cookman College and Florida Agricultural and Mechanical University in Tallahassee. The Governor of Florida gave an opening speech in which he praised the administrators of both schools and referred to them as "good" and "successful Negroes." At that time, there was a Civil Rights suit against the University of Florida Law School, filed by the NAACP—because the Law School did not want to admit Negroes. The governor went on to advise people in attendance to enjoy the game and avoid the "troublemakers" and "ill-advised Negroes" who were under the influence of the NAACP. The Governor described the NAACP as "radical" and "irresponsible."[27]

It is, however, interesting to note that although Mugo voiced the grievances of his people at that young age (he was then in his teens), he nonetheless held conservative views concerning the colonial situation in Kenya. He confessed that at the time he did not "believe that the Africans of Kenya were ready for complete independence."[28]

Having failed to be admitted to Makerere, Mugo joined the Medical Research Laboratory in Nairobi in 1945 as a trainee, and at the same time looked for the opportunity to travel abroad in search of advanced learning. In time, he was able to raise enough funds to go to India in 1949 to prepare for the Senior Cambridge Examination at St. Joseph's High School in Allahabad. Thereafter, in 1950, he trekked to the United States. It is not known for certain who sponsored his trip to America. However, he says emphatically that no government has sponsored his travels and academic wanderings among universities and colleges in America. All the expenses, he insists, were covered by "scholarships, friends, and self-help—working, doing various jobs on the campuses and employment in various restaurants and companies."[29]

It is apparent that Mugo considered St. Joseph's but a lay-by at the side of a long road to America. He assures us that his "mind was always about how to get to the United States." He noted, "I was restless while in India."[30] In fact, Mugo waited nervously for good news from his relative, Eliud Mathu, the first Kenyan to occupy an unofficial seat in the all-white Legislative Council (Legco). Mathu had sent, in 1948, a handwritten letter of recommendation on behalf of Mugo to St. Clair Drake at Roosevelt University. It did not take long for Mugo to leave for the United States. St Clair Drake welcomed him personally at the railway station in Chicago in the spring of 1950. Henceforward, an everlasting intimate friendship flowered between the two men. Mugo relished the relationship saying, "St. Clair Drake was very close to me. He was like my own brother from the same mother. I am so happy that he finally met my own mother in Kenya in 1963. I met Drake's mother in Stanton, Virginia, in December 1951. She also treated me as her own son."[31] Mugo confessed that at the beginning, he faced some difficulty adjusting to life in America, but Dr. Drake was always there helping him "to fit in the system." Mugo attended Summer School at Roosevelt University. The following year, Mrs. Mary McLeod Bethune, founder of Bethune-Cookman, offered him a partial scholarship at the University (College) for the academic year of 1950–1951. Mugo recalls with much joy that Dr. Bethune invited him "to a Christmas dinner in 1950, which I enjoyed very much. She was a dynamic lady who also loved the African students very much."[32] Nonetheless, he did not feel that his experience at the college was rewarding. He was saddened and disillusioned by the disinterest of the College President in African students.

Mugo studied history, political science, English literature, biology, and sociology at Bethune-Cookman. In the fall of 1951, he transferred to Lincoln University in Chester County, Pennsylvania, where he received a full scholarship. At Lincoln, Mugo felt at home. He describes his experience there as "wholesome." In his company were two Kikuyu close friends, Kariuki Karanja Njiiri and George Mbugua Kimani, as well as "one student from Southwest Africa (now Namibia), Mburumba Kerina, two (students) from Sierra Leone, and eight from Nigeria." Mugo noted that although the African students formed a close bond, they did not have an organization. Mugo stated, "I found, however, that the students from Nigeria, who were in the majority among African students, were a little bit unfriendly to other African students—especially the Ibos. This was, to me, unfortunate because the Ibo people of the eastern region of Nigeria had produced brilliant leaders like Azikiwe and others who were pan-Africanist in their outlook. Surprisingly, I found other students from Nigeria (apart from the Ibos) to be extremely friendly—especially the Yoruba."[33]

Once the Mau Mau revolution broke out in Kenya, Mugo and other Kenyan students in the United States were placed under constant surveillance. Upon the declaration of State of Emergency in Kenya in 1952, the United States Immigration Service decided to deport a number of Kenyan students, including Mugo Gatheru.[34] He was in his junior year at Lincoln when he received a letter from the Immigration Office in Philadelphia ordering him to leave the country within thirty days. This caused an uproar among Lincoln students who protested the deportation order. St. Clair Drake, as well as a host of liberal Americans, championed the "cause of Mugo" and fought the expulsion notices. For an undisclosed reason, Mugo was not prepared to discuss the case. In a correspondence in 2003 he wrote, "no observation about this incident."[35]

It was not however until 1957 that the Immigration Office finally rescinded its decision. Meanwhile, Mugo completed his studies at Lincoln in 1954 and obtained a B.A. degree in history and political science. He then left Pennsylvania for New York. He registered as part-time student for an M.A. degree in political science at New York University. At the same time, he worked for the New York Standard Manufacturing Company in Brooklyn making hampers, baskets and stools. He was subsequently employed as a clerk in the mailroom of Dun and Bradstreet, "a big company, a credit rating company." "The Management, especially in the mail room, liked me very much."[36] In 1958, Mugo graduated from New York University with an M.A. degree. In that same year, he married a white woman, Ms Dolores. It is possible that by then he had made up his mind not to return to Kenya.

America fascinated Mugo and many other African students so much so that they acquired citizenship and lived permanently in "exile." For one, Mugo was certainly impressed by the quality of life in New York City. He wrote:

> My experience in New York was wonderful. To live in a big city like New York City—one has to learn how to survive and that very quickly. I liked New York City very much. I formed the impression that New York City had everything: that if you do not find anything that you wanted in New York City, that thing does not exist anywhere in the world.[37]

Marriage to a white woman may yet be another reason for not returning home. Nevertheless, it must be noted that being wedded to white women did not necessarily preclude Kenyans, including *Mzee* Jomo Kenyatta himself, from making the journey back to their country of origin. Kenyatta was married to an English wife, Edna Clarke, from whom he had one son, Peter Magana Kenyatta. Professor Mugo was certain that Kenya would have welcomed his family with open arms. In fact, when he visited Kenya in 1980, accompanied by his wife and younger daughter, Wanjiku, he was warmly received by his relatives, old friends and people in general. Mugo, however, attests that there were three interrelated basic factors that forced him to stay in the west. These were family concerns, his disillusionment with Mboya's nepotism and fear of Mboya's wrath.

In November 1958, Mugo, accompanied by his wife, left New York for London ostensibly to study and train as a solicitor under the auspices of London Law Society.[38] William X. Scheinman, whom Mugo considered a friend, offered financial assistance that covered his tuition fees, board, and lodging. However, in 1960, Scheinman suddenly terminated his assistance at the behest, so Mugo alleges, of Tom Mboya. Mugo claims that Mboya "punished" him because of his from-afar campaign in support of Munyua Waiyaki, a Kikuyu politician, who was running against Mboya in Nairobi Central (Kamakunji) constituency in the 1960 general elections. Mugo says that Mboya's success or failure in that constituency depended on the Kikuyu, the overwhelming residents of Nairobi. Mugo wrote to his Kikuyu relatives and friends in the city asking them to vote for Waiyaki. He insists that his anti-Mboya campaign "was not because (Mboya) was a Luo, but because he did something in 1958, which Mugo did not like." Mugo explained that Mboya "spoke to a very large Negro group in Atlanta about the African problem in Kenya. The group was highly impressed. Some of the organizers in Atlanta were people like Dr. Horace Bond, Mugo' former friend and president of Lincoln University in Chester County, Pennsylvania. Immediately, after the meeting was over, Mboya was promised five scholarships, which were to be made available immediately for Kenyan students. In the end, Mboya allocated all these five scholarships to the Luo students—most of them members of his family and extended family."[39] In other words, Mboya, in the eyes of Mugo, practiced naked nepotism that a nationalist of his stature must shun without any reservations. Hence, he campaigned against Mboya. Mugo claims that when "Mr. Mboya learned that I was supporting Dr. Waiyaki, his political enemy . . . he asked William X. Scheinman to cut off all financial support, which he was offering to me." Scheinman immediately stopped his assistance.[40]

Undoubtedly, Mugo held personal animosity toward Tom Mboya. It would not be far from the truth to suggest that he expected to win one of the five scholarships offered to Mboya in Atlanta. Mugo was there, together with Dr. Njoroge Mungai, participating in arranging Mboya's itinerary. Both men were students at time and accompanied Mboya in his tours. He and Dr. Mungai were the two oldest and most prominent Kenyan students in the United States at the time. Mugo has been supporting himself for the last four years by working odd jobs. He was in dire need of financial assistance now that he had a family. That Mboya, whom Mugo considered a close friend, had overlooked him in the allocation of scholarships was a bitter pill to swallow. Worst still, Mugo received help not from his compatriot but from a white activist, William X. Scheinman. Hence, one could be correct to view his anti-Mboya campaign as no more than the settling of an old score.

Tom Mboya won the Nairobi seat easily. Mugo contemplated on what else Mboya, who was now "calling the shots" in Kenya, would do to him were he to return to the country. The drying up of Scheinman's financial assistance at the request of Mboya was disastrous enough. Mugo says, "this caused tremendous financial hardship to me." By then he had two or three children. So desperate was his situation that his wife was forced to work as a non-qualified pharmacist for St. Leonard Hospital in London for a couple of months in 1960. She then transferred to Hammersmith General Hospital. Mugo says of her with much adulation, "from 1960 to 1963, my wife, Dolores, was the bred-winner."[41] Toward the end of 1963, she abandoned her job at the hospital to look after the children. To maintain the family, Mugo discontinued his law studies, having passed Part I of the solicitors qualifying examination, to serve as a clerk for Lord Chancellor's Office in the High Court of Justice in 1964–1965. Thereafter, he worked as an articled clerk with a law firm, Gillhams Solicitors of West End in London until 1968. Mugo never took Part II of the qualifying examination.[42]

All the same, there was no reprieve from the hardship. Mugo grieved that "I had a wife and three very young children, and very, very little money. I could not make it in London. I regarded my wife and three children as number one, first priority."[43] However, rather than returning to Kenya, he desperately hunted for jobs in the USA. The thought of Kenya did not cross his mind because of the reasons mentioned above. Luckily, he was offered the position of Assistant Professor of African History at California State College, now California State University, in Sacramento. On August 25, 1969, the Mugo family arrived in the United States to settle permanently in California. In the mean time, Mugo obtained his J.D. degree from Northern California Law School, Sacramento, in 1988. He retired in May 2002 and now lives in Sacramento, which he considers as his "proper capital and home." At present, he is occupied with the writing of two books: "one on the political history of Kenya from 1898 to 1976 under the title, *The Moldings of the New Kenya,* (and) the second, a political novel under the heading, *The Red Feather in the Lake.*"[44]

One is, however, inclined to question the "fear of the wrath of Mboya" as an overriding justification for Professor Mugo's election to remain in "exile" considering that he would undoubtedly have had his Kikuyu friends, Dr. Waiyaki, Hon. Kariuki Njiiri, and Dr. Njorogi Mungai as protectors. Dr. Waiyaki (b. 1932) was a graduate of Fort Hare in South Africa, University of St. Andrews, Scotland, and Lund University, Sweden. He held the powerful positions of Parliamentary Secretary for Internal Security and Defense in the *Madaraka* cabinet, then of Assistant Minister in the Office of the President, Deputy Speaker of the National Assembly, Minister for Foreign Affairs (1974–1978), Minister of Industry (1979–1980), and Minister of Agriculture (1980). Moreover, Waiyaki was one of the two personal physicians of *Mzee* Jomo Kenyatta. Hon. Kariuki Njiiri, on the other hand, was Parliamentary Secretary for the Ministry of Resources, while Dr. Mungai, see below, the other personal physician of *Mzee* Jomo Kenyatta, was Minister for Health and Housing. At any rate, Mugo did not even visit Kenya until 1977, about eight years after the death of Mboya. This delay could have been the result of financial restraints. Hence, family considerations, fascination and assimilation into American life (including marriage to a white American woman) appear to be the real reasons behind Mugo's decision to live and raise his children in the United States.

Just as Mugo Gatheru elected or, according to him, was compelled by circumstance to seek employment and settle permanently in the United States, thus was the same reasoning of a few other Kenyan students who remained in the United States after graduation for a period of time to work in the host country before they finally returned to their homeland. Some of these students wanted to gain practical experience while others planned to earn money to take home with them. Of course, some students harbored the intention of staying permanently in America but after awhile went back to their country. They became, at long last, disillusioned with life in the west and longed for the comfort of life in the bosom of their own people. For example, Professor Robert Obudho, a Luo from South Nyanza, did not return immediately to Kenya upon receiving his Ph.D. degree in geography from Rutgers University. Obudho was one of the students in Mboya's airlift of 1961. He attended Cobleskill College, New York, and the University of New York, Sunny, from which institution he earned his B.Sc. degree in 1967. He returned to Kenya to join Nairobi University for one year. However, in 1968, the University sent him back to the United States. He attended Rutgers University where he obtained an M.A. degree in 1970 and a Ph.D. degree in 1974. Instead of returning promptly to his institution and country, Obudho remained at Rutgers as instructor and Assistant Professor until 1982. Thereafter (1982–1985), he held the position of Assistant Professor at State University of New York. After this long sojourn of fifteen years in the United States, Obudho finally went back home. He rejoined the teaching staff of the University of Nairobi, and now holds the position of Full Professor.[45]

At any rate, the earliest returnees from the United States were that handful of pioneer Kenyan missionary students who came to America in the first decades of the twentieth century. At the head of this batch was Molonkett Ole Sempele, the first Kenyan to study in America. Ole Sempele received his theological education in North Carolina and Boydton, VA. Upon his return to Kenya, he broke away from the AIM to found an independent African church. Ole Sempele was followed, a decade or so later, by Bishop Henry John Okullu who studied at Virginia Theological Seminary, and Bishop Thomas Johnson Kalume who attended Union Theological College.[46] We must also mention here Dr. Samuel Gakuhi Kibicho who first attended Carver School of Missions and Social Work before he moved to Louisville Presbyterian Theological Seminary and finally Vanderbilt University from 1960–1972. Dr. Kibichu returned to Kenya to become the Vice-Principal and thereafter Principal of St. Paul Theological College in Limuru. However, he joined the University of Nairobi in 1974 as lecturer, senior lecturer, and professor in the Department of Religious Studies.[47]

The second batch of Kenyans to return home from the United States was composed of trade union trainees. One of them was the celebrated trade union leader, Arthur A. Ochwada, a Luo, who was born in 1926 in Samia, Western Province. Ochwada, a graduate of Masino High School, began his career in the trade unions at an early age as Secretary of the East African Federation of Building and Construction Workers Union, a post that he held for nine years. In 1955, at the age of twenty-nine, he became the Deputy-Secretary for the Kenya Federation of Labor. It was while he was holding that position that he, together with William Kiwanuka and Patrick Mandawa, took a five-month advanced management course in Trade Unionism at Harvard University, and completed practical training in Detroit in 1958 under the auspices the AFL-CIO.[48] While in the United States, Ochwada cultivated close relationship with Asa Philip Randolph and corresponded with him regularly after his return to Kenya on matters concerning trade union activities. Upon his return to Kenya, Ochwada was elected General Secretary of the Trade Unions Congress, a position that he held from 1959 to 1961. In addition, he served as member of the Labor and Wages Advisory Board, the Christian Industrial Council, the Industrial Court, the National Wages Advisory Committee, and as member of the Executive Board of the International Confederation of Free Trade Unions. Like Tom Mboya, his trade unionist colleague, Ochwada entered the national political arena as one of the founders and the first Deputy General-Secretary of the Kenya African National Union (KANU). In 1963, he was elected Kenya representative to the East Africa Assembly, and in 1965, he was appointed chairman of the Agricultural Wages Council. Ochwada continued to serve his country as a veteran trade unionist, as Member of Parliament representing Busia South, and in various ministries in the cabinet of Mzee Kenyatta.[49]

Yet another renowned trade unionist who studied in the United States and returned home to participate in the modernization and development of the trade union movement and served his country in a number of capacities was Ochola Ogaye Mak'ayengo, a Lou from Ndhiwa, South Nyanza. Born in 1930, Ochola began his career as a clerk in Kenya Shell Co. but was soon hailed as the founder of the Kenya Petroleum Oil Workers Union, where he became the first Secretary-General (1956–1969). Meanwhile, he joined the University of Chicago under the auspices of the AFL-CIO and obtained a diploma in industrial relations. Subsequently, he returned to Kenya to fill the office of Secretary-General of Kenya African Workers Union, the office of Vice-President of Africa Chapter of the International Federation of Petroleum Workers, the office of Secretary-General of Railways and Harbors Union, and the office of Assistant Secretary-General of All Africa Trade Union Federation. Further still, just like his colleagues at the top of the trade union movement in Kenya, he ventured into open politics as a founding member of Kenya Peoples' Union (KPU), a move that led to his brief detention in 1969. That ordeal did not deter him from reentering the political field. In fact, after his release from detention, he succeeded in becoming a Member of Parliament representing Ndhiwa constituency for almost two decades. Additionally, he served as Assistant-Minister for Health, Assistant-Minister for Culture and Social Services, and Assistant-Minister for Foreign Affairs. He passed away in 1990, leaving behind a legacy of an industrious and dedicated trade unionist that rose from the rank of a junior clerk to one of the highest positions of responsibility in his country.[50]

The development of qualified, well-trained trade union personnel continued to be an urgent priority for Tom Mboya and the trade union leadership in Kenya. For that reason, the student airlifts of 1959, 1960 and 1961 brought to the United States a number of young Kenyans seeking high academic degrees in industrial management and labor relations, rather than just receiving a 'crash course' and practical training of short duration in trade union organization as was the general case in the past years. One of this new crop of trade union officers was Tom Diju Owuor, a Lou, who was born in 1936. One cannot but notice at this juncture the predominance of the Lou, the ethnic group of Tom Mboya, in the trade union movement in Kenya and consequently the predominance of Lou trade union trainees in receiving scholarships to study in the United States. To Mboya's critics, this fact lends credence to the allegation that Tom Mboya favored his kith and kin, the Lou. At any rate, Owuor arrived in the United States on the "Student Airlift" of 1961. He attended New York University (1961–1964) where he received a Bachelor degree, and thereafter (1964–1966) completed his MA studies in labor relations at Cornel University, Ithaca. Owuor returned to Kenya immediately following his graduation. He joined the Civil Service as a Labor Officer. Two years later, in 1967, he entered to the Private Sector as Personnel Manager of Uplands Bacon Factory Kenya Ltd., the first Kenyan to hold such a post. That move was in line with the

Kenyanization process of that enterprise that had been administered and controlled by British shareholders. Owuor remained with Uplands for three years. Thereafter, in 1969, he joined the semi-governmental company, Kenya Oil Industry, as its Industrial Relations Spokesman. At the same time, Owuor continued to serve in the Federation of Kenya Employees of which he became Chief Executive Officer from 1973 to 1976, and thereafter he became the Executive Director. He and his trade union colleagues who returned from their tour of study in the United States contributed mightily to the development of trade unionism in Kenya.[51]

Although the number of religious personalities and trade unionists who came to the United States for academic and training advancement was not that large, there is no record that any of them had remained in America. It appears that they all returned home to participate in the building of Kenya. Likewise, almost all the first Kenyans to receive higher education in the United States in Liberal Arts and the Sciences, with the exception of Professor Mugo Gatheru made their way back to Kenya. The first of this crop that completed its post-graduate education in Liberal Arts in the United States at the time when evangelical and vocational education was the rule of the day was Peter Mbiyu Koinange.[52] Koinange was born in 1907 in Kiambu in the heart of Kikuyu homeland. It was his father, Senior Chief Koinange, who paid for his trip and education in the United States. Mbiyu attended Hampton Institute, Wesleyan University, and finally received his MA degree from the University of Columbia Teachers College in 1936. He was thus the first Kenyan to complete post-graduate studies. On his way back to Kenya from the United States, he spent the best of two years (1936–1938) in Britain where he joined St. John's College, Cambridge, for one year and transferred to the University of London studying for a post-graduate diploma in education. However, he did not complete these studies. It was during his sojourn in Britain that he met and established close and everlasting relationship with an African-American student, Ralph Bunch, with Kwame Nkrumah, Milton Obote, and his countryman, Jomo Kenyatta. Although Kenyatta was opposed to the appointment of Mbiyu's father as Senior Chief by the colonial administration as well as to his collaboration with the colonial administration in Kenya, the two young nationalists remained close to each other until *Mzee* Kenyatta's death in 1978. Their intimate friendship solidified following the detention of Senior Chief Koinange by the colonial authorities at the height of Mau Mau insurgency.[53] When Kenyatta returned to the country, Mbiyu employed him as head of his Kenya Teachers College. Shortly thereafter, Kenyatta wedded Miss Grace Wanjiku, one of Mbiyu's sisters. The marriage sealed the close relationship between these twin pillars of might, Kenyatta and Mbiyu, in independent Kenya. It is thus not surprising that Mbiyu joined hands with his brother-in-law and other nationalists to form the Kenya African Union (KAU) and its successor, the Kenya African National Union (KANU). In 1963, Mbiyu became a member of the House of Representatives, representing Kiamba. He also served as Minister of State for African Affairs in the *Madaraka* cabinet, a position that was in tune with his strong Pan-Africanist sentiment that he apparently acquired at Hampton and through his association with African-American students, particularly Ralph Bunch, as well as with Kwame Nkrumah and others. Nkrumah was so impressed with Mbiyu's commitment to Pan-Africanism that he appointed him one of the Directors of the Bureau of African Affairs. In fact, while still at Hampton, Mbiyu became a member of Carter G. Woodson's organization, the Association for the Study of Negro Life and History.

In 1964, Kenyatta appointed Mbiyu Minister for Education, a post that was very close to Mbiyu's heart. But two years later Kenyatta brought him closer when he appointed him Minister of State in the Office of the President, a portfolio that he held until 1978, the year when Kenyatta passed away. As *nyapara,* meaning Prime Minister or the leading figure in the inner circle of authority, Mbiyu's word was as authoritative as that of *Mzee* Kenyatta himself. So powerful was he that all, even his colleagues in the cabinet, feared him. The story is told that when Kenyatta collapsed in Mombasa in the afternoon of August 22, 1978, he asked for Mbiyu just before he passed away. People wonder what might have happened to the succession had Mbiyu not left Mombasa for Nairobi to attend to personal matters a few hours before *Mzee* died. At any rate, during Moi's tenure as President, Mbiyu continued to play a role, albeit with much reduced power, in the political life of Kenya as Minister of Natural Resources for one year. However, he exited the circle of power when he lost his parliamentary seat in the general elections of 1979. He died two years later in 1981.

Hon. Mbiyu Koinange, the American-educated *Asomi*, left the legacy of an educator of the highest order. Immediately following his return to Kenya from the United States, he founded the Kenya Teachers College in Githunguri (1939) to provide teachers for the independent schools. In addition, he championed and campaigned very hard for sending Kenyans to the United States to receive higher education in its colleges and universities. One of the students that he inspired and helped to seek Liberal Arts education in the United States was his student and "protégé, Dr. Julius Gikonyo Kiano. As mentioned earlier, Dr. Kiano returned to Kenya as its first Ph.D. degree holder to join the Royal Technical College Nairobi. No Kenyan national had held such a position before him. Hence, Dr Kiano took the first step toward the grand scheme of Africanization of the Nairobi Campus and education in general.[54] Although Dr. Kiano left the college to participate in the nationalist movement, his services chartered the road map for qualified academicians to replace the white instructors who were now on their way out of Kenya. In fact, the Kenyanization of the Royal Technical College Nairobi and its expansion were two of the foremost priorities of Tom Mboya, Dr. Kiano and their colleagues who worked diligently to airlift Kenyan students to the United States in the period between 1957 and 1961. A number of these students returned to Kenya to serve in the departments and schools that would soon be created at the college, which would be upgraded to a full-fledged university in the very near future, as well as fill the positions vacated by the white faculty. Immediately following independence in 1963, the Royal College Nairobi became a constituent college of the University of East Africa. It was elevated to a full-fledged independent university by Act of Parliament in 1970.

Hon. Peter Mbiyu Koinange was one of several American-educated *Asomi* who held crucial portfolios in the *Madaraka* cabinet of 1963. The others included Hon. Samuel Ayodo, Minister of Local Government, Hon. Lawrence George Sagini, Minister of Natural Resources, and Dr. Julius Kiano, Minister of Commerce and Industry. Hon. Sagini (b. 1926), who hailed from the Luo, graduated from Kagumu Teachers College and Makerere. He attended Allegheny College in Meadville, Pennsylvania, on an Inter-American Institute of Labor scholarship. He graduated with a B.A. degree in 1959 and immediately returned to Kenya to fill the position of Education Officer and at the same time served as member of the steering committee of KANU. Consequently, he became one of the delegates that participated in the Lancaster House Conference of 1960. A year later (1961), he was elected to the Legislative Council as representative of Kisii. Hon. Sagini was then appointed Minister of Education, a portfolio that he held for two years (1962–1963). He was elected to Parliament in the national elections of 1963, and was duly appointed Minister of Natural Resources in the *Madaraka* cabinet. In 1964, *Mzee* Kenyatta appointed him Minister for Local Government. Hon. Sagini served Kenya in several capacities as a member of Parliament, the Council of Kenyatta University, and Chairman of the Council of the University of Nairobi. He also became the Director of the Maize and Produce Board and the Kenya Power and Lightening Co. Board. In addition, Hon. Sagini served as Board Member of a number of private companies including the East Africa Industries, Securicor Ltd., Elville House for the Depraved, as well as James Finly and Kenchick Ltd. He died in 1992. In 1995, the University of Nairobi conferred on him posthumously the Honorary Doctorate of Letters.[55]

On the other hand, Hon. Samuel Onyango Ayodo, also from the Luo, attended Maseno High School and Makerere. He graduated from Lincoln University in 1959 with a B.A. degree in education. He returned to Kenya to become a teacher in Kisii School. Within a year of his arrival, he was elected to the Legislative Council, and thereafter, in 1963, to the National Parliament. Hon. Ayodo then served in the Ministry of Local Government in the *Madaraka* cabinet. Later he became Minister of Wildlife and Tourism. Hon. Ayodo passed away in August 1998.[56]

The meteoric career of the American-educated *Asomi* who Africanized the University College of Nairobi testifies to the availability of positions for qualified Kenyans and of their swift rise to the top of the academic and administrative hierarchy following the departure of white instructors and administrative staff. By way of illustration, we will examine the profiles of two of these *Asomi,* Professor Philip Githinji and Professor Josephat Njunguna Karanja, both of whom hailed from the Kikuyu. Professor Githingi, brother of the incumbent President Mwai Kibaki, came to the United States in 1957 where he first attended Morgan State University in Baltimore. He then transferred to Purdue University, Indiana, from where he obtained a B.Sc. degree in mechanical engineering in 1960. Thereafter, Githingi attended California Institute of Technology and graduated with a M.Sc., degree in 1963. He returned to Kenya to join the teaching staff of the newly created Faculty (School) of Engineering. At the same time, Githingi pursued a Ph.D. degree, which he completed at Nairobi University in 1975. He then became Chairman and thereafter Dean of the Faculty of Engineering as well as Principal of the College of Architecture and Engineering. In 1985, he was appointed Deputy Vice-Chancellor of the University of Nairobi, and two years later Vice Chancellor of Kenyatta University.[57] Prior to his death he became the Regional Representative of the Commonwealth Higher Education Management Service.

Another American-educated elite, Professor Josephat Njunguna Karanja, enrolled at the University of Atlanta in 1957 after having spent a year at the University of New Delhi, India. He then attended Princeton University, NJ, where he received a Ph.D. degree in history in 1962. While still engaged in the writing of his dissertation, Karanja joined the faculty of Farleigh Dickinson University in New Jersey as lecturer in African studies. He then returned to Kenya to begin an active career that led him to serve in a number of capacities at the University College of Nairobi, the Ministry of Foreign Affairs, and in the political arena. He first joined Nairobi College as a lecturer. Towards the end of 1963, just over a year after his graduation from Princeton, Dr. Karanja was appointed as the first Kenyan High Commissioner to London, a position that he held until 1970. In that year, the

Nairobi College of the University of East Africa attained the status of a full-fledged university by an Act of Parliament. The Chancellor of the University, *Mzee* Jomo Kenyatta, appointed Dr. Karanja as its first Vice-Chancellor.[58] In 1986, Dr. Karanja made his entry onto the political stage as a Member of Parliament representing Githunguri constituency. A year later, he was appointed Assistant Minister for Research, Science, and Technology. In 1988, President Daniel Arap Moi raised him to the position of Vice-President. However, sixteen months later, he resigned his post after Parliament passed a vote of no confidence in him.[59] Parliament accused Dr. Karanja of furthering his own interests and those of his ethnic group, the Kikuyu, and of insubordination. It was alleged that whenever the President was on an official trip out of the country, he even "forced certain politicians to kneel before him to plead for mercy."[60] That parliamentary action ended Dr. Karanja's political career. He passed away in 1992.

Kenyan male students who studied in the United States during the period under consideration outnumbered by far their female counterparts. However, there is no evidence that any female student opted to remain in America. They all seem to have returned to their country of birth. Among them were Grace Njeri Wagema, Pamela A. Mboya, wife of Tom Mboya, and Dr. Wangari Muta Maathai. Ms Grace Wagema, who hailed from the Kikuyu, was born in Nairobi in 1925. Upon her graduation from Alliance High School in 1945, Ms Wagema was appointed Welfare Officer for East Africa Railways and Harbors. She was thus the first woman ever to hold such a position. However, she left her post three years later to study at Makerere. Subsequently, she became Headmistress of North Nyanza Home Craft Center. In 1959, Wagema arrived in the United States on the first Mboya airlift. She attended Howard University (1959–1963) where she received a B.A. degree in home economics. She returned to Kenya to become the first women to hold a senior position in the Ministry of Agriculture as Supervisor and shortly thereafter she was appointed as the Director of Home Economics and Agricultural Extension Department.[61]

Pamela Arua Odede, who changed her name to Pamela A. Mboya after her marriage to Tom Mboya, arrived in the United States on the same "Airlift." The *East African Standard* says that her wedding to Mboya followed her return in 1962 "was without doubt the social event of the year, remarkable for its style, glitterati guest list, and splendor."[62] Although Mboya represented Kamakunji, one of the poorest sections of Nairobi, the couple lived in style in the plush Lavington neighborhood, evidence of his unmatched appeal and popularity among workers, the youth, and the huge emigrant community.

Pamela Odede, a Luo, was born in Siaya in 1937. Having graduated from Makerere in 1959, she was immediately selected to travel to the United States. She was enrolled at Western College for Women in Oxford, Ohio where she received a B.A. degree in sociology. Once she returned to Kenya she served as the first female Executive Officer in Nairobi City Council Welfare Department. But within a year or so, she transferred to the lucrative position of Administrative Officer at Kenya Breweries Ltd. As a wife of Tom Mboya and one of the pioneer women to receive higher education, Mrs. Mboya soon emerged as one of the leading women in Kenya. So influential was she, that candidates for parliamentary seats in the national elections feverishly sought her support particularly in predominantly Luo constituencies.[63] Pamela Mboya gained the reputation of an outstanding sociologist through her services in local and international organizations. She served as committee member in both the National Council of Women of Kenya and the Y.M.C.A. She also served as chairperson of the board of governors of many schools. Moreover, she continues to serve as member of the Board of Directors of HelpAge International and as its representative in Kenya.[64] In addition, she is Vice-Chairman of HABITAT, the United Nations Human Settlement Program, a member of its Bureau Secretariat, and its permanent representative in East Africa. In 1998, President Moi invited her to head a committee to formulate a scheme for officers appointed to the newly established National Security Intelligence Service whose responsibility was to report to the President on issues concerning internal, external, and strategic security matters. Mrs. Mboya and her daughter, Susan Mboya, established the "Mboya Family Scholarship" program to honor the legacy of Mboya's drive to have Kenyan students and trade union officers receive their college education in the United States.

The 1960 "Student Airlift" also brought to the United States a young Kikuyu female student, Wangari Muta Maathai, whom *Time Magazine* named in its December 14, 1998, issue as one of the "Heroes for the Planet." Wangari (b. 1940) who graduated from Loreto Convent and Limuru High School obtained a B.Sc. degree in biology from Mt. St. Scholastica College in Atchison, Kansas, in 1964, and a M.Sc. degree from the University of Pittsburgh in 1965.[65] She was thus the first woman in East and Central Africa to gain a post-graduate degree. Wangari returned to Kenya early in 1966 saying "I knew that when I came . . . (to the USA) that I had to go back home . . . and make a contribution." She was immediately offered the position of Research Assistant in the Department of Veterinary Medicine at the University College of Nairobi. At the same time, she pursued a Ph.D. degree at the university. She earned it in 1971. Maathai was the first female Ph.D. holder in the region. She climbed up the academic ranks at the university to become an Associate Professor and Chairperson of the Department of Veterinary Anatomy. Once again, she was the first female to occupy such positions. Meanwhile, she became Director of the Red Cross Society and of the Council of Women of Kenya.[66]

In 1977, Dr. Wangari launched her worldwide known Green Belt Movement (GBM), "a grassroots organization that seeks to fight deforestation, desertification, and erosion in Kenya."[67] By the early 1990s, the movement, whose members were primarily women, succeeded in planting over twenty million trees. Hence, Wangari came to be known as the "Tree Woman." Furthermore, the movement not only endeavored to protect the environment but also worked to improve the quality of life in rural communities. The success of the GBM attracted the attention of the United Nations, European governments, and individual donors whose generous contributions permitted it to operate on a five million dollar budget.[68] Dr. Wangari addressed the UN General Assembly, delivered lectures at universities and colleges around the world, and spoke at forums from Brazil to Japan. She had since received numerous awards and prizes including "The Woman of the Year Award" in 1983, the "Right of Livelihood Award," known as the "Alternative Nobel Prize" in 1984, the "Better World Society Award" in 1986, the "Windsor Award for the Environment" in 1988, the "Woman of the World" in 1989, the "United Nations Environmental Program Global 500 Award" in 1989, the "Golden Environmental Prize" in 1991, and the "Golden Ark Award" in 1994. She received a Honorary Doctor of Law from Williams College in 1990 and Honorary Doctor of Agriculture from the University of Norway in 1997.[69]

However, Dr. Wangari and the GBM soon collided with the government of Kenya. In 1989, the Moi government decided to build a 62-story high-rise complex graced with a 30 foot statue of President Moi in *uhuru* Park in the heart of Nairobi. The tower would cost about $200 million. The funding was to be furnished by foreign financiers.[70] Dr. Wangari launched a well-orchestrated local and international campaign to prevent the construction of the building. She argued, "We can provide parks for rhino and elephants; why can't we provide open spaces for the people? Why are we creating an environmental havoc in urban areas." President Moi retaliated by calling her "a mad woman" who was leading "women with insects in their heads." He accused her of being "a threat to the order and security of the country." That accusation was followed by a character assassination debate in Parliament and public forums by various ministers who described her as "an ignorant and ill-tempered puppet of foreign masters . . . an unprecedented monstrosity."[71] She was threatened with the "mutilation of her genitals," ridiculed and called names, and her husband was pressured to sue for divorce. He was subsequently granted divorce on a trumped-up charge of adultery.[72] As a result of her fight and the support that she received from the National Museum of Kenya, the Association of Architects, and environmentalists world wide, the foreign investors withdrew their support for the project. Consequently, the project was shelved indefinitely. Nevertheless, matters flared once more between Dr. Wangari and the government over two environmental issues. The first was the allocation of 1000 hectare of Karura forest outside Nairobi to private developers to build luxury homes, and the second was the intended excision of Mau forest, homeland of the small Ogick ethnic group, for the benefit of a "politically connected" administrative official and his friends.[73] In both occasions, Dr. Wangari and her colleagues protested at the scene and were harassed and clubbed by police and hired thugs. She was arrested, beaten, interrogated, and incarcerated. A warrant was issued for the arrest of the hired thugs, but no trace of them was found. Dr. Wangari was, however, released after UN Secretary-Geberal, Kofi Anan, and the world community protested her detention.[74]

Dr. Wangari raised the level of her protest and confrontation with the authorities when she began to question the record of Moi's government concerning human rights, the rule of law, freedom of speech and assembly, and the general conduct of politicians. She ran against Moi in the presidential elections of 1997. However, her candidacy papers disappeared mysteriously a few days before the elections were held. Nevertheless, before the papers were found under the seat of the Chairman of the Elections Committee, news had gone out that she had withdrawn her candidacy. Dr. Wangari was elected to Parliament in the 2000 elections. On January 3, 2003, President Moi Kibaki appointed her Assistant Minister of Environment, Natural Resources, and Wildlife. The *East African Standard* commented on her appointment saying, "Maathai, an environmentalist of both local and international acclaim already carved a niche for herself on what ministry would properly suit her. Her appointment as the Assistant Minister for Environment, Natural Resources and Wildlife is rightfully planned."[75] In 2004, Dr. Wangari was rewarded for her environmentalist efforts with the Nobel Peace Prize.

Like their colleagues in other African nations at independence, most of the Kenyan university graduates from America and other countries were absorbed by the public rather than by the private sector for a number of reasons. First, employment opportunities in the public sector were far more numerous and readily available than in the private sector. That was due to the departure of the European civil servants and administrators. On the other hand, the private sector, small as it were, and with far less employment opportunities, remained in private European and Asian hands and to a great extent free from government interference. No nationalization of privately owned companies was initiated in Kenya. Hence, foreign employees did not abandon their positions and leave the country. Second, the private sector was deemed subordinate in all respects to the public sector. Hence, employment in the public sector carried with it more prestige and power. For example, for the graduate from the School of Law, being a magistrate was believed to be more rewarding than opening an attorney's office in downtown Nairobi, let alone in smaller towns. Certainly, government employment held the key to social standing, influence, and wealth. To show how keen African parents were to see their children work for the government it was often said in Sudan that "if one does not dine at the government table, one must feed on the leftover crumbs."[76] In Kenya, the *Asomi* who became government functionaries not only inherited absolute power but also the farms and plantations, as well as the businesses of the white settlers.

Of the few American-educated *Asomi* who joined the private sector following their return to Kenya, were Mwangi Maathai, Wilson Ndolo Ayah, Shadrack Kwasa, and Leonard Oliver Kibinge. Mwangi Maathai obtained a B.A. degree in sociology and history from Shaw University in 1963. He returned to Kenya and worked for Esso Oil Company and Kenya National Trading Corporation before he became Executive Manager of Marketing and then Director of Colgate Palmolive East Africa Ltd.[77] On the other hand, Wilson Ayah gained his M.Sc. degree in agricultural economics from the University of Wisconsin in 1961. He worked with Sterling Products for eight years (1961–1969). However, he abandoned the private sector to enter Parliament representing Kisumu Rural constituency. He was duly appointed Assistant Minister for the Treasury, and thereafter Minister for Water Development (1987–1990) and Minster of Foreign Affairs (1990–1992).[78] Likewise, Leonard Oliver Kibinge could not resist the lure of the Civil Service. Kwasa graduated from the University of Connecticut in 1960. Upon his return to Kenya, he was employed by the East Africa Tobacco Company Ltd. He did not spend more than a year at the company after which he joined the Foreign Service and was assigned to the Kenya Embassy in London and then Norway. Moreover, he became Undersecretary for the Ministry of Foreign Affairs and for the Ministry of Livestock Development.[79] The fourth Kenyan student, Shadrack Kwasa, holder of a Ph.D. degree from Howard University, took the position of Marketing Economist with Esso Oil Co. before he transferred to the Ministry of Foreign Affairs as Chief of Protocol (1964–1965). Thereafter, he became Head of the Price Control Department in the Treasury.[80] These profiles testify to the attraction and luster of the Civil Service, as well as to the abundance of employment opportunities in the public sector.

Yet, a few Kenyan *Asomi* reversed the equation. Having established a reputation as government officials, they duly left for the private sector to establish their own businesses. For example, Ng'the Njoroge who studied at Central State College, Wilberforce, Ohio, and Boston University, began his career upon his graduation in 1963 as an Assistant Secretary in the Ministry of Lands and Settlements. A year later, he moved to the Ministry of Foreign Affairs and climbed the ranks to become High Commissioner to Britain (1970–1979). He then retired from the Civil Service to open his private business in Nairobi.[81] Likewise, John Mukalasing Khaminwa, who obtained his L.L.B. from Dar-Es-Salam and a Masters degree from New York University, opened his own law firm after having joined the Civil Service for five years (1968–1973).[82] Another Kenyan, James Boro Karugi, graduate of Ohio State University (1962) and Lincoln Inn, London (1964), served in the Attorney-General's Chambers and advanced through the ranks to become Attorney-General. He retired from the Civil Service in 1981 to open his Private practice in Nairobi.[83] On the other hand, Zachariah Kinaiya, who studied at the University of Denver, returned to Kenya in 1960 to become Head Librarian at the Kenya Institute of Administration, the former Jeanes School. He left his position in 1981 for the lucrative Managing Director of Kenya Literature Bureau. However, he soon opened his own bookshop in Nairobi.[84]

The American-educated *Asomi* climbed up the ladder of the Civil Service with astonishing speed to occupy the high administrative positions that the colonial personnel had vacated. Since the majority of the *Asomi* joined the Civil Service, it would be sufficient to give brief reviews of the careers of a few of them to illustrate the urgency for a university educated cadre to Africanize the top-level posts in all departments. In 1963, Nicholas Murathe Mugo (Kikuyu) graduated from Lincoln University with a B.A. degree in history. He immediately found employment at the East Africa Common Services Organization. A year later, in 1964, he joined the Ministry of Foreign Affairs. Within nine years, he became Ambassador to Ethiopia (1973–1975), and thereafter Ambassador to France (1976–1977).[85] Another *Asomi*, Fredrick Ogweno Ouka (Luo), studied at Shaw University (1961–1964), and Syracuse University (1966–1967). He occupied the position of Assistant Secretary in the Treasury for four years (1967–1971). In the period between 1971 and 1977, Ouka served as Principal and then Chief Management Analyst for the East Africa Community. He rejoined the Civil Service in Kenya in 1977 as

Under Secretary for the Ministry of Defense.[86] Yet another *Asomi,* Christopher Kauara (Luhya), was appointed District Officer in 1964, a year after his graduation from Brooklyn College, New York. In 1968, he was elevated to the position of Under-Secretary for the Treasury.[87] Ms Dorcas Luseno (Kalanjin), a graduate of Spelman College and Columbia University, served as Women Education Officer before she became Deputy Director of Kenya National Council of Social Services in 1966.[88]

Simon Thuo Kairo (Kikuyu) attended Long Island University (1960–1961) before he transferred to Hutton College, South Dakota (1961–1963). He returned to Kenya to become Assistant Clerk in the Parliament, a diplomat, and finally Private Secretary to President *Mzee* Jomo Kenyatta.[89] Kyale Mwendwa, a graduate of Michigan State University (1961), was appointed District Education Officer upon his return to the country. The following year, he was promoted to Deputy Provincial Officer and immediately thereafter to Chief Education Officer in the Ministry of Education.[90] James Maina Wanjigi (Kikuyu) who attended the University of Connecticut and graduated with a M.Sc. degree in agricultural economics from Stanford University in 1961 and was appointed Agricultural Officer of Nyeri District upon his return in 1962. Two years later, he was elevated to the position of Deputy Director of Settlement and in the following year (1965) was promoted to the position of Director. In 1967, Wanjigi was transferred to the Industrial and Commercial Corporation where he served as Executive Director until 1969 when he entered Parliament representing Kamakunji (Nairobi Central) in a by-election following the assassination of Tom Mboya who had held that seat since 1957. Wanjigi was then appointed Assistant Minister of Agriculture, a position that he held for ten years (1969–1979), before he became Minister for Tourism, Minister for Environment, Natural Resources, and Tourism, and Minister for Cooperative Development and Marketing.[91]

Whenever the Africanization of the medical profession was mentioned, Kenyans instantly pointed to Dr. Njoroge Mungai (See Figure 4) as the Dean of physicians and the first Kenyan to qualify as an M.D. Dr. Njoroge, who graduated from the Presbyterian Church school, started his career as ground officer with East African Airways as a bus driver. However, his father, George Njoroge, a well-to-do businessman, sent him to study at Fort Hare University in South Africa from which institution, Njoroge obtained an M.Sc. degree in 1950. Thereafter, he traveled to the United States to attend Stanford University. He graduated in 1957 with a medical degree. He then completed his residency at King's County Hospital in New York City (1958–1959) and joined Columbia University as a scholar in Medicine for one year. At the end of 1959, Dr. Njorogi returned to Kenya as its first indigenous physician. Instead of joining the government hospital in Nairobi, he preferred to practice Medicine in his own mobile clinic traversing Nairobi, Thika and Embu serving the poor and destitute. He was quickly hailed as the American-educated "medicine man." When he filed as candidate to the House of Representatives for Nairobi West, his "flock" gave him a landslide victory. Dr. Njoroge was appointed Minister for Health and Housing in the *Madaraka* cabinet in 1963. Thereafter, he held a number of portfolios serving as Minister of Internal Security and Defense, Minister for Defense, Minister for Foreign Affairs, and Minster of Environment and Natural Resources. Dr, Njoroge was thus the longest serving member of the Kenyan cabinet. In September 2002, President Moi appointed him as a Personal Assistant. During the era of *Mzee* Jomo Kenyatta, Dr. Njoroge, who was a nephew of *Mzee,* served as his personal physician and confidant.[92]

A small number of Kenyan students elected to study Journalism, TV, Radio and Film. One of these was Hilary Bonface Ng'weno, from the Luhya, who first studied mathematics and nuclear physics at Harvard University before he transferred to Brandeis University where he took courses in film and international affairs. He returned to Kenya in 1962 to serve as a reporter with the Nation Newspapers Group Ltd., which was owned by the Aga Khan. Only two years later, in 1964, Ng'weno, at the age of 25, became the first African Editor-in-Chief of the *Nation*.[93] However, he resigned in 1965 to become a freelance journalist. In 1975, Ng'weno, or HBN as he came to be known in the media world, founded and edited the *Weekly Review* (WR), "the most influential and authoritative local weekly magazine in Kenya" for more than two decades.[94] From its first inaugural issue on February 8, 1975, the magazine "set the pace for all—politicians, business people, intellectuals, and all those Kenyans who needed to 'be in the know.'" Mutegi Njau, Investigative Editor of the *Nation,* says that the *Weekly Review* "introduced Kenyans to world-class analytical, interpretive journalism covering socio-economic and political issues, making it one of the most respected journals in this region."[95] Besides the *WR,* Ng'weno published the *Nairobi Times,* a weekly newspaper, *Echo,* a monthly magazine, and the *Financial Review.* In addition, he was the first African to be a columnist for *Newsweek.*

Ng'weno also ventured into TV, Radio and Recording industry with the establishment of Stellagraphics Ltd., and became a major shareholder in Stellavision, the third TV channel in Kenya. Ng'weno pushed to become a television producer. Unfortunately, according to Mutegi Njau, "he spread himself so thin on the ground."[96] His television production studio did not generate any revenue. By all accounts, it would take decades for such industry in Kenya to come of age. Worst still, it siphoned off much of the revenue from the *Weekly Review.* Moreover, the Moi government, according to Ng'weno himself, waged a covert war against the paper instructing "most parastatal (sic) organizations not to advertise with us. As a result, a lot of advertising has been cancelled . . . I do not know what the intentions of the Government actually are, whether to kill our newspapers or simply push us for something we have published."[97] Even the advertising agency, Beaver Marketing Ltd., whom Ng'weno contracted to shore up advertisement for the magazine, failed to produce anything. Ng'weno was thus forced to sell two of his papers. He sold the *Nairobi Times* to the ruling party, KANU, who changed its name to *Kenya Times,* and the *Financial Review* to one of his former employees. It is also reported that he even sold a few of the plots of land he had owned in order to remain solvent.

The government won its war of attrition. In the 1990s, readers of the magazine detected a steady transformation in Ng'weno "from being a critic of the system to an apologist." The *Weekly Revue,* which was once the pride of Kenya, drifted with its creator and "developed into just another of those weeklies that repeated what anybody who had glimpsed through the dailies already knew."[98] Furthermore, the readers were well aware of Ng'weno's flirtation with the Moi government. Riddled and squeezed by financial problems, Ng'weno befriended KANU's "bigwigs," accepted the chairmanship of a number of government bodies including the Kenya Wildlife Service and the Kenya Revenue Authority, and was a member of the group that "set up a think-tank to advise (KANU) how to organize and win the 1992 elections."[99] Little wonder that the circulation of the magazine plummeted from 50, 000 copies to as low a figure as 2,000. On May 14, 1999, the final issue of the *Weekly Review* was placed on the newsstands along Tom Mboya Street, the location where it was born.

Ng'weno, who refuses to talk with anyone about his experiences, has retired from the profession he so loved and nurtured to maturity. However, his school of journalism produced a host of remarkable journalists in Kenya. It is asserted, "some of the journalists who worked with Ng'weno hold senior positions in the media industry . . . some of them have since joined the world of academia, while others are consultants with various international organizations."[100] Wachira Waruru, the Managing Director of Kenya Broadcasting Corporation, says of Ng'weno, "he was my mentor, my teacher, my trainer and a role model until today. I have never known a better teacher and trainer than Hilary . . . I joined the *Weekly Review* as an intern from the university, and upon completion of my stint, he recruited me as a writer. I owe what I am today to Hilary." Kwendo Opanga, Executive Editor of the *East Africa Standard* states, "I am a journalist because there was Hilary Ng'weno and the *Weekly Review* and later the weekly broadsheet, *Nairobi Times*." Likewise, Professor Absalom Mutere of the United States International University says, "Hilary knew Fleet Street; he knew *New York Times;* he had vast knowledge of what happened in Western media. Hilary brought a new brand of journalism in Kenya."[101] Such was the influence of the American experience on Hilary Bonface Ng'weno, doyen of journalism in East Africa.

Yet another Kenyan who elected to take the media as a profession was Nyoike F. Njoroge, a Kikuyu who studied at Kendall Junior College, Everston, Illinois (1956–1961). Njoroge returned to Kenya to work as Lab Technician with Technicolor Corporation. Three years later, in 1964, he transferred to the Voice of Kenya as a producer/director and in 1965 was promoted to Head of the Kenya television services. Njoroge has since become the General Manger of Kenya Film Corporation.[102]

Tom Mboya, Asa Philip Randolph, Horace Bond, Frank Montero, William X. Scheinman, Dr. Julius Gikonyo Kiano, George Houser, President John R. Kennedy, Congressman Charles Diggs and others who played the most significant role in having Kenyan students receive university education in the United States hoped that all the students returned to their home country once they completed their studies to participate in its development. There is no evidence to show that any of the pioneer Kenyan trade union officers and university students who went to the United before 1958, other than Professor Mugo Gatheru, remained behind. Yet, at independence in 1963, there were less than 500 Kenyans with university degrees from overseas, for during the colonial period (1895–1963), the authorities did not encourage, indeed deliberately neglected high education in the country. The 500 or so Kenyans who held university degrees, together with those who were airlifted to America in 1959, 1960, and 1961 constituted the "core of the Civil Service" in independent Kenya.[103] They replaced the colonial personnel that had run and exploited the country for more than half a century. Of course, some students stayed in the United States either temporarily or permanently. This problem, the "brain drain," continues to plague Africa to the present day.

Chapter Six
Conclusion

Education in Kenya, and in all human societies for that matter, has always been a catalyst for change and the dominant factor in the preservation of values and culture. In Kenya, as well as in other African nations, education has its roots in what western scholars consistently refer to as 'informal or traditional education' to distinguish it from 'formal education' that was imported into Africa by white missionaries and colonial administrations. In the traditional system, students learned how to live with their environment. Astute students moved through apprenticeship and initiation processes to the top of the social hierarchy to become members of the Council of Elders. All the time, students were schooled in the customs and traditions that made the society what it was. The age groups (warrior groups) were the custodians and defenders of the heritage of the people and the land. Hence, when the British invaded Kenya, the warrior groups of the Nandi, for example, fought gallantly for nearly seven years in defense of their territory before the British invading forces treacherously murdered their leader. Henceforward, the British colonial administration banned all such ancient organizations. The dismantling of the warrior groups was the first breach in the fortress of traditional Africa.

Yet, Kenya, particularly along its *Swahili* coast, was influenced by Islamic education for centuries before the arrival of the British. Out of the *Kuranic* schools emerged a sizeable group of scholars and *muallimous* (educators). Islamic education on the coast merged smoothly into "traditional education." Consequently, it preserved the *Swahili* culture, the child of a marriage between the original Bantu and Islamic culture. Importantly, Islamic education preserved the first indigenous written language of East Africa, that is, *Kiswahili,* which is now the lingua franca of the region and the official language, besides English, of Kenya. Of the well-known *Swahili* scholars that Islamic education in Kenya gave birth to, one may mention

Professor Ali Mazrui and Professor Ahmad Idha Salim. Although these professors, like many of their classmates, were expected to attend *Al-Azhar* Islamic University in Cairo after they had left the *Kuranic*/Arabic schools, they were handpicked, together with other students from chiefly families, by the colonial authorities to pursue 'formal education' in western institutions. At present, Professor Mazrui (Ph.D. Oxford) is the Albert Schwietzer Chair at Africana Studies in Binghamton, New York, while Professor Salim (Ph.D. School of Oriental and African Studies, University of London) is Kenyan Ambassador to the Sultanate of Oman. However, both traditional and Islamic education were overshadowed to a great extent by "formal education," which made its appearance with the arrival of European missionaries, and the establishment of the first mission station/school, ironically at Rabai close to Mombasa, the citadel of Islamic education. Steadily, Christian missionary education penetrated into the interior where mission schools were erected everywhere. These schools produced African evangelists who took the Bible to their people. Education in missionary schools focused on studying the Bible, reading and writing in the English language, and in an assortment of vocational training. Likewise, the African-American school, the Jeanes School assisted Kenyans in industrial training. Furthermore, a handful of Kenyan students who graduated from the mission schools became the first batch of Kenyan students to receive advanced studies overseas in black seminaries in the United States.

White missionary education, however, demanded that the African make a complete break with his heritage. However, it hardly provided the African converts with up-ward mobility in the church hierarchy. Consequently, African graduates of missionary schools broke away from the establishments of their mentors to form independent African churches that brought Christ to Africans through a medium that they knew and respected. That was the beginning of the assertion of Africanity and the birth of nationalism in Kenya. Missionary education helped Kenyans to take the first step along the difficult road to independence. Indeed, the first nationalist organization in Kenya that challenged the authority of the British, the Young Kikuyu Association, was founded and led by the father of Kenyan nationalism, Harry Thuku, graduate of missionary schools.

The colonial administration provided the second type of 'formal education' in Kenya through the establishment of government run schools. This too was yet another factor in the emergence of the western-educated elites in the country. To meet its demand for a semi-skilled labor force for the white man's plantations and to fill junior posts in the administration, the colonial authorities opened primary and secondary schools in Kenya. After a series of meetings, the various committees and commissions that were formed by the authorities arrived at the conclusion that a technical college be established in Uganda to train students from Kenya, Uganda, Zanzibar and Tanganyika in mechanics, carpentry, and building. Makerere Technical College was accordingly opened in 1922 with 14 students. Later, Makerere added more courses in agriculture, veterinary science and medical care. Students with Cambridge school certificates spent two years at Makerere where they obtained "A" level degrees. Makerere helped prepare a handful of East African students who pursued higher education at the undergraduate level in the United States, India, Britain and in other countries. In 1956, the colonial administration established the Royal Technical College Nairobi. A third college was founded in Dar Es-Salam in 1961. Graduates from the two institutions, like those from Makerere, sought university degrees overseas.

If missionary education produced independent African churches, it also fostered, together with government education, the emergence of independent Kenyan schools, the most prominent of which was at Githinguri in the heartland of Kikuyu country. Githinguri, Makerere, Nairobi, and Dar-Es-Salam, as well as the host of public, missionary and independent schools produced Kenyan elites, the *Asomi,* who looked for higher education abroad. At the head of Kenyans who reached out for the United States to help their fellow citizens receive college degrees was the charismatic nationalist, Tom Mboya. As general Secretary of the Kenya Federation of Trade Unions, Mboya cultivated a close relationship with the leadership of the AFL-CIO and the African-American Civil Rights Movement, as well as with the heads of Historically Black Colleges, white activists, philanthropists, and politicians. He secured assistance from African-American organizations, such as the American Society of African Culture as well as other organizations like the American Committee on Africa, the Phelps-Stokes Fund, and the African-American Students Foundation, the Joseph Kennedy Foundation and the Department of State. Assistance was also sought from Civil Rights leaders, such as Asa Randolph, Martin Luther King Jr. and Congressman Charles Diggs; from educators, such as Horace Bond; from white activists, such as William X. Scheinman and George Houser; from film stars, Harry Belafonte and Sidney Poitier; and from the super sportsman, Jackie Robinson. These institutions, organizations, and individuals succeeded in offering scholarships to Kenyan students and trade unionists to study and train in the United States. Mboya benefited greatly from the Cold War politics as the government of the United States extended a helping hand in the hope that Kenyan students educated in American colleges and universities would, upon their assumption of political power, succeed in stopping the tide of communism that was surging toward the continent and build an Africa dedicated to the ideals of western democracy. The African-American leadership had also another agenda emerging from the ideals of Pan-Africanism. The leadership saw the struggle of Africans for independence and the struggle for equality and the destruction of racism in the United States as one fight against a common enemy, the white man. A mature, well-educated, highly skilled nationalist leadership in Africa would be yet another weapon in the "black arsenal" to combat white colonialism and racism.

Ever since Kenya fell to the British in 1895, white administrators occupied the top positions in the country. Moreover, white settlers and European businessmen controlled the political and economic life of Kenya. Thus, at independence, the colonial administration in Kenya left behind an administrative structure, an economy, a political system, an infrastructure, primary and secondary schools, as well as two junior colleges, Nairobi and Edgerton, of its own creation. While in authority, the Colonial Office controlled and staffed these institutions and establishments. Once the British left the country, Kenya was forced to find, indeed create, manpower of superior quality to replace the colonial cadre. The task before Kenya, that is building a nation, was enormous, serious, and challenging.

The local colleges were not equipped to meet the challenge. They did not possess the teaching staff and the facilities to produce the huge army of administrators and professionals desperately needed by the emerging nation. In fact, when the British evacuated Kenya, they left just about 500 Kenyans with university degrees from abroad. The solution then rested on two essential avenues: expansion of local colleges and up-grading them to university level, and sending students in greater numbers to study overseas in the United States and other countries. In reality, expansion in higher education at the local level naturally took a long time. Hence, to meet the immediate and urgent needs, Kenyans sought the assistance of foreign countries, particularly the United States. Henceforth, students from Kenya, more than from other African countries, received the lion's share of American scholarships and financial assistance. The overwhelming majority of them returned home to build their country. Graduates of American universities, both undergraduates and graduates, served their homeland as educators, politicians, members of parliament, businessmen, administrators, journalists, communication specialists, lawyers, judges, physicians, and in other professions. They continue to participate in the running of their country.

Appendix

TABLES

Table 1	African Students, Showing Academic Status by Fields of Major Interest in 1965	130
Table 2	Africans Students Showing Financial Support and Academic Status in 1965	132
Table 3	Estimated Outputs from Overseas and East African Colleges, 1964–1970	133
Table 4	Universities in Africa	137
Table 5	145 Institutions participating in the African Scholarships Program of American Universities	142
Table 6.1	Number of African Students in the United States, 1950–1964	148
Table 6.2	Number of African Students in the United States, 1965–1974	149
Table 7	African Students, Showing Home Country, Gender, Year Studies in United States Began, Financial Support, Academic Status	150
Table 8	Kenyan Students: Gender and Academic Status, 1955–1974	151

FIGURES

Figure 1	Mbiyu Koinange	152
Figure 2	Dr. Julius Gikonyo Kiano	153
Figure 3	Dr. Wangari Maathai	154
Figure 4	Dr. Njoroge Mungai	155
Figure 5	Map of Kenya	156

Table 1. African Students, Showing Academic Status by Fields of Major Interest in 1965

	Home Country										
	Ethiopia	Ghana	Kenya	Liberia	Nigeria	Sierra Leone	Somalia	South Africa	Tanzania	Uganda
Agriculture										
Undergraduate	1	9	36	4	114	6	8	4	12	9
Graduate	9	8	5	3	28	1	1	16	2	5
Other	1	–	3	–	12	–	–	1	22	3
Business Administration										
Undergraduate	21	11	52	36	88	7	3	12	11	5
Graduate	4	12	5	4	10	–	–	19	1	1
Other	2	2	3	11	11	–	–	6	7	2
Education										
Undergraduate	4	3	37	15	29	11	8	4	12	2
Graduate	25	4	8	33	38	8	–	11	4	1
Other	3	1	1	5	3	–	3	1	4	–
Engineering										
Undergraduate	12	27	35	20	220	9	14	21	21	20
Graduate	12	17	4	1	37	1	–	28	2	1
Other	5	1	1	6	17	–	2	3	1	–

Appendix

Humanities									
Undergraduate	19	15	58	31	83	21	4	36	33	17
Graduate	7	10	9	14	29	3	–	36	8	3
Other	4	7	6	4	13	–	2	15	2	5
Medical Sciences									
Undergraduate	8	21	38	10	95	5	2	28	12	10
Graduate	8	6	11	3	31	1	–	7	2	1
Other	5	–	3	2	9	1	–	7	–	–
Physical and Natural Sciences									
Undergraduate	12	21	114	14	132	14	11	11	58	31
Graduate	18	18	24	9	57	13	1	51	9	9
Other	5	4	4	1	5	1	4	1	2	1
Social Sciences									
Undergraduate	37	38	241	43	190	29	35	23	50	59
Graduate	34	33	61	21	112	15	2	33	18	16
Other	4	3	9	10	3	3	1	10	11	17
All Other									
Undergraduate	1	–	2	5	1	–	–	–	1	4
Graduate	1	–	–	–	1	–	–	–	–	–
Other	1	–	1	–	–	–	–	–	–	–
No Answer	3	11	3	10	4	–	–	6	–	1

Source: *"Open Doors"* International Institute of Education, 1965, Table 2, pp. 22-23

Table 2. African Students Showing Financial Support and Academic Status in 1965

	Home Country										
	Ethiopia	Ghana	Kenya	Liberia	Nigeria	Sierra Leone	Somalia	South Africa	Tanzania	Uganda
Financial Support										
U.S. coll/univ & gov't	8	6	22	1	24	3	–	21	7	7
U.S. coll/univ & foreign	12	4	47	5	63	6	–	7	34	19
Private	27	40	131	32	153	13	2	54	31	28
Private & foreign govt	5	5	22	1	16	2	–	7	9	6
Private & U.S. gov't	8	1	33	4	10	3	–	1	8	5
No answer	28	37	43	67	107	12	12	50	8	16
Academic Status										
Undergrad	115	146	614	180	954	102	85	140	210	157
Grad working r unspecified/no degree	20	18	11	20	51	10	2	47	7	2
Grad working master's degree	81	63	92	60	185	26	2	79	32	30
Grad working doctoral degree	20	27	24	11	108	6	–	76	7	6
Special	26	20	20	33	73	4	13	41	44	24
No answer	4	8	13	11	11	1	–	7	5	4

Source: "*Open Doors, 1965,*" Report on International Exchange-Institute of International Education, pp. 16-17.

Table 3. Estimated Outputs from Overseas and East African Colleges, 1964–1970

Area of Studies	Total in school (East Africa)	Total in school (Overseas)	Grand Total	Average Graduating Per Year	Estimated Total Output 6 Plan Years	Adjusted for Wastage "No Return"
Accountancy	4	97	101	25	150	128
Public Administration & Political Sciences	–	134	134	45	270	216
Architecture and Building	19	15	34	7	42	36
Town Planning	–	5	5	1	6	5
Agriculture, Agronomy and Dairy & Farm Management	33	97	130	43	258	219
Arts Degree (B.A.)	163	249	412	137	822	699
Chemistry	3	49	52	17	102	87
Commerce and Business Administration	27	43	70	23	138	118
Dentistry (5 Years)	–	16	16	3	18	15
Economics and Agricultural Economics	9	151	160	53	318	270

(continued)

Table 3. Estimated Outputs from Overseas and East African Colleges, 1964–1970 *(continued)*

Area of Studies	Total in school (East Africa)	Total in school (Overseas)	Grand Total	Average Graduating Per Year	Estimated Total Output 6 Plan Years	Adjusted for Wastage "No Return"
Education, Secondary Teacher	28	394	422	106	636	509
Chemical Engineering	–	15	15	4	24	20
Civil Engineering	6	74	80	20	120	96
Electrical Engineering	7	57	64	16	96	77
Mechanical Engineering	8	57	65	16	96	77
Forestry	–	10	10	3	18	16
Geology	–	2	2	1	6	5
Law	92	85	177	44	264	211
Librarians	–	5	5	2	12	11
Medicine, Physician, Surgeon	73	231	304	51	306	214
Mining Engineering	–	1	1	–	2	2
Pharmacy	–	46	46	12	72	58
Science General (B.Sc.)	93	223	316	105	630	535

Appendix 135

Social Science, Philosophy & Anthropology	7	73	80	27	162	138
Veterinary	21	44	45	11	66	53
Zoology	2	24	26	9	54	46
Personnel Management	–	3	3	2	12	11
Aeronautical Engineering	–	20	20	5	30	24
Journalism	–	15	15	5	30	26
Mathematics	1	38	39	13	78	66
Statistics	–	3	3	1	6	5
Biology	–	34	34	11	66	56
Engineering (not specified)	54	126	180	45	270	216
Agricultural Engineering	–	9	9	2	12	10
Marine Engineering	–	3	3	1	6	5
Radio & TV Engineering	–	27	27	7	42	34
Telecommunication Engineering	–	11	11	3	18	6
Survey— Quantity	17	3	20	5	30	24
Land	15	2	17	5	30	24

(continued)

Table 3. Estimated Outputs from Overseas and East African Colleges, 1964–1970 (continued)

Area of Studies	Total in school (East Africa)	Total in school (Overseas)	Grand Total	Average Graduating Per Year	Estimated Total Output 6 Plan Years	Adjusted for Wastage "No Return"
Music	–	8	8	3	18	16
Divinity & Nunnery	–	48	48	12	72	58
Nursing & Midwifery	–	379	379	95	570	466
Home Economics and Occupational Therapy	28	39	67	22	132	112
Public Health	–	3	3	2	12	11
Radiography and Occupational Therapy	–	20	20	7	42	36
Physics	2	25	27	9	54	46
Art	15	23	38	10	60	48
Navigation	–	16	1	1	–	2
Soil Scientist	–	1	7	2	12	12
Botany	–	7	7	2	12	12
Total	727	3,040	3,767	0511	6,310	5,199

Ministry of Economic Planning and Development, *High-Level Manpower Requirements and Resources in Kenya, 1964-1970.* (Nairobi: Government of Kenya Printing, 1965), 111-12.

Table 4. Universities in Africa

States	Universities	Year founded	No. of students '63
Algeria	University of Algiers	1879	2,500 (est.).
Burundi	University of Usumbura (formerly the University of Ruanda-Urundi, est. 1960).	1963	85.
Cameroon	Universite' Federale du Cameroun, Yaounde	1962	518.
Congo (Leopoldville)	Lovanium University, Leopoldville Universite officielle du Congo (formerly Universite' de l'Etat, Elisabethville).	1954	1,200.
Ethiopia	Haile Selassie I University, Addis Ababa (incorporating University College of Arts and Sciences, established 1950).	1961	1,093.
Ghana	University of Ghana, Legon (formerly University College of Ghana, est. 1948).	1961	1,300.
	Kwame Nkrumah University of Science and Technology, Kumasi (formerly Kumasi College of Technology, established 1951). University College of Cape Coast	1961	150.
Ivory Coast	University of Abidjan (incorporating the Center of Higher Education, est. 1959).	1963	1,035.

(continued)

Table 4. Universities in Africa *(continued)*

States	Universities	Year founded	No. of students '63
Kenya	University of East Africa (Kenya Component: The University College, established 1956, Nairobi)University of East Africa (Kenya Component: The University College, established 1956, Nairobi)	1963	478.
Liberia	University of Liberia, Monrovia—	1951	350 (est.).
	Cuttington College, Suacoco (originally founded 1888 but closed from 1929 to 1948).	1961	150.
Libya	The Libyan University	1955	1,500.
Morocco	University of Rabat—	1957	Not available
	Qarawayin University, Fez	859	Do.
Nigeria	University College Ibadan—	1948	1,779 (1962).
	University of Nigeria, Nsukka (Incorporating Enugu branch of the Nigeria College of Arts, Sciences and Technology).	1960	1,200 (1962).
	Ahmandu Bello University, Zaria (incorporating Zaria branch of the Nigerian College of Arts, Science and Technology).	1962	425 (1962).
	Ahmandu Bello University, Zaria (incorporating Zaria branch of the Nigerian College of Arts, Science and Technology).	1962	425 (1962).

	University of Ife (incorporating Ibadon branch of the Nigerian College of Arts, Science and Technology)[1].	1961	244 (1962).
	University of Lagos	1962	130 (1962).
Rwanda	University of Butare	1963	50.
Senegal	University of Dakar	1957	2,006.
Sierra Leone	University College of Sierra Leone, Freetwon (formerly Fourah Bay College, established 1827).	1960	435.
South Africa	University of Cape Town,[1]	1918	5,010 European (1962); 475 non-European[2].
	University of Nata,[1] Durban and Pietermartizeburg (including non-white medical school in Durban-founded 1951).	1909	3,164 European (1962); 475 non-European[2]
	University for Christian Higher Education,[1] Potchefsroom (established As college 1869).	1951	1,901 (1962).
	The University of the Orange Free State[1] (established as college 1855)	1950	2,125 (1962).
	Rhodes University,[1] Grahamstown (established as college 1904).	1951	1,062 European (1962); 106 non-European[2].

(*continued*)

Table 4. Universities in Africa (continued)

States	Universities	Year founded	No. of students '63
	University of Stellenbosch[1]	1916	4,818 (1962).
	University of Pretoria[1] (established as college 1908)	1930	9,368
	University of the Witwatersrand,[1] Johannesburg	1922	5,662 European (1962); 222 non-European.[2]
	University of South Africa (correspondence courses serving all races).	1873	9,920 European 2,175 non-European; 1,117 postgrads of all races.
	University College of Zululand	1959	131 non-European.
	University College of Fort Hare	1923	196 non-European.
	University of North, Turfloop	1959	228 non European.

Southern Rhodesia	University College of the Western Province	1960	321 colored.
	University College for Indians, Durban	(³)	670
	University College of Rhodesia and Nyasaland, Salisbury	1955	480 (including 11 Africans).
Sudan	University of Khartoum (formerly Gordon Memorial College, established 1902)	1956	2,200.
Tanzania	University of East Africa (Tanganyika component: University College of Dares Salaam, established 1961).	1963	84.
Tunisia	University of Tunis (incorporating the Institute of Higher Studies, established 1945, and Zitouna University).	1960	3,298.
	University of East Africa (Uganda component: Makeere University College, Kampala, established 1950).	1963	749

Key: [1] Restricted to Europeans by law since 1959
[2] Non-European students enrolled in courses prior to 1959 and allowed to complete studies.
[3] Not available.

Source: Subcommittee on Africa, Committee on Foreign Affairs, *African Students and Study Programs in the United States* (Washington, D.C.: U.S. Government Printing Office, 1965), 25-26.

Table 5. 145 Institutions participating in the African Scholarships Program of American Universities

State	College/University	College Fund	Scholarship Program
Alabama	Taledega College	X	
	Tuskegee Institute	X	
California	California Institute of Technology		
	Claremont Men(s College		
	Harvey Mudd College		
	Mills College		
	Occidental College		
	Pomona College		
	Seripps College		
	Stanford University		
	University of California at Los Angeles		
	University of California		
	University of Southern California		
Colorado	Colorado College		
	Colorado State University		
	Connecticut College for Women		
Connecticut	University of Colorado		
Connecticut	Wesleyan University		
	Yale University		
District of Columbia	Catholic University of America		
	Georgetown University		
	Howard University		
Florida	Bethune-Cookman College	X	
Georgia	Atlanta University	X	
	Clark College	X	
	Morehouse	X	
	Paine College	X	
	Spelman College	X	

Appendix 143

Table 5. 145 Institutions participating in the African Scholarships Program of American Universities *(continued)*

State	College/University	College Fund	Scholarship Program
Indiana	Purdue University		
	University of Notre Dame		
Iowa	Cornell College		X
	Grinnel College?		
	State University of Iowa		
Kansas	University of Kansas		
Louisiana	Dillard University	X	
Louisiana	Xavier University	X	
Maine	Bowdoin College		
	Colby College		
Maryland	Johns Hopkins University		
	Goucher College?		
Massachusetts	Boston University		
	Brandales University		
	Clark University		
	Harvard University		
	Mount Nolyoke College		
	Radcliffe College		
	Smith College		
	Tufts College		
	Wellesley College		
	Williams College		
Michigan	Michigan State University		
	University of Michigan		
Minnesota	Carleton College		
	Macalester College		

(continued)

Table 5. 145 Institutions participating in the African Scholarships Program of American Universities *(continued)*

State	College/University	College Fund	Scholarship Program
	Saint Olaf College		
	University of Minnesota		
Minnesota	Carleton College		
	Macalester College		
	Saint Olaf College		
	University of Minnesota		
Mississippi	Tougaloo Southern Christian College	X	
Missouri	University of Missouri		
Nebraska	University of Nebraska		
New Hampshire	Dartmouth College		
	University of New Hampshire		
New Jersey	Douglass College		
	Princeton University		
	Rutgers, The State University		X
	Alfred University		
New York	Barnard College		
	Brooklyn College of Pharmacy of Long Island University		X
	Cantaisu College?		X
	Colgate University		
	Columbia University		
	Cornell University		
	Kimira College		X
	Fordham University		
	Hamilton College		
	Hobart College		X
	Ithica College		X

Appendix 145

Table 5. 145 Institutions participating in the African Scholarships Program of American Universities *(continued)*

State	College/University	College Fund	Scholarship Program
New York	Nanhattanville College of the Sacred Heart		
	New York University		
	?Institute of Technology		
	University of Rochester		
	Vasser College		
	William Smith College		X
North Carolina	Barber-Scotia College	X	
	Bennet College	X	
	Davidson College		
	Livingstone College	X	
	St. Augustine(s College	X	
	Shaw University	X	
Ohio	Antioch College		
	Baldwin-Wellace College		X
	Denison University		X
	Heidelberg College		X
	Kenyon College		
	Marietta College		X
	Miami University		
	Mount Union College		X
	Muskingum College		
Ohio	Oberlin College		
	Ohio State University		
	Ohio Wesleyan University		X
	Western Reserve University		
Oregon	Oregon State College		

(continued)

Table 5. 145 Institutions participating in the African Scholarships Program of American Universities *(continued)*

State	College/University	College Fund	Scholarship Program
	Read College		
	University of Oregon		
Pennsylvania	Albright College		X
	Alleghany College		X
	Bryn Mawr College?		
	Buchnell University		
	Drezel Institute of Technology		
	Harverford College		
	Lafayette College		
	Lehigh University		X
	Lincoln University	X	
	Pennsylvania State University		
	Swarthmore College		
	University of Pennsylvania		
	Waynesburg College		X
	Brown University		
Rhode Island	Pembroke College		
South Carolina	Benedict College	X	
Tennessee	Fisk University	X	
	Knoxville College	X	
	Lane College	X	
	LeMoyne College		
Texas	Bishop College	X	
	Huston-Tillotson College	X	
	Texas College	X	
	Wiley College	X	
Vermont	Bennington College		
	Middlebury College		

Appendix 147

Table 5. 145 Institutions participating in the African Scholarships Program of American Universities *(continued)(continued)*

State	College/University	College Fund	Scholarship Program
Virginia	Hampton Institute	X	
	St. Paul(s College	X	
	Virginia Union University	X	
Washington	University of Washington		
	Washington State University		
Wisconsin	Lawrence College		
	Marquette University		
	University of Wisconsin		

Source: Papers of Congressman Charles Diggs, Moorland-Spingarn Research Center, Howard University, Washington, D.C. Box 194 Folder 15.

Table 6.1. Number of African Students in the United States, 1950–1964

Home Country	1950-51	1954-55	1956	1957	1958	1959	1960	1961	1962	1963	1964
Ethiopia	41	62	110	151	151	145	170	171	176	171	220
Ghana				153	135	150	167	160	201	246	279
Kenya	5	19	22	17	32	73	156	332	543	697	775
Liberia	98	188	146	172	210	205	170	166	180	219	285
Nigeria	249	268	226	222	192	209	258	343	552	813	1140
Sierra Leone	45	27	23	31	37	47	39	60	94	114	147
Somalia							11	8	35	59	76
South Africa									256	312	344
Tanzania											
Uganda	1	4	6	10	21	26	29	40	102	127	159

Source: "*Open Doors*" Institute of International Education

Appendix

Table 6.2. Number of African Students in the United States, 1965–1974

Home Country	1965	1966	1967	1968	1969	1970	1971	1972	1973	1974
Ethiopia	226	294	323	361	422	540	759	883	1046	1289
Ghana	282	306	368	374	407	539	647	745	871	946
Kenya	774	712	681	586	523	492	534	499	540	568
Liberia	315	291	282	299	295	337	372	381	431	436
Nigeria	1382	1570	1732	1790	1790	1851	2333	3077	4092	4817
Sierra Leone	149	155	179	189	221	241	312	355	463	552
Somalia	102	91					60	55		403
South Africa	390	409	464	477	481	457	445	417	418	
Tanzania		259	246	225	207	215	238	217	256	272
Uganda	223	215	239	229	225	257	263	244	262	252

Source: "*Open Doors*," Institute of International Education

Table 7. African Students, Showing Home Country, Gender, Year Studies in United States Began, Financial Support, Academic Status

Home Country	Total	Gender		Year studies begin in United States				Financial Support			
		Male	Female	1964-65	1963	1962 and before	No answer	U.S. Gov't	Foreign Gov't.	Self	U.S. College Univ.	U.S. College Univ. Private
Total	6,855	5,951	894	1,900	1,371	2,287	1,297	1,735	927	887	635	451
Ethiopia	266	226	40	101	60	58	47	111	3	26	18	10
Ghana	282	251	31	68	57	93	64	29	48	46	44	22
Kenya	774	661	113	188	134	371	81	131	12	106	96	131
Liberia	315	230	85	106	52	69	88	71	69	52	5	8
Sierra Leone	149	7	52	33	34	63	19	29	16	27	22	16
South Africa	390	330	60	136	88	89	77	33	10	102	86	19
Somalia	102	100	2	32	22	25	23	82	3	2	5	1
Tanzania	305	251	54	98	67	118	22	112	7	20	27	42
Uganda	223	190	33	93	46	61	23	85	23	5	21	8

Source: *"Open Doors"* Institute of International Education

Appendix

Table 8. Kenyan Students: Gender and Academic Status, 1955–1974

Kenya	Total	Male	Female	Under-graduate	Graduate MA	Graduate unknown	Graduate Ph.D.	Special Student	Did not specify
1955	19	19	–	12	4			3	–
1956	22	21	1	17	2			3	–
1957	17	16	1	10	5			2	–
1958	32	31	1	16	15			1	–
1959	156	136	20	118	23			10	5
1960	156	136	20	118	23			10	5
1961	332	289	43	283	33			11	5
1962	543	477	66	487	33			18	5
1963	697	609	88	609	48	15	10	14	1
1964	775	671	104	619	65	13	22	42	14
1965	774	661	113	614	92	11	24	20	13
1966	712	613	99	183	66	3	10	26	3
1967	681	585	96	469	124	29	43	13	3
1968	586	490	96	353	112	47	49	21	4
1969	523	434	89	315	85	45	58	15	5
1970	492	391	91	260	96	51	58	13	14
1971	534	426	97	294	85	80	56	10	9
1972	499	385	87	269	51	103	40	9	27
1973	540	429	94	312	77	99	27	11	14
1974	568	435	110	314	54	121	29	9	41

Source: "*Open Doors*," Institute of International Education

Figure 1. Mbiyu Koinange

Source: General Records of the Department of State, National Archives, MD, RG 59, Box 2418.

Appendix

Figure 2. Dr. Julius Gikonyo Kiano

Source: General Records of the Department of State, National Archives, MD, RG 59, Box 2418

Figure 3. Dr. Wangari Maathai
Photo Credit: Martin Rowe

Appendix 155

Figure 4. Dr. Njoroge Mungai

Source: General Records of the Department of State, National Archives, MD, RG 59, Box 2418.

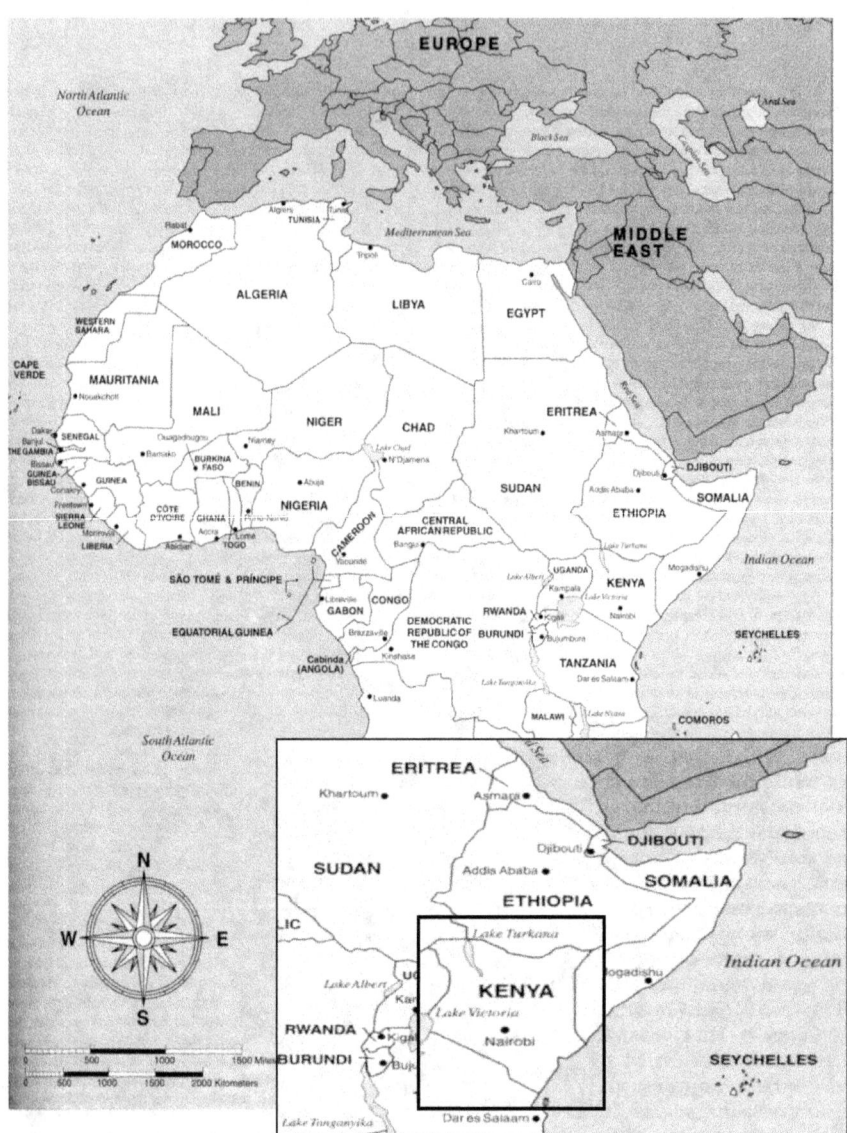

Figure 5. Map of Kenya

Source: Adapted from Wayne Edge ed. Global Studies Africa, 11/e. McGraw Hill/Dushkin. Dubuque, Iowa, 2003.

Notes

NOTES TO CHAPTER ONE

1. Interview with Dr. Kiano, Nairobi, 23 June 1999.
2. Ibid.
3. Arab traders, like traders from Persia, India, Indonesia, and China came to East Africa in search of tortoise shells, ivory, rhinoceros horns, gold, leopard skins, and slaves. They traded or bartered these items with metal tools, utensils, swords, cowry shells, and beads. For more information on the East African/Indian Ocean trade, particularly the slave trade see Edward Alpers, The East African Slave Trade, Nairobi, East African Publishing House, 1967, Deryck Scarr, Slaving and Slavery In The Indian Ocean, Baltimore: St. Martin's Press, 1993, Joseph E. Harris, The African Presence in Asia: Consequences of the East African Slave Trade, Evanston: Northwestern University Press, 1971.
4. 4 Ralph Uwechue, ed. 1996, Africa Today, 3rd ed., Africa Books Limited, p. 854.
5. Kevin Shillington, A History of Africa, New York, St. Martin's Press, 1995, p. 128. See Roland Oliver, The Missionary Factor in East Africa, London, Longmans, Green and Co., 1952.
6. Ioan Davies, *African Trade Unions,* Middlesex, England, 1966, pp. 194–195.
7. Interview with Dr. Kiano, Nairobi, 23 June 1999.
8. It is generally accepted that the first black intellectual to move Pan-Africanism to practical application was W.E.B. DuBois. Other distinguished black intellectuals who promoted Pan-Africanism were Martin R. Delany, Alexander Crummell, and Edward Wilmot Blyden, George Padmore, and Henry Sylvester Williams. Williams planned a preliminary Pan-African Conference where the actual term Pan-Africanism seems to have been coined. The first Pan-African Conference was set up in 1919 by W.E.B. DuBois and others in Paris. After World War II African and African-American intellectuals and leaders used the ideology of Pan-Africanism as an expression of the struggle for independence and equal

rights. Black nationalism emphasized African origins and identity, black pride, self-help, self-reliance in the building of African-American communities. In some degree it also infers the notion or desire to establish a black nation in Africa or some part of the United States. Some great proponents of this philosophy were Paul Cuffe, W.E.B. DuBois, Marcus Garvey, and Malcolm X. Although Marcus Garvey's organization, the Universal Negro Improvement Association, was the largest mass movement of people of African decent in the history of the world perhaps the best-known leader was Malcolm X. African nationalism developed as a result of European colonization of Africa, colonial laws, unfair working conditions, and a discriminatory system accompanied by burdensome taxes. Of the noted African figures who promoted this ideology were Harry Thuku, Kwame Nkrumah, and Jomo Kenyatta.

9. Ronald Walters, *PanAfricanism in the African Diaspora: An Analysis of the Modern Afrocentric Political Movements,* Detroit, Wayne State University Press, 1993, p. 41.
10. Joseph E. Harris, *Global Dimensions of the African Diaspora,* Washington, D.C., Howard University, 1993, p. 3.
11. P. Olisanwuche Esedebe, Pan-Africanism: The Idea and Movement, 1776–1963, Washington, D.C.: Howard University Press, 1982, p. 2.
12. Kenneth King, *Pan-Africanism and Education: A Study of Race Philanthropy and Education In The Southern United States Of America and East Africa,* Oxford, Clarendon Press, 1971, p. 3.
13. The *Washington Post,* October 9, 2003, p. A24.
14. See Martin Staniland, *American Intellectuals and African Nationalists, 1955–1970,* New Haven, Yale University Press, 1991.
15. See, Daniel N. Sifuna, *Development of Education in Africa: the Kenyan Experience,* Nairobi, Initiatives Publishers, 1990 and James R. Sheffield, *Education in Kenya: A Historical Study,* New York, Teachers College Press, 1973.
16. George E. Urch, "Education and Colonialism in Kenya," in *History of Education Quarterly,* 11, 3 Autumn, 1971.
17. Magnus O. Bassey, *Western Education and Political Domination in Africa: A Study in Critical and Dialogical* Pedagogy, London, Bergin and Garvey, 1999.
18. M.G. Capon, *Towards Unity in Kenya: the Story of Co-operation Between Missions and Churches in Kenya, 1913–1947,* Nairobi, Christian Council of Kenya, 1962.
19. Sylvia M. Jacobs, ed., *Black Missionaries and the Missionary Movement in Africa,* London, Greenwood Press, 1982.
20. Leroy Fitts, *The Lott Carey Legacy of African American Missions,* Baltimore: Gateway Press, 1994.
21. Kenneth King, *Pan-Africanism and Education: A Study of Race Philanthropy and Education in the Southern United States of America and East Africa,* Clarendon Press, Oxford University Press, 1971.
22. Tom Mboya, *Freedom and After,* Boston, Little Brown and Company, 1963; David Goldsworthy, *Tom Mboya: The Man Kenya Wanted to Forget,* 1982;

Alan Rake, *Tom Mboya: A Young Man of New Africa,* Garden City, New York: Doubleday, 1962.

NOTES TO CHAPTER TWO

1. The terms traditional and pre-colonial education are used interchangeably to describe the education system in Kenya prior to the arrival of the Europeans.
2. J.D. Fage, "The Development of African Historiography, in J. Ki-Zerbo, ed., *UNESCO General History of Africa,* vol. 1, p. 30.
3. Daniel N. Sifuna, *Development of Education in Africa: The Kenya Experience,* p. 3.
4. J.E. Otiende, "Education Since the Early Times," in William R. Ochieng, ed., *Themes in Kenyan History,* Nairobi, Ohio University Press, 1990, p. 145.
5. Mugo Gatheru to Jim Harper, October 31, 2003.
6. Jomo Kenyatta, *Facing Mount Kenya: The Tribal Life of the Gikuyu,* New York, Vintage, 1962, p. 96.
7. Mokubung Nkomo, ed. *Pedagogy of Domination: Toward a Democratic Education in South Africa,* Trenton, New Jersey, Africa World Press, Inc. 1990, p. 19. Also refer to, Godfrey Muriuki, *A History of the Kikuyu, 1500–1900,* Nairobi, Oxford University Press, 1974, pp. 8–9.
8. Sifuna, *Development of Education in Africa,* pp. 4–5.
9. Barbara B. Lloyd, "Education and Family Life in the Development of Class Identification Among the Yoruba," in Peter C. Lloyd, ed., *The New Elites of Tropical Africa,* London, Oxford University Press, 1966, p. 164.
10. Daniel Sifuna, *Development of Education In Africa,* p. 9.
11. Fred Fluitman, ed., *Training for the Informal Sector,* Geneva, International Labor Office, 1989, p. 20.
12. Timothy Regan, "Philosophy of Education in the Service of Apartheid: The Role of Fundamental Pedagogics' in South African Education," *Educational Foundations,* 4, no. 2, 1990, 65.
13. David G. Scanlon, "The Bush School," *Phi Delta Kappan,* 61 no. 4, January 1960, p. 148 and Godfrey Muriuki, *A History of the Kikuyu,* pp. 118–119.
14. James R. Sheffield, *Education in Kenya: An Historical Study,* New York, Teachers College Press, 1973, p. 3. Also see, Jomo Kenyatta, *Facing Mount Kenya: The Traditional Life of the Gikuyu,* London, Heinemann, 1979, p. 112 and Muriuki, *A History of the Kikuyu,* 112 and Louis S.B. Leaky, *The Southern Kikuyu Before 1903,* New York, Academic Press, 1977, p. 2.
15. Generally speaking it took five to nine years of experience to qualify for the rank of a junior warrior. Muriuki, *A History of the Kikuyu,* p. 120 and Leakey, *The Southern Kikuyu,* p. 711.
16. Leakey, *The Southern Kikuyu,* p. 711.
17. Muriuki, *A History of the Kikuyu,* p. 127–128.
18. H.A. Mwanzi, "African Initiative and Resistance in East Africa, 1880–1914," in G. Mokhtar, ed., *General History of Africa vol. II: Ancient*

Civilizations of Africa, Paris, United Nations Educational, Scientific, and Cultural Organization, 1986, p. 154.
19. Muriuki, *A History of the Kikuyu,* pp. 121–122.
20. Crawford Young, *The African Colonial State in Comparative Perspective,* New Haven, Yale University Press, 1994, pp. 36–37. Young defines the African colonial state using the guidelines of the development of European states. He argues that the early modern state was absolutist as rulers created standing armies and professional bureaucracies; royal writ and law penetrated the territory; flows of revenue beyond the circumscribed income from royal estates secured the treasuries. Machiavelli, Bodin and Hobbes were the philosophers of absolutism and provided the normative text through which the early modern states achieved recognition and claimed legitimation. He asserts that states must have most but not necessarily all of the nine attributes he outlines in his text. The attributes are territory, population, sovereignty, power, law, state as nation, state as an international actor, state as idea, and states as historical actor. Young argues that no rule is clearer than the percept that no State may lawfully attempt to exercise its sovereignty of another. The population is subordinate to the laws of the state and organized into a formal set of statuses. A state that loses its territory or population ceases to exist. Sovereignty calls for complete independence and self-government of a territory existing as an independent state. The territory now known as Kenya was not centralized and not considered a nation-state by European standards. Nevertheless, the ethnic groups, specifically, the Kikuyu, with their council of elders, were able to possess many of the previously mentioned attributes outlined by Young. Godfrey Muriuki noted in "The Kikuyu in the Pre-Colonial Period," in Bethwell A. Ogot, *Kenya Before 1900,* Nairobi, East African Publishing House, 1976. Also refer to, S.N. Eisenstadt, "African Age Groups: A Comparative Study," *Africa,* 24 August 1954, pp. 100–112.
21. M. El-Fasi and I. Hrbek, "The Coming of Islam and the Expansion of the Muslim Empire" in M. El-Fasi and I. Hrbek, eds. *General History of Africa vol. III: Africa from the Seventh to the Eleventh Century,* Paris: United Nations Educational, Scientific, and Cultural Organization, 1988, 40.
22. Aziz Batran, *Islam and Revolution in Africa,* Battleboro, Vermont, Amana Books, 1984, 13.
23. Ibid., See Aziz Batran, *Islam and Revolution* for the rise of the *Kharijites* and their persecution by the *Umayyads.* The *Kharijite,* meaning those who withdrew from the armies of the fourth Caliph, Ali (d. 661), in the course of his struggle for the leadership of the *umma* with Muawya, the patriarch of the *Umayyads,* developed a novel political ideology. They insisted that the *imamate* (leadership of the *umma*) was grounded on popular consensus. Any qualified Muslim irrespective of social status or race had the right of becoming the imam (even if he were a Black slave). This ideology rejected categorically the dynastic system of the *Umyyads* and their successors, the *Abbasids.* Hence, the *Kharijites* fell victim to outrageous persecution by the ruling dynasties.

24. See for example, E.W. Bovil, *The Golden Trade of the Moors,* London, Oxford University Press, 1968 and R.C.C. Law, "The Garamantes and Trans-Saharan Enterprise in Classical Times, *Journal of African History,* 3, 1967, 181–200; Anthony G. Hopkins, *An Economic History of West Africa,* New York: Columbia University Press, 1973; and J.D. Fage, *A History of West Africa,* London, Cambridge University Press, 1969.
25. John O. Hunwick and Obad A. Saodei, eds., *Timbuktu and the Songhay Empire: Al-Sa'di's Ta'rik al-Sudan Down to 1613 and Other Contemporary Documents,* Leiden, Boston, Brill, 1999.
26. See, John Ralph Willis, ed., *The Cultivators of Islam,* London, Frank Cass, 1979; "The Passion of Al-Hajj Umar" and Aziz Batran, "The Nineteenth-Century Islamic Revolutions in West Africa" and M. Ly-Tall, " "Massina and the Tordbe (Tukuloor) Empire Until 1878 and Y. Person, "States and Peoples of Senegambia and Upper Guinea" in Jacob Fustus Ade F. Ajayi, ed., *General History of Africa vol. VI: Africa in the Nineteenth Century Until the 1880's,* Paris, United Nations Educational, Scientific, and Cultural Organization, 1998. Also refer to, Aziz Batran, *The Qadiryya Brotherhood in West Africa and the Western Sahara: The Life and Times of Shaykh al-Mukhtar al-Kunti, 1729–1811,* Rabat, Publications de l'Institute des Etudes Africaines, 2001; and Jamil M. Abun-Nasr, *The Tijaniyya, A Sufi Order in the Modern World,* London, Oxford University Press, 1965.
27. F.T. Masao and H.W. Mutoro, "The East African Coast and the Comoro Islands" in *General History of Africa: Africa from the Seventh to the Eleventh Century vol. III,* Paris, United Nations Educational, Scientific, and Cultural Organization, 1988, pp. 586–615. The actual date of the arrival of Islam in Kenyan is currently under debate. However, some Muslim scholars, including Sheikh Muhammad bin Sarif Al-Bajdh, note that Islam came to East Africa during the tenure of the Umayyad caliph, Abdul-Malik bin Marwan. This date was confirmed by Dr. Mark Harton of Oxford. His research at Shanga, on Pate Island confirms the eighth century as the time when Islam began to make its appearance on the coast of Kenya.
28. William R. Ochieng, ed., *Themes in Kenyan History,* Nairobi, Ohio University Press, 1990, 149. A *sheikh* is defined as a Muslim leader or religious official.
29. Henry A. Giroux, *Teachers as Intellectuals: Toward a Critical Pedagogy of Learning,* Westport, Bergin & Garvey, 1988, pp.101–102.
30. Philip G. Albach and Gail P. Kelly, eds., *Education and Colonialism,* New York, Longman, 1978, p. 212.

NOTES TO CHAPTER THREE

1. European writers define western education as formal or modern education because it takes place in formalized classroom setting or institution. On the other hand, they refer to African education as informal or traditional since it occurs in a variety of environments including the home, during apprenticeship, initiation ceremonies, through myths, folklore, or legend.

2. Geoffrey Parrinder, *Religion in Africa,* New York, Praeger Publishers, 1969, p. 103.
3. Ibid., pp. 104–109.
4. J.D. Fage, *A History of West Africa,* Cambridge, the University Press, 1969, p. 55.
5. I.N. Kimambo, "The East African Coast and Hinterland, 1845–80" in Adi Ajayi, *UNESCO General History of Africa,* vol. VI, 1989, pp. 264—265.
6. J.D. Fage, *A History of Africa,* London, Routledge, 1995, p. 260.
7. Kimambo, "The East African Coast and Hinterland, 1845–80," p. 263.
8. The *mijikenda,* or nine villages/"tribes," included the *Chonyi, Digo, Duruma, Giriama, Jibana, Kambi, Kauma, Ribe and Rabai.* For a brief history of Rabai see *Rabai to Mumias: A Short history of the church of the Province of Kenya,* by Provincial Unit of Research Church of the Province of Kenya, Nairobi, Uzima, 1994. Rabai was also given the name Frere after Sir Bartle Frere who advised the CMS to establish a mission station at the village. Sir Bretle Frere was sent by the British government in 1872 to negotiate a treaty prohibiting the slave trade with the Sultan of Zanzibar.
9. K. Asare Opoku, "Religion in Africa During the Colonial Era" in A. Adu Boahen, ed., *UNESC O General History of Africa,* vol. VII, Paris, 1985, p. 527.
10. Neely Tucker, *Descendants Hold To Ex-Slaves' Dream,* Detroit Free Press, 5 November 1997, p. 15.
11. The establishment of Sierra Leone and Liberia were a direct result of the abolition of slavery and the slave trade. Sierra Leone was founded in 1787 as a settlement of four hundred free Blacks from England. In the 1790's more free Blacks from Nova Scotia arrived. These two groups were somewhat integrated and came to be known as "Creoles." In 1808, the British took over the settlement. The Anti-Slavery Squadron used it as a base for settling freed Blacks who were released from captured slave ships. Liberia, on the other hand, was founded in 1822 by freed Blacks from the United States of America. The resettlement was organized by the American Colonization Society, which held the belief that the increasing number of Blacks in the Southern States threatened keeping other Blacks in bondage.
12. James R. Sheffield, *Education in Kenya: A Historical Study,* New York, Teachers College Press, 1973, p. 9.
13. Joseph E. Harris, *The African Presence In Asia: Consequences of the East African Slave Trade,* Evanston, Northwestern University Press, 1971, pp. 73–76; Neely Tucker, *Descendants Hold To Ex-Slaves' Dream,* p. 15.
14. Walter Williams, *Black Americans and the Evangelization of Africa, 1877–1900,* Madison, University of Wisconsin Press, 1982, p. 141.
15. K. Asare Opoku, "Religion in Africa During the Colonial Era," p. 525.
16. Of the early missionary schools in Kenya, one may mention Maseno, Budo, Saint Austin's, Thogoto, Kijabe, Mangu, and Siyiapie.
17. Colin Reed, *Pastors, Partners, and Paternalists: African Church Leaders and Western Missionaries in The Anglican Church In Kenya, 1850–1900,* Leiden, New York: E.J. Brill, 1997, p. 121.

18. Owallo is said to have had a vision in 1907 in which he was taken to Heaven by the Arch- Angel, Gabriel. While in heaven, he noticed that the Popes, Europeans as well as Asians were not allowed entry. He therefore came to the conclusion that the white and Asian led churches were not for Africans. Hence, he founded *Nomiya* that mixed Christianity with Luo traditional practices.
19. K. Asare Opoku, "Religion in Africa During the Colonial Era," p. 531.
20. For Black Theological Institutes see G.F. Richings, *Evidence of Progress Among Colored People,* 8th edition, Philadelphia, 1902.
21. Kenneth King, *Pan-Africanism and Education: A Study of Race Philanthropy and Education in the Southern States of America and East Africa,* New York, Oxford University Press, 1971, p. 245.
22. The *Nation,* February 4, 2004. Archbishop Festo Olang died on February 3, 2004. He was 95 years old and had made great contributions to the church in Kenya. For more information see, "Bishop Olang End of Illustrious Ministry" in the *Nation* February 4, 2004.
23. *Sunday Standard,* September 7, 2003; *Catholic Information Service For Africa,* Issue No. 255, September 5, 2003, pp. 1–7.
24. *Catholic Information Service For Africa,* Issue No. 255, September 5, 2003, pp. 1–7.
25. *Sunday Standard,* September 7, 2003.
26. *East Africa Standard,* December 15, 2003.
27. Ibid.
28. Ibid.
29. 29 Mugo Gatheru to Jim Harper, October 31, 2003.
30. 30 K. Asare Opoku, "Religion in Africa During the Colonial Era," p. 525.
31. The British intended to use the East Coast of Africa in order to control the ocean routes to India through exerting informal control over the region. However, at the end of the nineteenth century, they changed their policy to outright control as more European nations competed with them for the acquisition of African territories.
32. William R. Ochieng, ed., *Themes In Kenyan History,* Nairobi, Ohio University Press, 1990, p. 127.
33. See Ronald Robinson and John Gallagher, *Africa and the Victorians: The Climax of Imperialism In The Darker Continent,* New York, St. Martin's Press, 1961; Roland Oliver, *History of East Africa,* Oxford, Clarendon Press, 1976; Peter N. Stearns, ed., *The Encyclopedia of World History,* sixth ed., New York, Houghton Mifflin Company, 2001. Frederick Lugard is generally considered to be the architect of British Indirect Rule, that is, governing Africans through indigenous authorities. He applied this policy in Nigeria during his tenure as Governor of the colony from 1901 to 1906.
34. Kenneth Ingham, *A History of East Africa,* New York, Praeger, 1965, 51.
35. The construction of the Ugandan railway in the period between1895 and 1901 opened the interior for unprecedented settler colonization of the region.

36. George Bennett, *Kenya: A Political History: The Colonial Period*, London, Oxford University Press, 1963, p. 12. Colonial policy makers in Britain were in agreement that the surest and best way for exploiting the resources of the region was alienation of Kenyan and Ugandan Highlands to white settlers after the South African example. Little wonder that, at the beginning, Whites in South Africa, more so than those from mainland Britain, were intensely enthusiastic to settle in the Protectorate. Ancestral land was seized by white settlers and the indigenous rightful owners were herded into reserves or forced to work as squatters in white farms.
37. J.S. Mangat, *A History of Asians In East Africa, 1886–1945*, Oxford, Clarendon Press, 1969, pp. 84–87. The Indian community made important contributions to the economy of East Africa as traders forming the foundation of the emerging Indian *bazaars* in East Africa.
38. Sir Andrew Cohen, *British Policy In Changing Africa*, Evanston, Northwestern University Press, 1959, p. 16.
39. Ochieng, *Themes In Kenyan History*, p. 149. Furthermore, the Frazer Commission urged the Administration to provide more grant-in-aid assistance to missionary schools.
40. Daniel N. Sifuna, *Development of Education in Africa: The Kenyan Experience*, p. 52. The debate regarding the form of education appropriate for Kenyans was similar to the debate between Booker T. Washington and W.E.B. DuBois over the form of education best for African-Americans. In general, in Africa as well as in the United States vocational education was considered an inferior form of education by both parents and students.
41. Mugo Gatheru to Jim Harper, October 31, 2003.
42. Ibid.
43. 43 Sheffield, *Education in Kenya*, p. 23.
44. *Carnegie Reporter*, vo. 2, No. 1, 2002.
45. *East African Standard*, December 2, 2003. The philosophy of "teaching the dignity of labor" was exposed by Blacks during this period when the primary focus for educational instruction was industrial or vocational. Blacks believe that they could build character and maintain a high level of dignity through hard work and service. Refer to, Louis Harlan, ed., *The Booker T. Washington Papers vol. 3 1889–1895*, Urbana, University of Illinois Press, 1974, p. 315.
46. Ibid.
47. Darlene Clark Hine, William C. Hine, and Stanley Harrold, eds., *The African-American Odyssey*, New Jersey, Prentice Hall, 2003, p. 338. Hampton Normal and Agricultural Institute was founded in 1868 and was directed for decades by Samuel Chapman Armstrong, a white missionary with strong paternalistic inclinations. In accordance with the dominant philosophy of the time, Hampton embraced concepts such as hard work, diligence, and Christian morality. It stressed learning trades such as shoemaking, carpentry, tailoring, and sewing but placed little emphasis on critical or independent thinking. Students were instructed to conform to middle-class values and were cautioned against involvement in politics.

One of Hampton's graduates was Booker T. Washington, who not only became one of America's leading advocates of industrial education but also founded Tuskegee Institute, which, like Hampton, focused on vocational education.

48. William Seraile, "Black American Missionaries in Africa, 1821–1925" in Social Studies, 63, October 1972, pp. 198–202.
49. Kenneth King, "The American Negro as Missionary to East Africa: A Critical Aspect of African Evangelism" in *African Historical Studies,* vol. 31, 1970, pp. 5–22. King argues that some missionary societies no longer employed African-American missionaries by the beginning of the twentieth century. According to him, even the less determined investigator would prove that this was the result of discriminatory missionary policies.
50. Ibid., 5–22
51. E.S. Atieno-Odhiambo, "Politics and Nationalism in East Africa, 1919–35" in A. Adu Boahen, ed., *UNESCO General History of Africa,* vol. VII, p. 671.
52. R.D. Ralston, "Africa and the New World" in A. Adu Boahen, ed., *UNESCO General History of Africa,* vol. VII, pp. 755–759.
53. Ibid., p. 756.
54. King, "The American Negro as Missionary to East Africa: A Critical Aspect of African Evangelism," p. 11.
55. Sylvia M. Jacobs, "The Historical Role of Afro-Americans in American Missionary Efforts in Africa" in Sylvia M. Jacobs ed., *Black Americans and the Missionary Movement in Africa,* Westport, Connecticut, Greenwood Press, 1982, pp. 5–25.
56. George Shepperson and Thomas Price, *Independent Africa: John Chilembwe and the Origins, Setting and Significance of the Nyasaland Native Rising of 1915,* Edinburgh, Edinburgh University Press, 1987, p. 80. Also see, Mekki Mtewa, "Problems of Oedipal Historicism: The Saga of John Chilembwe–the Malawian," in *Journal of Black Studies,* vol. 8, December 2, 1977, pp. 227–250.
57. Kenneth King, "Africa and the Southern United States: Some Notes on J.H. Oldham and American Negro Education For Africans" *Journal of African History,* X, April 1969, 659–677.
58. Ibid., p. 143.
59. Vincent Harlow and E.M. Chilver, eds., *History of East Africa,* Oxford University Press, 1965, p. 222.
60. King, "The American Negro as Missionary to East Africa: A Critical Aspect of African Evangelism," p. 8.
61. Max Yergan Papers, Moorland-Spingarn Box 206-1 Folder 27. Also see, Jesse Edward Moorland, "The Young Men's Christian Association and the War," *Crisis,* XV, December 3, 1917, pp. 65–68.
62. For more information on Max Yergan see David Anthony, "Max Yergan in South Africa: From Evangelist Pan-Africanist to Revolutionary Socialist," in African Studies Review, 34, s, September, 1991.
63. Atieno-Odhiambo, "Politics and Nationalism in East Africa, 1919–35,," p. 650.3.

64. Welbourn, *East African Rebel*, p. 159.4.
65. For further information on Bishop Daniel William Alexander see, Morris Johnson, *Archbishop Daniel William Alexander and the African Orthodox Church,* Rowman and Littlefield, U.K., 1999.
66. Robert T. Vinson, "In the Time Of the Americans: Garveyism in Segregationist South Africa, 1920-1940" Ph.D. Dissertation, Howard University, 2001.6.
67. For more information on Mbiyu Koinange see Chapter Five.
68. Interview with Dr. Kiano, Nairobi, June 29, 1999.8.
69. *News and Letters,* Chicago, January-February, 1998.
70. For more information regarding Dr. Kiano see Chapter Four.1.
71. Atieno-Odhiambo, "Politics and Nationalism in East Africa, 1919-35," pp. 665-672.
72. Ibid., p. 669.
73. George Bennett, "The Development of Political Organizations in Kenya," *Political Studies,* no. 2, June 1957, pp. 119-122.
74. *Kipande* or forced labor was imposed by the Colonial Authorities on all adult males to serve in settler plantations and public facilities.

NOTES TO CHAPTER FOUR

1. Eric Asby, *Universities: British, Indian, African: A Study in Ecology of Higher Education,* Cambridge, Harvard University Press, 1966, p. 198.
2. Godfrey N. Brown, "British Educational Policy in West and Central Africa," in *The Journal of Modern African Studies,* 2 no. 3 1964, pp. 365-377.
3. Asbv, *Universities: British, Indian, African,* pp. 215-223.
4. Tuskegee Registry. See also Kenneth King, *Pan-Africanism and Education: A Study of Race Philanthropy and Education in he Southern States of America and East Africa,* Oxford, Clarendon Press, 1971, pp. 1-2.
5. Mohammed Jama, Tuskegee Registry, Memo to Mr. Scott regarding Mohammad Jama, 10 October, 1916; Booker T. Washington Papers, Library of Congress, Washington D.C. Box 312.
6. Roosevelt to E.J. Scott (Secretary to Tuskegee Institute) 13 October, 1916, the R.R. Morton Papers, General Correspondence, 1916, Tuskegee Institute Archives.
7. See Chapter Five for a detailed information on Mbiyu Koinange.
8. Interview with Dr. Kiano, Nairobi, Kenya, June 29, 1999.
9. Ibid.
10. Macharia Munene, "United States and Anti-Colonialism in Kenya, 1895-1963," in *African Review of Foreign Policy,* vol. 12, March, 1999, p. 12.
11. Edmond J. Dorez to Department of State, 22 August, 1957, Records of the Department of State, Decimal File 1955-1959, National Archives, MD, RG 59, Box 2141.
12. Interview with Dr. Kiano, Nairobi, Kenya, June 29, 1999.
13. Ibid.

14. Daily Nation, August 9, 2003.
15. Other similar organizations were likewise established. They included the Luo Union, NAU of the Akamba, the Abaluhya Association, the Kalenjin Association, and the Maji-Kenda Association. Although these associations began as welfare and cultural organisations, they quickly assumed a political character and were led by cliques of western-educated politicians. In time, these ethnic organisations became so powerful that they threatened the national unity that KANU represented. Hence, in July 1980, President Moi dissolved these organisations. See O.P. Ogot, "The Politics of Populism," in Ogot and Ochieng, *Decolonization and Independence in Kenya*, pp. 195–197.
16. Interview with Dr. Kiano, Nairobi, Kenya, June 29, 1999; See also, *African Biographies (Bonn-Bad)*, 1967 entry 3; R. Segal, p. 141–142; J. Dickie and A. Rake, 1973 p. 199; *Joe: Election Review*, 1974 p. 8, 43; *Weekly Review Election Handbook*, 1979, p. 37; *Weekly Review, Guide to Politics in Mbiri*, 1979, pp. 31–40; M. Nzioki and M.B. Dar, 1983, p. 317; Citation on Dr. Julius G. Kiano, on conferment of Hon D. Litt., University of Nairobi, 1st December 1997, p. 9.
17. *East African Standard*, August 13, 2003.
18. *Daily Nation*, August 9, 2003.
19. Mugo Gatheru to Jim Harper, October 31, 2003.
20. *Harambee* is a *Kiswahili* word meaning self-help.
21. Marco Publishers (Africa) Limited, *Who's Who in East Africa, 1967–1968*, 1968, p. 121.
22. See Chapter Five.
23. Ashby, *Universities: British, Indian, African*, pp. 477–478.
24. Ibid., p. 198; J.F. Ajayi, *The African Experience With Higher Education*, London, James Currey, 1996, p. 53.
25. Atieno Odhiambo, "The Formative Years: 1945–1955" in Bethwell Ogot and William Ochieng, eds., *Decolonization and Independence in Kenya, 1940–1993*, London, James Currey, 1995, pp. 27–31.
26. Ibid., p. 34.
27. Michael Twaddle, "The Struggle for Political Sovereignty in Eastern Africa" in Ali Amamin Mazuri and Christophe Wondji, eds., *UNESCO General History of Africa*, vol. VIII, pp. 235–236.
28. The ex-servicemen were Kenyan soldiers who served in the British army in India, Burma, Ceylon, the Middle East and Europe. They played the most vital role in training the Mau Mau Land and Freedom Army. Their militant leaders were Bildad Kaggia, J.D. Kali, and Dedan Kimathi. See P. Ogula, "A Biography of ex-Senior Chief Mukundi of Samia and Bunyala," in *Kenya Historical Review*, 2, no. 2 1974, p. 185.
29. Atieno Odhiambo, "The Formative Years: 1945–1955" in Bethwell Ogot and William Ochieng, eds., *Decolonization and Independence in Kenya*, pp. 27–35.
30. Bethwell Ogot, "The Decisive Years, 1956–63" in Bethwell Ogot and William Ochieng, eds., *Decolonization and Independence in Kenya*, pp. 51–55.

31. Ibid., p. 41. Among the loyal chiefs were Chief Waruhiu, Chief Githu, Chief Kanyua, Chief Njonjo and Chief Nderi. The loyal western-educated elites included Parmenas Karitu, David Wanguhu, David Waruhiu, and Reuben Karari.
32. Ibid., p. 58.
33. E.S. Atieno-Odhiambo, "The Formative Years, 145–55" in Bethwell A. Ogot and William R. Ochieng, eds., *Decolonization of Kenya, 1940–1993*, pp. 38–39.
34. Ogot, "The Decisive Years," p. 52. The district parties that emerged were: The Mombasa African Democratic Union, the Abagusii Association of South Nyanza District, the Taita African Democratic Union, the African District Association of East Nyanzathe, Nakuru African Progressive Party, the Abaluhya People's Association, the Nyanza North African Congress, and the Nakuru District Congress.
35. The eight Districts were Nairobi Constituency, Ukambani Constituency, the Coast Constituency, Central Province, Nyanza South, Nyanza North, Central Nyanza, and Rift Valley.
36. Interview with Macharia Munene of the United States International University Nariobi, Kenya, 29, 1999.
37. George Houser to Jim Harper, November 11, 2003.
38. Ibid.
39. Ibid.
40. Ibid.
41. Ibid
42. Ibid. Mboya spoke six languages fluently: Suba, Luo, Kikuyu, Kamba, Kiswahili and English.
43. Ibid.
44. C.H. Millard to George Meany, 23 August 1957, letter, Papers of the Brotherhood of Sleeping Car Porters, Manuscript Division, Library of Congress, Box 97 Folder 1 Africa.
45. "CIA Plotted Odinga's Removal From Office," in the *Sunday Nation*, July 2, 2000.
46. C.H. Millard to George Meany, 23 August 1957, letter, Papers of the Brotherhood of Sleeping Car Porters, Manuscript Division, Library of Congress, Box 97, Folder 1 Africa.
47. Planning Document, the Papers of the Brotherhood of the Sleeping Car Porters, Library of Congress, Manuscript Division, 4 September, 1957, Box 97, Folder 1 Africa.
48. "The Emergence of Africa, Report to the President by Vice-President on his trip to Africa," White House Release, April 7, 1957. See also Waldemar Nelson, *The Graet Powers and Africa,* New York, Praeger Publishing, 1969, p. 266.
49. "CIA Plotted Odinga's Removal From Office," in the *Sunday Nation*, July 2, 2000.
50. Papers of the Brotherhood of Sleeping Car Porters, Library of Congress Manuscript Division, Box 97, Folder 1 Africa.

51. Tom Mboya to George Meany, 11 March 1958, letter, Papers of the Brotherhood of Sleeping Car Porters, Manuscript Division, Library of Congress, Box 97, Folder 1 Africa.
52. Arnold Zack, *Labor Training in Developing Countries,* Pall Mall, 1964, pp. 150–152.
53. George Brown to Asa Philip Randolph, 28 February 1958, Letter, Papers of the Brotherhood of Sleeping Car Porters, Manuscript Division, Library of Congress, Box 97, Folder 1 Africa.
54. Asa Philip Randolph was not only a proponent of African-American rights, he also advocated for the independence of African nations. During the 1940s and 1950s, Randolph became a prominent spokesperson for African-American Civil Rights. He pressured two United States Presidents, Franklin D. Roosevelt and Harry S. Truman, to pass legislation to alleviate discrimination in the United States government and the military. For example, in 1947, President Truman called for a peacetime draft. However, the orders of Truman did not include a provision against segregation. In response, Randolph established the Committee Against Jim Crow in Military Service and Training to lobby for integration in the armed forces. The name was later changed to the League for Non-Violent Disobedience Against Military Segregation. The organization threatened that African-Americans would otherwise refuse to register for the draft or to serve in the military when called. In June 1948, Randolph testified before the Senate Armed Services Committee. Subsequently, President Truman issued an executive order barring discrimination in the military.
55. Asa Philip Randolph to Tom Mboya, December 1, 1961, Letter, Papers of the Brotherhood of Sleeping Car Porters, Manuscript Division, Library of Congress, Box 98, Folder 1 Africa.
56. George Houser to Jim Harper, November 11, 2003.
57. Dr. Julius Gikonyo Kiano to A. Philip Randolph, 28 February 1958, letter, Papers of the Brotherhood of Sleeping Car Porters, Manuscript Division, Library of Congress, Box 97, Folder 1, Africa.
58. Asa Philip Randolph to Andrew M. Mwinamo, 21 December 1959, letter, Papers of the Brotherhood of Sleeping Car Porters, Manuscript Division, Library of Congress, Box 98, Folder 1 Africa.
59. For more information see Bethel, Leonard L., "The Role of Lincoln University (Pennsylvania) in the Education of African Leadership: 1854–1970," Ph.D. Dissertation, Rutgers University, 1975.
60. Tom Mboya to *Sunday Post,* 28 August 1959, Press Release, Papers of Charles Diggs, Manuscript Division, Moorland-Spingarn Research Center, Howard University, Box 194, Folder 15.
61. Charles Diggs to James K. Penfield, 16 July 1959, letter, General Records of the Department of State, National Archives, MD, RG 59, Box 2141 also refer to J.C. Satterthwaite to Charles Diggs, 22 July 1959, letter, General Records of the Department of State, National Archives, MD, RG 59, Box 2141.
62. George Houser to Jim Harper, November 11, 2003.
63. *New York Times,* Late Edition, East Coast, July 25, 1999, section 1, p. 31.

64. Ibid.
65. Mugo Gatheru to Jim Harper, October 31, 2003.
66. Ibid.; *New York Times,* Late Edition, East Coast, July 25, 1999, section 1, p. 31.
67. Interview with Dr. Kiano, Nairobi, Kenya, June 29, 1999.
68. *Sunday Nation,* August 10, 2003.
69. George Houser to Jim Harper, November 11, 2003.
70. William X. Scheinman to Charles Diggs, 29 June 1959, letter, Papers of Charles Diggs, Moorland-Spingarn Research Center, Howard University, Washington D.C., Box 194, Folder 15.
71. Tom Mboya to *Sunday Post,* 28 August, 1959, Press Release, Papers of Charles Diggs, Box 194, Folder 15.
72. Charles Diggs to James K. Pefield, 16 July 1959, Letter, General Records of the Department of State, National Archives, MD, KG 59, Box 2141.
73. Ibid.
74. Charles Diggs to James K. Pefield, 16 July 1959, Letter, General Records of the Department of State, National Archives, MD, KG 59, Box 2141; J.C. Satterthwaite to Charles Diggs, Letter, General Records of the Department of State, National Archives, MD, KG 59, Box 2141.
75. William X. Scheinman to Charles Diggs, 27 July 1959, letter, Papers of Charles Diggs, Jr., Manuscript Division, Moorland-Spingarn Research Center, Howard University, Box 194 Folder 15; Charles Diggs to William B. Macomer, Jr., 12 August 1959, letter, Papers of Charles Diggs, Jr., Manuscript Division, Moorland-Spingarn Research Center, Howard University, Box 194, Folder 15.
76. "American Scholarship Help for Kenya" 6 September 1959, Press Release, Papers of Charles Diggs, Manuscript Division, Howard University, Washington D.C., Box 194 Folder 15.
77. Charles Diggs to Robert G. Storey, 8 July 1959, letter, Papers of Charles Diggs, Jr., Manuscript Division, Moorland-Spingarn Research Center, Howard University, Washington D.C., Box 194, Folder 15.
78. Horace Mann Bond to John A. Davis, 20 May 1959, letter, The Horace Mann Bond Papers, Part II, Subject Files, 1926–1971, M6541, Reel 11.
79. "American Scholarship Help for Kenya" 6 September 1959, Press Release, Papers of Charles Diggs, Manuscript Division, Howard University, Washington, D.C. Box 194 Folder 15.
80. Ioan Davies, *African Trade Unions,* Middlesex, England, Penguin Books Ltd., 1966, pp. 194–195.
81. "The Facts on Grant To African Students Airlift," September 1960, memorandum, Papers of Charles Diggs, Moorland-Spingarn Research Center, Howard University, Washington, D.C. Box 194 Folder 15.
82. Ibid.
83. For a full discussion see Mansfield I. Smith Ph. D. dissertation, "The East Africa Airlifts of 1959, 1960 and 1961," Syracuse University, 1966.
84. United States Congress, Committee on Foreign Relations, "Transportation of 250 East African Scholarship Students," Congressional Record, August, 1960.

85. Democratic National Committee, 8 August 1960, press release, Papers of Charles Diggs, Jr., Moorland-Spingarn Research Center, Howard University, Washington D.C., Box 194 Folder 15.
86. "The Facts on Grant To African Students Airlift," September 1960, memorandum, Papers of Charles Diggs, Moorland-Spingarn Research Center, Howard University, Washington D.C., Box 194 Folder 15.
87. Interview with Professor Godfrey Muriuki, University of Nairobi, Kenya, June 23, 1999; Interview and personal communication with Michael Kamau, United States Embassy, Nairobi, Kenya, June 15, 1999. The Kikuyu criticism of Tom Mboya was articulated by Dr. Mugo Gatheru, a Kikuyu graduate of American Universities. See Chapter Five below.
88. African-American Students Foundation, 1960 Students Airlift, 1960, report, Papers of Charles Diggs, Jr., Manuscript Division, Moorland-Spingarn, Howard University, Washington D.C, Box 194, Folder 15.
89. Crossroads Africa was established in 1958 to involve African, American, and Canadian College students in work camps in the new nations of Africa. However, in 1964, it expanded its activities in cooperation with the Bureau of Educational and Cultural Affairs of the Department of State to launch the African Youth Leadership Program under which eight African youth leaders from four West African countries were brought to the United States. The following year, twenty-five participants from twelve East, West, and Central African nations came to America. Customarily, the Youth Leadership Program takes place during the summer.
90. Department of State, March-September 1961, report, Papers of Charles Diggs, Moorland-Spingarn Research Center, Howard University, Washington, D.C., Box 207 Folder 26.
91. For a good discussion of the "Airlifts" see, Smith, Mansfield Irving, "The East Africa Airlifts of 1959, 1960, 1961," Ph.D. Dissertation, Syracuse University, 1966.
92. Being the Chairman of the All-Africa People's Conference in Accra in 1958, "put Mboya at par with the good and great of the African continent such as Prime Minister Kwame Nkrumah of Ghana and President Julius Nyerere of Tanzania." *East African Standard,* December 2, 2003. Mboya was then 28 years old.
93. Ibid.
94. *East African Standard,* December 2, 2003.
95. Ibid., December 3, 2003.
96. Tom Mboya, "Last Words from a Murdered African Leader: The American Negro Cannot Look to Africa for an Escape," *New York Times Magazine,* 13 July 1969, 30.

NOTES TO CHAPTER FIVE

1. See Tables 1 and 2 of African students showing academic status by fields of major interest and financial support.
2. Kariuki K. Njiiri to President of the United States, 5 June 1962, letter, General Records of the Department of State, Decimal File 1960–1963, RG

59, Box 1058; Richard B. Freund to Kariuki Njiiri, 22 June 1962, letter, General Records of the Department of State, Decimal File 1960–1963, RG 59, Box 1058.
3. Committee on Foreign Affairs, African Students and Study Programs in the United States, Washington, D.C.: U.S. Government Printing Office, 1965, p. 41.
4. See Table 7 Outputs from Overseas and East African colleges.
5. Ministry of Economic Planning and Development, *High-Level Manpower Requirements and Resources in Kenya, 1964–1970,* Nairobi, Government of Kenya Printing, 1965, No. iii.
6. *The Chicago Tribune,* January 5, 1992. As a result of her contribution to sustainable development, democracy, and peace Dr. Wangari Maathai became a recipient of the Nobel Peace Prize in 2004.
7. Ministry of Economic Planning and Development, *High-Level Manpower Requirements and Resources in Kenya,* 1964–1970, Nairobi: Government of Kenya Printing, 1965, iii.
8. Willard Quincy Stanton to Secretary of State, 25 May 1945, letter, General Records of the Department of State, Decimal File 1940–1945, RG 59, Box 6215. Stanton was the American Consulate in Nairobi, Colony of Kenya.
9. These statistics of population and students were taken from the UNESCO final report which was given at a conference of African States on the development of education in Africa in May 1961.
10. Colony and Protectorate of Kenya, *Education Department Triennial Survey, 1955–1957,* Nairobi: Government of Kenya Printer, 1958, p. 29.
11. Tom Mboya to Editor of *Sunday Times,* 28 August 1959, letter, Papers of Charles Diggs, Moorland-Spingarn Research Center, Howard University, Washington D.C.
12. For a detailed list of African Colleges and Universities and enrollment in 1963, see Table 1.
13. J.F. Ade Ajayi, *The African Experience With Higher Education,* London, James Currey, 1996, pp. 97–98.
14. Interview with Dr. Aziz Batran, April, 2002.
15. Thanks to the new universities and foreign scholarships by 1981 the number of graduates in Kenya jumped to the staggering 9,000.
16. See Table 5 for the institutions that participated in the African Scholarship Program of American Universities and United Negro College Fund participants in 1961.
17. See Table 3 for the number of African Students studying in the United States from 1950–1978 & Table 4 showing home country, gender, and financial and academic year of studies in the United States.
18. Committee on Foreign Affairs, African Students and Study Programs in the United States, Washington, D.C., U.S. Government Printing Office, 1965, 1.
19. See Table No. 1, Institute of International Education, "Open Doors Report on International Educational Exchange," Washington DC, United States Government Printing, 2002, p. 9.

20. Joseph B.K. Ulayeneza to American Cousulate, 4 April 1957, letter, General Records of the Department of State, Decimal File 1955–1959, RG 59, Box 2141.
21. Marshall Wright to Senator Herbert Humphrey, 12 July 1972, letter, General Records of the Department of State, Subject Numeric Files, Culture and Information 1970–1973, RG 59, Box 403.
22. Dean Rusk to American Embassy in Nairobi, Kenya, 6 December 1968, telegram, General Records of the Department of State, Central Policy Files, Culture and Information 1967–1969, RG 59, Box 365.
23. American Embassy, Nairobi, Kenya, to Department of State, 13 December, 1968, airgram, General Records, Central Foreign Policy Files, Culture and Information, 1967–1969, RG 59, Box 365.
24. American Embassy, Nairobi, Kenya, to Department of State, 8 April, 1968, airgram, General Records of the Department of State, Numeric Files, Political and Defense 1970–1973, RG 59, Box 2418.
25. This crisis continues to beleaguer Africa to the present day. *The Ghanian Chronicle,* November 22, 1999.
26. Mugo Gatheru to Jim Harper, October 31, 2003.
27. Ibid.
28. Ibid.
29. Ibid.
30. Ibid
31. Ibid.
32. Ibid.
33. Ibid.
34. R. Mugo Gatheru, *A Child of Two Worlds,* London, Routledge & Kegan Paul, 1964, p. 169–184.
35. Mugo Gatheru to Jim Harper, October 31, 2003.
36. Ibid.
37. Ibid.; Mugo says the his book, *Child of Two Worlds,* London, Routledge and Kegan Paul, 1964, reflects who he is. My impression of him is that he is indeed a man of divided loyalty and passion—a man with one foot planted in the country of his birth, Kenya, and the other foot firmly placed in his adopted home, the United States of America. Although Mugo visited Kenya three times, that is, in 1977, 1978, 1980 on sabbatical leave, he has retired in Sacramento, California.
38. Ibid. To qualify as a solicitor one had to pass Part I and Part II of the solicitors qualifying examination. In addition, one had to serve as an articled clerk with a solicitors' law firm for three years in order to gain practical experience.
39. Ibid.
40. Ibid.
41. Ibid.
42. Ibid.
43. Ibid.
44. Ibid.

45. *Nairobi Varsity Focus,* 1995, p. 17; Own C.V., 1997. Professor Obudho authored a number of books including *Demography, Urbanization and Spatial Planning in Kenya; Issues in Resource Management and Development in Kenya,* with J.B. Ojwng; *Urbanization in Kenya: A Bottom-up Approach to Development; Periodic Markets; Urbanization and Regional Planning: A case Study from Kenya,* with Peter Walker; *Development of Urban Kenya* with Salah El-Shaikhs; and *Slum and Squatter Settlements in Sub-Saharan Africa* with Constance C. Mhlang.
46. For more information on both leading Church figures see Chapter Four above.
47. *Africa Who's Who,* 1981, p. 581.
48. See Chapter 4.
49. *Who's Who in East Africa,* p. 125.
50. *Daily Nation,* November 7, 1990, p. 1–2.
51. *IIE Report on Kenya Graduates,* 1965, p. 10; *Africa Who's Who,* 1981, p. 942.
52. See Chapter Three above.
53. The authorities and white settler community described this once loyal chief as "the evil genius of Mau Mau." For more information on Chief Koinange see Jeff Koinange, *Koinange-wa-Mbiyu:Mau Mau's Misunderstood Leader,* The Book Guild Ltd., Sussex, England, 2000.
54. See Chapter Four above for more information on Dr. Kiano.
55. *Nairobi Varsity Focus,* November 1995 and 1996, p. 35) "Citation on Conferment of Hon. Dr. Litt," *University of Nairobi,* December, 1995, p. 12; *Weekly Review,* March 1979, p. 5; Nzioki and Dar, 1983, p. 83; *Macro,* 1963, p. 153.
56. *Who's Who in East Africa,* p. 12.
57. *The Weekly Review,* June 5, 1987, p. 13; *Kenyatta University News,* No. 2, August 1987, p. 2.
58. *The Weekly Review* June 5, 1979, p. 10.
59. *East Africa Standard,* May 2, 1989; *Kenya Periodicals,* 1990, p. 40.
60. "Prominent Kenyans Who Served Under Moi," in *East Africa Standard,* September 12, 2003.
61. Macro, 1968, p. 169; "Reporter," July, 1963, p. 31.
62. *East African Standard,* December 2, 2003.
63. *The East African Standard,* May 22, 2002.
64. HelpAge is a London based non-profit organization that works with and for disadvantage old people world-wide.
65. The *East African Standard,* January 4, 2003, says that Dr. Wangari received her Masters degree with assistance "from the African-American Institute of New York." She received her Masters degree in Biological Sciences from the University of Pittsburgh in 1966.
66. The *Daily Nation,* January 4, 2003; M. Likmani, *Women of Kenya,* 1991, p. 18; *Weekly Viva Magazine,* July 1984, pp, 10; *Africa Who's Who,* 1981, p. 754.
67. See for example, *United Nations Studies at Yale,* September, 1995; *Goldman Prize,* San Francisco, 1999.

68. Several chapters of the movement rose in Ethiopia, Tanzania, Malawi, Uganda, Lesotho, and Zimbabwe.
69. The *Daily Nation,* January 4, 2003; *Jubillee 2000 Coalition,* Kenya, 2000.
70. The *Daily Nation,* January 4, 2003.
71. *In Context,* A Quarterly Of Humane Sustainable Culture, 1991, pp. 1–9; *One World,* November 7, 2003, pp. 1–7.
72. Ibid.
73. *The Daily Nation,* March 7, 2001; *Kabissa-Fahamu Newsletter,* March 16, 2001.
74. Ibid.
75. The *East African Standard,* January 4, 2003.
76. Interview with Dr. Batran, Washington D.C., June 12, 2002.
77. Amin and Moll, 1975; *Weekly Review,* May 19, 1975, p. 10; *Africa Who's Who,* 1981, p. 681; *Kenya Periodicals Ltd.,* 1992, p. 41.
78. *Weekly Review,* August 21, 1987; *The East Africa Standard,* March 10, 1990, pp. 1–2; *Kenya Periodicals Ltd.,* 1992, p. 39.
79. *Africa Who's Who,* 1081, p. 608; Nzioki and Dar, 1983, p. 95.
80. Nzioki and Dar, 1968, p. 68.
81. *Africa Who' Who,* 1981, p. 797; *Inside Kenya Today,* December 1970, pp. 29–40.
82. *Weekly Review,* May 22, 1987, p. 15, June 12, 1987, pp. 19–11; Macro, 1968, p. 65.
83. Macro, 1968, p. 60; *Weekly Review,* July 12, 1985, p. 13.
84. Nzioki and Dar, 1983, p. 78; *Maktaba,* vol. 8 (1–2), 1984, p. 73.
85. Macro, 1968, p. 103, Nzioki and Dar, 1983, p. 347.
86. *Africa Who's Who,* 1981, p. 940.
87. Kay. E. . 1970, p. 155.
88. Macro, 1968, p. 82.
89. Amin and Moll, 1975; Macro, 1968, p. 57.
90. Nzioki and Dar, 1983 p. 324; Macro, 1968, p. 114.
91. Weekly Review, January 19, 1993, p. 6; January 17, 1882, p. 8; *Reporter,* July 2, 1965, p. 29; Macro, 1968, p. 86; *Weekly Review Election Handbook,* 1979, p. 50; Nzioli and Dar, 1983, p. 28.
92. Daily Nation, September 13, 2002; *African Biographies,* profile 7; Africa Books Ltd., London, 1991, p. 1197; *Who's Who in East Africa,* Macro, p.106.
93. The *Daily Nation* was launched in October 1960 with a predominantly British staff from London's Fleet Street. The newsroom was dominated by Britons including John Platter, Brian Marsden, Michael Chester, Brian McDermott, Peter Hinchliffe, Brian Tetley, Neil Graham, Peter Darling, Allen Armstrong, Buddy Trevor, and John Eames. See the *Daily Nation,* July 28, 2001.
94. *East African Standard,* December 6, 2003.) Ng'weno authored two books: *The Men from Pretoria,* a fiction novel, and *The Day Kenyatta Died.* Both books were published by Longman.
95. *The Daily Nation,* May 29, 1999.

96. Ibid.
97. *East African Standard,* December 6, 2003.
98. *The Daily Nation,* May 29, 1999.
99. Ibid.
100. *East African Standard,* December 6, 2003.
101. Ibid.
102. Nzioki and Dar, 1983, p. 82; *Africa Who's Who,* 1981, p. 797.
103. Interview with Julius Kiano, Nairobi, June 29, 1999.

Bibliography

BOOKS

Abdul-Raheem, Tajudeen, ed. *Pan-Africanism: Politics, Economy, and Social Change in the Twenty-first Century.* New York: New York University Press, 1996.

Abun-Naser, Jamil M. *A History of the Maghrib.* New York: Cambridge University Press 1975.

Adams, C.C. and Marshall Talley. *Negro Baptists and Foreign Missions.* Philadelphia, Pennsylvania: National Baptist Convention, U.S.A., 1994.

Alpers, Edward. *The East African Slave Trade.* Nairobi: East African Publishing House, 1967.

Altbach, Philip G., and Gail P. Kelly, eds. *Education and Colonialism.* New York: Longman, 1978.

Amin, Mohamed. *Tom Mboya: A Photographic Tribute.* Nairobi: East African Publishing House, 1969.

Azevedo, Mario. *African Studies: A Survey of Africa and the African Diaspora.* Durham, NC: Carolina Academic Press, 1998

Barrett, David B., George K. Mambo, Janice McLaughlin, and Malcolm J. McVeigh. *Kenya Churches handbook: The Development of Kenyan Christianity, 1498–1973.* Kisumu, Kenya: Evangel Publishing House,

Bassey, Magnus O. *Western Education and Political Domination in Africa: A Study in Critical and Dialogical Pedagogy.* London: Bergin and Garvey, 1999.

Batran, Aziz. *Islam and Revolution in Africa.* Battleboro, Vermont: Amana Books, 1984.

Bennett, George. *Kenya: A Political History: The Colonial Period.* London: Oxford University Press, 1963.

Berman, Edward. *Education in Africa and American: A History of the Phelps-Strokes Fund, 1911–1945.* New York: Teachers College, Columbia University Press, 1969.

Bidwell, Sidney. *Red, White and Black Race Relations in Britain.* London: Gordon and Cremonesi, 1976.

Bohannan, Paul and Philip Curtin. *Africa and Africans.* Prospect Heights: Illinois, 1995.

Bond, Horace Mann. *Education for Freedom: A History of Lincoln University, Pennsylvania.* Princeton, New Jersey: Princeton University Press, 1976.

Boyte, Sara Evans. *Tom Mboya of Kenya: A Case Study of the Interactions of Politics and Ideology in Emerging Africa.* Theses, M.A. Duke University, 1968.

Capon, M.G. *Towards Unity in Kenya: The Story of Co-operation between Missions and Churches in Kenya 1913–1947.* Nairobi: Christian Council of Kenya, 1962.

Castle, E.B. *Growing Up in East Africa.* London: Oxford University Press, 1966.

Cohen, Sir Andrew. *British Policy in Changing Africa.* Evanston: Northwestern University Press, 1959.

Coleman, James S. *Education and Political Development.* Princeton, New Jersey: Princeton University Press, 1965.

Conniff, Michael L. and Thomas J. Davis. *Africans in the Americas: A History of the Black Diaspora.* New York: St. Martin's Press, 1994.

Conyers, James L. *Carter G. Woodson: A Historical Reader.* London: Garland Publishing, 2000.

Curtin, Philip D. *Africa and the West: Intellectual Responses to European Culture.* Wisconsin: University of Wisconsin Press, 1972.

Davies, Ioan. *African Trade Unions.* Middlesex, England: Penguin Books Inc., 1966.

Diop, Cheiika Anta. *African Origin of Civilization: Myth or Reality.* New York: Lawerance Hill, 1974.

DuBois, W.E.B. *The Souls of Black Folk.* Nashville, Tennessee: Fisk University Press, 1979.

Esedebe, P. Olisanwuche. *Pan-Africanism: The Idea and Movement, 1776–1963.* Washington, D.C.: Howard University Press, 1982.

Elliott, Charles. *The East African Protectorate.* London: Edward Arnold, 1905.

Fafunwa, Babs A. *History of Education in Nigeria.* London: George Allen and Unwin, 1974.

Fredrickson, George M. *A Comparative History of Black Ideologies in the United States and South Africa.* New York: Oxford University Press, 1995.

Fitts, Leroy. *Lott Carey: First Black Missionary to Africa.* Valley Forge: Judson Press, 1978.

"———." *The Lott Carey Legacy of African American Missions.* Baltimore: Gateway Press, 1994.

Fluitman, Fred. *Training For the Informal Sector.* Geneva: International Labor Office, 1989.

Freire, Paulo. *Cultural Action For Freedom.* Cambridge, MA: Harvard Educational Review, 1970.

Gatheru, R. Mugo. *Child of Two Worlds.* London: Routledge and Kegan Paul, 1964.

Giroux, Henry A. *Teachers As Intellectuals: Toward a Critical Pedagogy of Learning.* Westport, Ct: Bergin and Garvey, 1988.

Goldsworthy, David. *Tom Mboya, the Man Kenya Wanted to Forget.* Nairobi: Heinemann, 1982.

Goggin, Jacqueline. *Carter G. Woodson: A Life in Black History.* Baton Rouge and London: Louisiana State University Press, 1993.

Bibliography

Gordon, Colin, ed. *Power/Knowledge: Selected Interviews and Other Writings, 1972–1977*. New York: Pantheon Books, 1980.
Harlow, Vincent and E.M. Chilver, eds. *History of East Africa*. Oxford: Oxford University Press, 1965.
Harris, Joseph E. *The African Presence in Asia: Consequences of the East African Slave Trade*. Evanston: Northwestern University Press, 1971.
"———." Global Dimensions of the African Diaspora. Washington, D.C.: Howard University, 1993.
. *Africans and Their History*. New York: Meridian, 1998.
Hawting, G. R. *The First Dynasty of Islam: the Umayyad Caliphate A.D. 661–750*. Carbondal: Southern Illinois University Press, 1987.
Herskovits, Melville. *The Human Factor in Changing Africa*. New York: Knopf, 1962.
Hine, Darlene Clark, William C. Hine, and Stanley Harrold, eds. *The African-American Odyssey*. New Jersey: Prentice Hall, 2003.
Hrbed, I. ed. *General History of Africa: Africa from the Seventh to the Eleventh Century*. Berkeley: University Press of California, 1992.
Ingham, Kenneth. A History of East Africa. New York: Praeger, 1962.
Jacobs, Sylvia M. *Black Americans and the Missionary Movement in Africa*. London: Greenwood Press, 1982.
Jones, Thomas Jesse. *Education in Africa: A Study of West, South, and Equatorial Africa by the African Education Commission*. New York: Phelps-Stokes Fund, 1921.
Jong, Albert De. *Mission and Politics in Eastern Africa: Dutch Missionaries and African Nationalism in Kenya, Tanzania and Malawi 1945–1965*. Nairobi, Kenya: Paulines Publications Africa, 2000.
Kaplan, Irving. *Area Handbook for Kenya*. Washington, D.C.: U.S. Government Printing Press, 1967.
Karenga, Maulana. *Introduction to Black Studies*. Los Angeles, California: University of Sankore Press, 1993.
Kenyatta, Jomo. *Facing Mount Kenya: The Tribal Life of the Gikuyu*. New York: Vintage, 1962.
"———." *Facing Mount Kenya: The Traditional Life of the Gikuyu*. London: Heinemann, 1979.
King, Kenneth. *Pan-Africanism and Education: A Study of Race Philanthropy and Education in the Southern United States of American and East Africa*. Clarendon Press: Oxford University Press, 1971.
Kritzeck, James and William H. Lewis, eds. *Islam in Africa*. New York: Van Nosrand-Reinhold, 1969.
Koinange, Jeff M. *Koinange-Wa-Mbiyu: Mau Mau's Misunderstood Leader*. Sussex, England: Book Guild Ltd., 2000.
Langley, J. Ayodele. *Pan-Africanism and Nationalism in West Africa, 1900-1945: A Study in Ideology and Social Classes*. Oxford: Clarendon Press, 1973.
Lauren, Paul Gordon. *Power and Prejudice: The Politics and Diplomacy of Racial Discrimination*. Boulder and London: Westview Press, 1988.
Leaky, Louis S.B. *The Southern Kikuyu Before 1903*. New York: Academic Press, 1977.

Lewis, David Levering. *W.E.B. DuBois: Biography of a Race 1868–1919.* New York: Henry Holt and Company, 1993.

"———." *W.E.B. DuBois: The Fight for Equality and the American Century 1919–1963.* New York: Henry Holt and Company.

Lewis, L.J. *Educational Policy and Practice in British Tropical Areas.* London: Nelson and Sons, 1954.

Lloyd, Peter C. *The New Elites of Tropical Africa.* London: Oxford University Press, 1966.

Mangat, J.S. *A History of Asians in East Africa, 1886–1945.* Oxford: Clarendon Press, 1969.

Martin, Sandy D. *Black Baptists and African Missions: The Origins of a Movement 1880–1915.* Georgia: Mercer University Press, 1989.

Martin, Tony. *The Pan-African Connection: From Slavery to Garvey and Beyond.* Dover, Massachusetts: Majority Press, 1984.

Mboya, Tom. *The Challenge of Nationhood: A Collection of Speeches and Writings.* London: Heinemann Books, 1970.

"———." *Freedom and After.* Boston: Little Brown and Company, 1963.

Meier, August, John Bracey, Jr. and the late Elliott Rudwick. Black Protest in the Sixties. New York: Markus Wiener Publishing, 1991.

Monanyi, Clara. *Ronald Ngala: Teacher with a Mission.* Nairobi: Sasa Sema Publications, 2001.

Munene, Macharia. *The Truman Administration and the Decolonization of sub-Saharan Africa.* Nairobi: Nairobi University Press, 1995.

Munene, Macharia and J.D. Olewe Nyunya and Korwa Adar, eds. *The United States and Africa: From Independence to the End of the Cold War.* Nairobi: East African Educational Publishers Ltd., 1995.

Muriuki, Godfrey. *A History of the Kikuyu, 1500–1900.* London: Oxford University Press, 1974.

Murphy, E. Jefferson. *Creative Philanthropy: Carnegie Corporation and Africa 1953–1973.* New York: Teachers College Press, Columbia University, 1976.

Nelson, Harold D. *Kenya: a Country Study.* Washington, D.C.: United States Printing Office, 1984.

Nielsen, Waldemar A. *The Great Powers and Africa.* New York. Prager Publishers, 1969.

Nkomo, Mokubung. *Pedagogy of Domination: Toward a Democratic Education in South Africa.* Trenton, N.J.: African World Press, 1990.

Nnolim, Charles E. *The Role of Educatin in Contemporary Africa.* New York: Professors World Peace Academy, 1988.

Nwauwa, Apollos. *Imperialism, Academe and Nationalism: Britain and University Education for Africans 1860–1960.* London: Frank Cass, 1997.

Ochieng, William R. Themes in Kenyan History. Ohio University Press: James Currey, 1990.

"———." *History of Kenya.* London: MacMillan Publishers, 1985.

Odinga, Oginga. Not Yet Uhuru: an Autobiography of Oginga Odinga. London, Heinmann, 1967.

Ogot, Bethwell A. *Kenya Before 1900.* Nairobi: East African Publishing House, 1976.

Ogot, Bethwell and William R. Ochieng, eds. *Decolonization and Independence in Kenya 1940–93*. London: James Currey, 1995.
Olela, Henry. *Beyond Those Hills*. London: Evans Brothers, 1966.
Oliver, Roland. *The Missionary Factor in East Africa*. London: Longman Green and Co., 1952.
"——." *History of East Africa*. Oxford: Clarendon Press, 1976.
Othieno, Antipa N. *An Outline of History of Education in East Africa, 1844–1925*. Teachers College: Columbia University, 1963.
Padmore, George. *Pan-Africanism or Communism*. Garden City, New York: Doubleday, 1971.
Park, Eunjin. "White" Americans in "Black" Africa: Black and White American Methodist Missionaries in Liberia, 1830–1875. London: Routledge, 2001.
Paterson, Thomas G. and Stephen G. Rabe. *Imperial Surge: The United States Abroad, the 1890s-Early 1900s*. Toronto: D.C. Heath and Company, 1992.
Phipps, William. *William Sheppard: Congo's African American Livingstone*. Louisville, Kentucky: Geneva Press, 2002.
Polatrick, Florence T. *Shapers of Africa*. New York: J. Messner, 1969.
Price, Slater W. *My Third Campaign in East Africa*. London: William Hunt and Co., 1891.
Rake, Alan. *Tom Mboya: A Young Man of New Africa*. Garden City, New York: Doubleday, 1962.
Ranger, Terrance. *Emerging Themes in African History*. Nairobi: East African Publishing House, 1968.
Reed, Colin. *Pastors, Partners, and Paternalists: African Church Leaders and Western Missionaries in the Anglican Church in Kenya, 1850–1900*. Leiden: New York: E.J. Brill, 1997.
Richards, Charles and James Place. *East African Explorers*. London: Oxford University Press, 1960.
Robinson, Ronald and John Gallagher. *Africa and the Victorians: The Climax of Imperialism in the Darker Continent*. New York: St. Martin's Press, 1961.
Roelker, Jack R. *Mathu of Kenya: A Political Study*. California: Hoover Institution Press, 1976.
Ross, W. Macgregor. *Kenya From Within*. London: Allen and Unwin, 1927.
Sagini, Meshack. *The African and The African American University: A Historical and Sociological Analysis*. London: University Press of America, 1996.
Scarr, Deryck. *Slaving and Slavery in the Indian Ocean*. Baltimore: St. Martin's Press, 1993.
Sheffield, James R. *Education in Kenya: A Historical Study*. New York: Teachers College Press, 1973.
Shepperson, George and Thomas Price. *Independent African: John Chilembwe and the Origins, Setting and Significance of the Nyasaland Native Rising of 1915*. Edinburgh: University Press, 1987.
Shillington, Kevin. *History of Africa*. New York: St. Martin's Press, 1995.
Sifuna, Daniel N. *Development of Education in Africa: The Kenyan Experience*. Nairobi: Initiatives Publishers, 1990.
Skinner, Elliott. *Beyond Constructive Engagement: United States Foreign Policy Toward Africa*. New York: Paragon House Publishers, 1986.

Soja, Edward W. *The Geography of Modernization in Kenya: A Spacial Analysis of Social, Economic, and Political Change.* Syracuse: Syracuse University Press, 1968.
Staniland, Martin. *American Intellectuals and African Nationalists, 1955–1970.* New Haven: Yale University Press, 1991.
Trimingham, John S. *A History of Islam in West Africa.* London: Oxford University, 1962.
"——." *Islam in the Sudan.* New York: Praeger, 1968.
"——." *Islam in Ethiopia.* London: Oxford University Press, 1952.
"——." *The Influence of Islam in Africa.* New York: Praeger, 1968.
Thuku, Harry. *Harry Thuku an Autobiography.* London: Oxford University Press, 1970.
Waldsemar, Neilson. *The Great Powers of Africa.* New York: Praeger, Publisher, 1969.
Walters, Ronald. *Pan Africanism in the African Diaspora: An Analysis of the Modern Afrocentric Political Movement.* Detroit: Wayne State University Press, 1993.
Wandira, Asavia. *The African University in Development.* Braamfontein, Johannesburg: Zenith Printers, 1977.
Welbourn, F.B. *East African Rebels: A Study of Some Independent Churches.* London: SCM Press, 1961.
Williams, Walter L. *Black Americans and the Evangelization of Africa 1877–1900.* Wisconsin: University of Wisconsin Press, 1982.
Young, Crawford. *The African Colonial State in Comparative Perspective.* New Haven: Yale University Press, 1994.

ARTICLES

Adeleke, Tunde. "Black Americans and Africa: A Critique of the Pan-African and Identity Paradigms." *International Journal of African Historical Studies,* 31, 3 (1998): 505–536.
Ajayi, J.F. Ade. "Nineteenth Century Origins of Nigerian Nationalism." *Journal of the Historical Society of Nigeria* 2, no. 2 (1961): 196–210, 197.
Anthony, David H. "Max Yergan in South Africa: From Evangelical Pan-Africanist to Revolutionary Socialist." *African Studies Review* 34, 2 (September, 1991): 27–55.
Beck, Ann. "Colonial Policy and Education in British East Africa, 1900–1950." *Journal of British Studies,* 5, 2 (May 1966), 115–138.
Bennett, George. "The Development of Political Organizations in Kenya." *Political Studies,* no. 2 (June 1957): 119–122.
Berman, Edward H. "Tuskegee—In—Africa." *Journal of Negro Education* 41, 2 (Spring 1972): 99–112.
"——." "African Responses to Christian Mission Education." *African Studies Review* 17, 3 (December, 1974): 527–540.
Buxton, T.F. Victor. "A Social Effort in East Africa." *Journal of the Royal African Society* 10, 39 (April 1911): 342–344.

Coleman, James S. "The Problem of Political Integration in Emergent Africa." *Western Political Quarterly* 8, 1 (March, 1955): 44–57.
Contee, Clarence. "The Emergence of DuBois as an African Nationalist." *Journal of Negro History* 54, 1 (January 1969): 48–63.
Court, David. "The Education System as a Response to Inequality in Tanzania and Kenya." *Journal of Modern African Studies* 14, 4 (December, 1976): 661–690.
Davis, Jackson. "The Christian Mission in Africa: International Conference held at Le Zonte, Belgium, September 14–20, 1926." *Social Forces* 5, 3 (March, 1927): 483–487.
Emerson, Rupert. "Pan-Africanism." *International Organization,* 16, 2, Africa and International Organization (Spring 1962), 275–290.
Eisenstadt, S.N. "African Age Groups: A Comparative Study." *Africa* 24 (August 1954): 1000–112.
Geiss, Imanuel. "Pan-Africanism." *Journal of Contemporary History* 4, 1 (January 1969): 187–200.
Giroux, Henry A. "Rethinking Education Reform In The Age of George Bush." *Phi Delta Kappan* 70 no. 9 (1989): 728.
Jacobs, Sylvia M. "James Emman Kewgyir Aggrey: An African Intellectual in the United States." *Journal of Negro History* 81, (Winter-Autumn, 1996): 47–61.
Kheir, Sheikh Abdallah A. "Islam and Muslims in Kenya." *Journal of Islamic Guidance* 5 (no. 1 1999):
King, Kenneth. "The American Negro as Missionary to East Africa: A Critical Aspect of African Evangelism." *African Historical Studies* 3, (January 1970): 5–22.
"———." "Africa and the Southern United States: Some Notes on J.H. Oldham and American Negro Education for Africans." *Journal of African History* 10, 4 (1969): 659–677.
"———." "The American Negro as Missionary to East Africa: A Critical Aspect of African Evangelism." *African Historical Studies* 3, 1 (1970): 5–22.
"———." Africa-Related Material in Black American Colleges and the Phelps-Stokes Fund of New York." *African Historical Studies* 3, 2 (1970): 419–426.
"———." "James E.K. Aggrey: Collaborator, Nationalist, Pan-African." *Canadian Journal of African Studies* 3, 3 (Autumn, 1969): 511–530.
"———." African Students in Negro American Colleges: Notes on the Good African." *Phylon* 31, 1 (1st Quarter, 1970), 16–30.
Marable, W. Manning. "Booker T. Washington and African Nationalism." Phylon 35, 4 (4th Quarter, 1974): 398–406.
Marks, Shula. "The Ambiguities of Dependence: John L. Dube of Natal." *Journal of Southern African Studies* 1, 2 (April, 1975): 162–180.
Mazuri, Ali A. "Africa Between Nationalism and Nationhood: A Political Survey." *Journal of Black Studies,* 13, 1 (September 1982): 23–44.
Moorland, Jesse Edward. "The Young Men's Christian Association and the War." *Crisis* XV 2 (Dec. 1917): 65–68.
"———." "The Young Men's Christian Association Among Negroes." *Journal of Negro History* 9, 2 (April, 1924): 127–138.

Morris, Milton D. "Black Americans and the Foreign Policy Process: The Case of Africa." *Western Political Quarterly* 25, 3 (September, 1972): 451–463.

Mtewa, Mekki. "Problems of Oedipal Historicism: The Saga of John Chilembwe-the Malawian." *Journal of Black Studies* 8, 2 (December, 1977): 227–250.

Nantambu, Kwame. "Pan-Africanism Versus Pan-African Nationalism: An Afrocentric Analysis." *Journal of Black Studies* 28, 5 (May 1998): 561-574.

Nicol, Davidson. "Africa and the U.S.A. in the United Nations." *Journal of Modern African Studies* 16, 3 (September, 1978): 365–395.

Nichols, William J. "A Report on Kenya." *Transition* 0, 36 (1968): 22–25.

Read, Margaret. "Education and Cultural Traditions." *Institute of Education* (1950): 9.

Reid, George. "Missionaries and West Africa Nationalism." *Phylon* 39, 3 (3rd Quarter, 1978): 225–233.

Richards, Yevette. "African and African-American Labor Leaders in the Struggle Over International Affiliation." *International Journal of African Historical Studies* 31, 2 (1998): 301–334.

Regan, Timothy. "Philosophy of Education in the Service of Apartheid: The Role of 'Fundamental Pedagogics' in South African Education." *Educational Foundations* 4, (no. 2 1990): 65.

Scally, Anthony, Anson Phelps Stokes, the Freeman Publishing Co., and Carter G. Woodson, eds. "Phelps-Stokes Confidential Memorandum for the Trustees of the Phelps-Stokes Fund Regarding Dr. Carter G. Woodson's Attacks on Dr. Thomas Jesse Jones." *Journal of Negro History* 76, (Winter-Autumn, 1991), 48–60.

Sanders, Edith R. "The Hamitic Hypothesis: Its Origin and Functions in Time Perspective." *Journal of African History* 10 (April 1969): 521–532.

Scanlon, David G. *"The Bush School."* Phi Delta Kappan 61, 4 (January 1960): 148.

Seraile, William. "Black American Missionaries in Africa, 1821–1925." *Social Studies* 63, (October 1972): 198–202.

Shepperson, George. "Pan-Africanism and "Pan-Africanism": Some Historical Notes." *Phylon* 23, 4 (4th Quarter 1962): 346–358.

Tucker, Neely. "Descendants Hold To Ex-Slaves Dream." *Detroit Free Press* 5, (November 1997): 15.

Tunteng, P. Kiven. "George Padmore's Impact on Africa: A Critical Appraisal." *Phylon* 35, 1 (1st Quarter. 1974): 33–44.

Urch, George E. "Education and Colonialism in Kenya." *History of Education Quarterly* 11, 3 (Autumn, 1971): 249–264.

William, Seralie. "Black American Missionaries in Africa, 1821–1925." *Social Studies* 63, (October 1927): 198–202.

Williams, Michael. "Pan-Africanism and Zionism: The Delusion of Comparability." *Journal of Black Studies* 21, 3 (March 1991): 248–371.

"———." "Nkrumahism as an Ideological Embodiment of Leftist Thought Within the African World." *Journal of Black Studies* 15, 1 (September,1984): 117–134.

Williams, Walter. "Ethnic Relations of African Students in the United States, with Black Americans, 1970–1900." *Journal of Negro History* 65, 3 (Summer 1980), 228–249

"———." "Black Journalism's Opinions about Africa during the Late Nineteenth Century." *Phylon* 34, 3 (3rd Quarter, 1973) 224–235.
Young, Crawford. "United States Policy Toward Africa: Silver Anniversary Reflections." *African Studies Review* 27, 3 (September, 1984): 1–17.

DISSERTATIONS AND THESES

Bassey, Magnus O. "The Politics of Education in Nigeria: The Case of Government Take-Over of Schools in the Cross River and Kano States" Ph.D. Dissertation, 1989.
Bethel, Leonard L. "The Role of Lincoln University (Pennsylvania) in the Education of African Leadership: 1854–1970" Ph.D. Dissertation, Rutgers University, 1975.
Hayslett, James E. "A Study of the Evolution, Substance, and Problems of American Foreign Policy for Africa, 1945–1961" M.A. Thesis, Howard University, 1963.
Martin, L.A. "Education In Kenya Before Independence: An Annotated Bibliography" M.A. Thesis, Syracuse University, 1969.
Repashy, Allen James. "The Reactions of Kenyan Returnees to Their Educational Experiences Abroad" Ph.D. Dissertation, University of California at Los Angeles, 1966.
Smith, Mansfield Irving. "The East Africa Airlifts of 1959, 1960, and 1961" Ph.D. Dissertation, Syracuse University, 1966.
Vinson, Robert T. "In the Time of the Americans: Garveyism in Segregationist South Africa 1920–1940" Ph.D. Dissertation, Howard University, 2001.

KENYAN AND AMERICAN NEWSPAPERS

The Chicago Defender
Crisis
Daily Nation
East African Times
Liberator
Negro World
New York Times
Pittsburgh Courier
Washington Post

ARCHIVAL RESOURCES

Congressional Record
Kenya Ministry of Economic Planning and Development Report, 1964–1970
Records of the American Society of African Culture (unpublished), Howard University, Washington, D.C.
Records of the American Committee on Africa, Duke University, North Carolina
Papers of Charles Diggs, Jr. (unpublished), Howard University, Washington, D.C.

Papers of Max Yergan, Howard University, Washington, D.C.
Papers of Horace Mann Bond, Duke University, North Carolina
Papers of the Brotherhood of Sleeping Car Porters, Library of Congress, Washington, D.C.
General Records of the Department of State, Subject Numeric File 1970–73, Political and Defense RG 59
General Records of the Department of State, Decimal File 1940–41, RG 59, National Archives II, College Park, Maryland
General Records of the Department of State, Decimal File 1945–49, RG 59, National Archives II, College Park, Maryland
General Records of the Department of State, Decimal File 1940–44, RG 59, National Archives II, College Park, Maryland
General Records of the Department of State, Decimal File 1960–63, RG 59, National Archives II, College Park, Maryland
General Records of the Department of State, Decimal File, 1955–59, RG 59, National Archives II, College Park, Maryland

INTERVIEWS AND PERSONAL COMMUNICATIONS

Aziz Batran, interview by author, tape recording, Howard University, Washington, D.C.
Michael Kamau, personal communication with author, Nairobi, Kenya, June 15, 1999.
Julius Gikonyo Kiano, interview by author, tape recording, Nairobi, Kenya, June 29, 1999.
Macharia Munene, personal communication with author, Nairobi, Kenya, June 29, 1999.
Godfrey Muriuki, personal communication with author, Nairobi, Kenya, June 23, 1999.
R. Mugo Gatheru, personal communication with author, Sacramento, California, October 31, 2003.

George Houser, personal communication with author, New York City, New York, November 11, 2003.

Index

A

AASF, *see* African American Students Foundation (AASF)
AAU, *see* Association of African Universities (AAU)
Abdallah, Muhammad ibn, 27
Abshire, David M., 16
ACOA, *see* American Committee on Africa (ACOA)
Adi, Hakim, 7
AEMO, *see* African Elected Members Organization (AEMO)
AFGRAD, *see* African Graduate Fellowship Program (AFGRAD)
AFL-CIO, *see* American Federation of Labor and Congress of Industrial Organization (AFL-CIO)
African-American Civil Rights Movement, 127
African-American factor, 47–53
African-American missionaries, 13, 48–49
African American Students Foundation (AASF), 15, 81
African "brain drain," 101–102
 beginning of, 99
African education, 30–31
African Elected Members Organization (AEMO), 73
African Graduate Fellowship Program (AFGRAD), 97–98
African Inland Church, 39
Africanization
 colonial administration, 101–124
 of Kenya, 91–92
 medical profession, 121–122
African Labor College, 77
African Methodist Episcopal Church (AME), 49
African Methodist Episcopal Zion (AMEZ), 49
African Orthodox Church (AOC), 54
African Scholarship Program (ASPAU), 97–98
African Scholarships Program of American Universities
 institutions participating, 142–147
African students
 academic status, 130–131
 demographics, 150
 financial support, 132
 United States, 148–149
African Students Airlifts, 15, 16, 81
Africa universities, 137–141
Aga Khan University, 96
Age groups, 25–27
Age sets, 25–27
Aggrey, James, 4, 48, 60
Alexander, Bishop, 54
Amalgamated Clothing Workers, 75–76
AME, *see* African Methodist Episcopal Church (AME)
American actors, 74
American Committee on Africa (ACOA), 17
 founding, 19
American education Asomi
 returning home 1958–1963, 91–124
American Federation of Labor and Congress of Industrial Organization (AFL-CIO), 75–76
American government scholarships, 91–101

187

American Society of African Culture
    (ASAC), 15
AMEZ, see African Methodist Episcopal
    Zion (AMEZ)
Anglican Church Missionary Society, 3
Antioch College, 62
Antony of Nubia, 33
AOC, see African Orthodox Church (AOC)
Apprenticeship, 24–25
Arabic, 22
Arab Muslim armies, 28
Argwings-Kodhek, 71–72
Asabyya, 30
ASAC, see American Society of African
    Culture (ASAC)
Askias, 29
Asomi, 2
    education, 47
        abroad, 127
    Garveyism, 7
    reaction, 53–58
    rise, 33–58
ASPAU, see African Scholarship Program
    (ASPAU)
Asquith Commission, 56
Asquith Commission Report of 1943, 60
Association of African Universities (AAU),
    95
Ayah, Wilson Ndolo, 119
Ayodo, Samuel Onyango, 114

B
Bantu, 29
Bargash, Sayyed, 34
Beauttah, Jones, 42
Beecher Commission, 45
Bethune, Mary McLeod, 104
Bilad El-Sudan, 28
Bombay Africans, 35, 36–37
Bombay Slaves, 36
Bond, Horace, 106
Bond, Horace Mann, 17, 65, 78–79
Boothe Joseph, 50
Boydton Academic and Bible Institute, 60
Breakaway Churches, 41
British colonialism
    resistance to
        Nandi, 26
Brotherhood of the Sleeping Car Porters, 17,
    75–76, 77
Bunche, Ralph, 55, 78

C
Capricorn African Society, 71
Carter, Gwen, 63
Cash crops, 44
Channon Report, 60
Chhani, Sehmi, 88–89
Children
    community responsibility, 30
Chilimbwe, John, 50, 51
Christianity, 33
Church Missionary Society (CMS), 3,
    34–35, 37, 58
Church of Scotland, 49
Church of Scotland Mission, 50
Church of the Ancestors, 38
CMS, see Church Missionary Society (CMS)
Coffee, 44
Columbia University Teachers College, 62
Community responsibility
    children, 30
Congress of Racial Equality (CORE), 74
CORE, see Congress of Racial Equality
    (CORE)
Council of elders, 26
CSNA, see Cultural Society of New Africa
    (CSNA)
Cultural Society of New Africa (CSNA), 16,
    63, 65
Currie Report, 59–60

D
de Gama, Vasco, 2
de la Warr Commission, 55
de la Warr Report, 59–60
Diaspora, 5–6
Diggs, Charles, 15–16, 82–83, 86
Dini ya Nsambwa (Church of the Ances-
    tors), 38
Dini ya Roho (Holy Ghost Church), 38
Division of labor
    parents, 23
Dubinsky, David, 75–76
DuBois, W.E.B., 6, 49, 60

E
East Africa, 52
    colleges
        outputs, 133–136
    students
        statistical data, 14
East African Association, 61

Index

Education
  Asomi, 47
  elders, 23–24
  government, 33–58
  Kenya, 8, 12–14
  missionaries, 33–58
  parents, 23–24
  Sempele, Molonkett Ole, 8–9
  United States, 59–89
Education abroad
  Asomi, 127
"Education Drive"
  Kenyan overseas, 17–18
Egerton College, 66, 96
Elders
  education, 23–24
Elliot Commission Report of 1945, 60
European missionaries
  Kenya, 3

F

Fasting during *Ramadan*, 27
Folk tales, 23–24
Fort Jesus, 2–3
Frazer, J. Nelson, 44
Frazer Commission, 44–45

G

Garvey, Marcus, 54, 60
Garveyism
  Asomi, 7
Gatheru, Reuel John Mugo, 19, 46, 102–109
  education, 22–23
  U.S. education, 64–65
GBM, *see* Green Belt Movement (GBM)
GEMA, *see* Gikuyu-Embu-Meru Association (GEMA)
Gender
  Kenyan students, 151
Gender roles, 23
Gicheru, James
  Kenyan independence, 73
Gikuyu-Embu-Meru Association (GEMA), 64
Githinji, Philip, 114
Goat Oath, 70
Gordon, Walter A., 78
Government education, 33–58
Government workers, 119
Green Belt Movement (GBM), 117
Group (taifa), 30

H

Hadith (traditions of Prophet Muhammad), 30
Hajj (pilgrimage to Mecca), 27
Hamerton, Atkins, 34
Hampton Institute, 62
Harambee, 65
Helstein, Ralph, 75–76
Higher education
  United States, 59–89
Hillman, Sidney, 75–76
Holy Ghost, 38
Holy Ghost Church, 38
Holy Ghost Fathers, 3
Houser, George, 19
Howard University, 15

I

IBEAC, *see* Imperial British East Africa Company (IBEAC)
ICFTU, *see* International Confederation of Free Trade Unions (ICFTU)
IMAC, *see* Independent Maasai African Church (IMAC)
Imazigh, 28
Imperial British East Africa Company (IBEAC), 43
Independent African Church, 9, 38, 61
  founding, 38
Independent Kenya Teachers College, 59
Independent Maasai African Church (IMAC), 38–39
Industrial education, 61
Initiation set, 25–27
Initiation system, 25–27
Institute of International Education, 98
International Confederation of Free Trade Unions (ICFTU), 76
International Ladies Garment Workers' Union, 75–76
International Missionary Council, 51
Islam, 33
Islamic education, 61
  influence
    Kenya, 21–31, 125–126
Islamic law, 30

J

Jasomi, *see* Asomi
Jeanes School, 47, 48, 59
Jesuits, 33

Jesus, 33
Jihad, 29
Jomo Kenyatta University, 96
Jones, Jesse, 51
Jones, William, 37
Joroho (Holy Ghost), 38
Joseph, 33
Journalism, 122–123
Juma, Muhammad, 61, 62

K

Kabaka of Buganda, 43
Kabarak University, 96
Kabete Independent School, 59
KADU, see Kenya African Democratic Union (KADU)
Kagumu Teachers College, 66
Kairo, Simon Thuo, 121
Kalume, Thomas Johnson, 40, 41, 109
KANU, see Kenya African National Union (KANU)
Karanja, Josephat Njunguna, 114–115
Karanja, Kariuki, 91–92
Karugi, James Boro, 120
KAU, see Kenya African Union (KAU)
Kauara, Christopher, 121
Kavirondo Taxpayers Welfare Association (KTWA), 57
KCA, see Kikuyu Central Association (KCA)
Kennedy, John F., 66, 91, 97
  student transportation, 85–86
  Tom Mboya, 88
  Tom Mboya meeting, 80
Kenya, 1
  Africanization of, 91–92
  education, 8, 12–14
  educational opportunities under colonial rule, 93–94
  European missionaries, 3
  female students in the United States, 115
  Islamic education, 21–31
  Islamic education influence, 125–126
  manpower needs, 92
  map, 156
  missionaries, 3
  missionary schools, 46
  missionary universities, 96–97
  traditional education, 22–23
  women's education, 92–93
Kenya African Democratic Union (KADU), 73

Kenya African National Union (KANU), 64, 73, 109
  formation, 112
Kenya African Union (KAU), 68
  formation, 112
  slogan, 71
Kenya Broadcasting Corporation, 123
Kenya Education Drive, 1
Kenya Independence Movement (KIM), 64
Kenyan independence, 73
Kenyanization
  Royal Technical College, 113
Kenyan nationalism, 68
Kenyan overseas "Education Drive," 17–18
Kenyan student
  first in America, 4
Kenyan students
  employment, 118–119
  gender, 151
  returning from United States, 108–109
Kenyan trade unionists, 84
Kenya Peoples' Union (KPU), 110
Kenya Teachers College, 62, 112
Kenyatta, Jomo, 4, 42, 55, 57, 111–112
  cabinet, 64
  education, 22–23
  Kenya nationalism, 68
  Tom Mboya assassination, 88
  U.S. education, 65
Kenyatta, Peter Magana, 105
Kenyatta University College, 96, 97
Khaminwa, John Mukalasing, 120
Kharijites, 28
Kiama (council of elders), 26
Kiambu Mafia, 88
Kiano, Julius Gikonyo, 1, 5, 42, 55
  Kenyan independence, 73
  photograph, 153
  U.S. education, 62, 63, 64, 65
Kibicho, Samuel Gakuhi, 109
Kibinge, Leonard Oliver, 119
Kikuyu, 24
Kikuyu Central Association (KCA), 57
Kikuyu Independent School Organization (KISA), 53, 54, 65
Kikuyu Karanja Education Association (KKEA), 53, 54
Kikuyu students, 86
KIM, see Kenya Independence Movement (KIM)

Index

Kimani, George Mbugua, 65
   U.S. education, 64–65
King, Coretta Scott, 62, 78
King, Martin Luther
   letters from Tom Mboya, 17
King of Buganda, 43
Kiriri Women's University of Science and Technology, 96
KISA, *see* Kikuyu Independent School Organization (KISA)
Kiswahili, 2, 22, 30
Kiwanuka, William, 77, 109
KKEA, *see* Kikuyu Karanja Education Association (KKEA)
Koinange, Mbiyu, 4, 5, 42, 55
Koinange, Peter Mbiyu, 55, 111–112, 113
   photograph, 152
   U.S. education, 62, 63
Koran, 30
Koranic schools, 21, 30, 31
KPU, *see* Kenya Peoples' Union (KPU)
Krapf, Johann, 3
KTWA, *see* Kavirondo Taxpayers Welfare Association (KTWA)
Kuranic schools, 125–126
Kwasa, Shadrack, 119–120

L

Lancaster House Constitutional Conference on Kenya, 91
Langley, J. Ayodele, 6
Legends, 23–24
Literary education, 61
Livingston, David, 34
Lockwood, John, 67
London Law Society, 105
London Missionary Society, 34

M

Maathai, Mwangi, 119
Maathai, Wangari Muta, 93, 116
   photograph, 154
Machakos, 44
MacKenzie, Robert, 42
Mackinnon, William, 42–43
Macmillan, Harold, 73
Madaraka cabinet, 112–113
Madaraka Day, 2, 73
Madrasas (Koranic schools), 21, 30, 31
Maghrib, 28
Mahatma Ghandi Academy, 67

Mak'ayengo, Ochola Ogaye, 109–110
Makerere College, 56, 62, 66, 127
   East Africans students attending, 94
Makerere Government Institute, 59
Makodollah, George King, 101
Mandawa, Patrick, 77, 109
Marabouts, 28
Mary, 33
Mathu, Eliud Wambu, 68, 70
Mati, Bernard, 73
Mau Mau
   organized labor, 69
Mau Mau Layer, 71–72
Mau Mau Revolution, 3, 68–71
Mazrui, Ali, 31, 102, 126
Mboya, Pamela, 19, 115–116
Mboya, Tom, 1, 9, 15, 42, 92, 95
   assassination of, 88–89
   biographical studies, 13–14
   combating communism, 88
   criticism of, 86
   education, 19, 127
   fundraising, 82–83
   graduation, 47
   Kenyan independence, 73
   letters to Martin Luther King, 17
   Mau Mau Revolution, 72
   punishing Mugo, 106
   student transportation, 85
   trade unions, 5, 76–79, 110
   U.S. education, 62
   U.S. trip, 74–77, 81–82
McCaray, George, 77
McCarthy, John Joseph, 40
Meany, George, 75–76
Mecca, 27
Medical profession
   Africanization, 121–122
Mijikenda (nine groups), 35
Millard, C.H., 76
Missionaries, 13
   education, 33–58
   Kenya, 3
Missionary schools, 126
   Kenya, 46
Missionary universities
   Kenya, 96–97
Moi, Daniel, 42, 47, 72
   Kenyan independence, 73
Moi University, 96, 97
Montero, Frank, 81

Morrow, Fredrick, 78
Mosques, 21
Mugo, Nicholas Murathe, 120
Muliro, Masinde, 72
Mungai, Njoroge, 106
   photograph, 155
Muriuki, Godfrey, 25
Murray, Philip, 75–76
Musa, Mansa, 29
Muslims, 29
Muslim scholars (mualimou), 30
Mutual Education in Cultural Exchange of 1961, 16
Mwalimou (teacher), 10, 30
Myths, 23–24

N

NAACP, National Association for the Advancement of Colored People (NAACP)
Nairobi, 44
   Royal College, 67
   Royal Technical College, 63, 95
   University of, 67, 96
Nairobi District African Congress (NDAC), 72
Nairobi People's Convention Party (NPCP), 72
Namisi, Rosa, 40
Nandi
   resistance to British colonialism, 26
National Association for the Advancement of Colored People (NAACP), 63
National Baptist Convention (NBC), 49, 50
NBC, see National Baptist Convention (NBC)
NDAC. see Nairobi District African Congress (NDAC)
Negro World, 54
Ngala, Ronald Gideon, 72
   Kenyan independence, 73
Ng'weno, Hilary Bonface, 122–123
Nine groups, 35
Nixon, Richard, 76, 78, 85
Njenga, Nahashon Njiguna, 88
Njiiri, Kariuki, 5, 42, 65
   U.S. education, 62, 63, 64
Njogu, Peter, 99–100
Njoroge, George, 121–122
Njoroge, Nyoike F., 124
Nomiya Luo Mission, 38

Northey, Edward, 50
NPCP, see Nairobi People's Convention Party (NPCP)
Nyende, Simon, 57

O

Obanga, Beneah Apolo, 68
Obudho, Robert, 108
Ochwada, Arthur, 77, 109
Odede, Pamela Arua, 115–116
Odinga, Oginga Jaramogi, 42, 72, 88
   Kenyan independence, 73
   U.S. education, 64
Odongo, Alfa, 38
Oguda, L.G., 72
Okatch, Thaddeus, 99–101
Okiwiri, Jonathan, 42, 57
Okullu, Henry John, 40–41, 108
Olang, Festo, 39
Oldham, Joseph Houldsworth, 51
Omulo, Reuben, 57
"Open Doors" reports, 17
Operation Jock, 69
Organized labor
   Mau Mau, 69
Orgoiyoy, 26
Orr, James R., 45
Otiende, Joseph D., 92
Otunga, Maurice Michael, 39
Ouka, Fredrick Ogweno, 120
Owallo, John, 38
Owuor, Tom Diju, 110–111

P

Padmore, George, 60
Pan-Africanism, 3, 5–7, 7, 68
Parents
   division of labor, 23
   education, 23–24
Phelps-Stokes Commission, 45, 47, 48, 51, 59, 60, 72
Pilgrimage to Mecca, 27
Pioneer Business Institute, 62
Pororiet, 26
Prince Henry, 34
Providing to poor and needy, 27

R

Rabai community, 35–36
Racial prejudice, 36
Randolph, Asa Philip, 75–76, 77–78

Index

Rebmann, Johann, 3, 35
Research methods, 14–19
Reuther, Walter, 75–76
Riika (initiation set), 25–27
Ritual prayer, 27
Robinson, Jackie, 85
Roosevelt, Theodore, 61
Royal College of Nairobi, 67
Royal Technical College, 63, 96
    Kenyanization, 113
    Nairobi, 95

S

Salat (ritual prayer), 27
Salim, Ahmad Idha, 126
Salim, Ahmad Idhra, 31
Saoum (fasting during *Ramadan*), 27
Scheinman, William X., 79–80, 105–106
    Tom Mboya friendship, 80
Scholars (marabouts), 28
Scott, E.J., 61
Scott, Michael, 74–75
Scottish Free Church (SFC), 42, 43
Sempele, Molonkett Ole, 4, 108
    conversion, 39
    education, 8–9
    founding Independent African Church, 38
    U.S. education, 60–61
Sentogo, Z.K., 56
SFC, *see* Scottish Free Church (SFC)
Shahada, 27
Sharia (Islamic law), 30
Simon of Cyrene, 33
Smith College, 63
St. Augustine, 33
St. Joseph's Collegiate School, 65
St. Mark, 33
Stanford University, 62
Student Airlifts, 63, 87

T

Taifa, 30
Teacher, 10, 30
    shortages, 8
Tertulian of Carthage, 33
Thogoto Missionary School, 60
Thuku, Harry, 4, 42, 126
    arrest, 57
    East African Association, 61
    nationalism, 58

Torchbearers Association, 70
Trade unions, 5, 76–79, 110
    development of personnel, 110
Traditions of Prophet Muhammad, 30
Tuskegee, 61

U

Ugandan Railway, 43
Ulayeneza, Joseph B. K., 99–100
Umayyads, 28
Umma, 28
United Auto Workers, 75–76
United Packinghouse Workers, 75–76
United States
    higher education, 59–89
United States Agency for International Development (USAID), 97–98
United States International University, 96
United Steelworkers, 75–76
Unity (asabyya), 30
Universal Negro Improvement Association (UNIA), 54
University of California at Berkeley, 62
University of London, 67
University of Nairobi, 67, 96
USAID, *see* United States Agency for International Development (USAID)

V

Vocational education, 47

W

Wagema, Grace, 115
Wangari, Maathai, 64
Wanjigi, James Maina, 121
Washington, Booker T., 52
Waswahili, 30
Weekly Review, 122
Western-Educated Elites in Kenya, 9
Women's education
    Kenya, 92–93

Y

Yergan, Max, 15–16, 52–53
Yohari, Juma, 61
Young Kavirondo Association (YKA), 57
Young Men's Christian Association (YMCA), 52

Z

Zakat (providing to poor and needy), 27

For Product Safety Concerns and Information please contact our EU representative GPSR@taylorandfrancis.com
Taylor & Francis Verlag GmbH, Kaufingerstraße 24, 80331 München, Germany

www.ingramcontent.com/pod-product-compliance
Lightning Source LLC
Chambersburg PA
CBHW061832300426
44115CB00013B/2344